# VINES AND
# GROUND COVERS

BY PHILIP EDINGER AND THE EDITORS OF SUNSET BOOKS

SUNSET BOOKS · MENLO PARK, CALIFORNIA

# EXTERIOR DECORATION

If you think of the garden as a space to be decorated, you'll find vines and ground covers an essential part of the design. These finishing touches can give your landscape an extraordinary beauty—and, at the same time, hide less attractive parts of the garden from view.

In this book, you'll meet a selection of plants to bring charm and variety to shady groves or sunny slopes, arching arbors or tall, straight fences. From see-though screens to solid walls, from Aubusson-dense carpets to rippling seas of foliage, the multitude of vines and ground covers here are well worth working into your exterior decor.

## SUNSET BOOKS

Vice President, Sales: Richard A. Smeby
Editorial Director: Bob Doyle
Production Director: Lory Day
Art Director: Vasken Guiragossian

**Staff for this book:**

Managing Editor: Suzanne Normand Eyre
Copy Editor and Indexer: Rebecca LaBrum
Photo Researcher: Tishana Peebles
Production Coordinator: Patricia S. Williams
Special Contributors: Lisa Anderson, Jean Warboy

Art Director: Alice Rogers
Illustrators: Lois Lovejoy, Catherine M. Watters
Map Design and Cartography: Reineck & Reineck, San Francisco
Computer Production: Fog Press

Cover: *Clematis,* large-flowered hybrid. Photography by Marion Brenner.
Border photograph *(Nepeta × faassenii)* by David McDonald.

First printing January 1999
Copyright © 1999 Sunset Publishing Corporation, Menlo Park, CA 94025.
First edition. All rights reserved, including the right of reproduction in whole or in part in any form. Library of Congress Catalog Card Number: 98-86304.
ISBN 0-376-03821-7

Printed in the United States

For additional copies of *Vines and Ground Covers* or any other *Sunset* book, call our distribution partners at Leisure Arts, 1-800-526-5111.

## PHOTOGRAPHERS

**Marion Brenner:** 56 bottom, 62 middle, 92 top left, 95 bottom, 99 top left; **Kathleen Brenzel:** 46 top; **David Cavagnaro:** 1, 3 bottom, 15 middle left, 22 middle left, 29 top, 29 bottom, 35 top right, 38 middle, 41 top left, 41 top right, 44 bottom, 47 bottom, 49 top right, 50 top right, 51 top left, 51 bottom left, 66 top right, 67 left, 69 top right, 70 bottom right, 72 top right, 79 bottom, 84 top right, 91 top right, 96 top left, 96 right, 98 middle, 100, 105 bottom left, 106 top right, back cover bottom left; **R. Cowles:** 102; **Claire Curran:** 68 top left, 71 left, 92 bottom right, 93 bottom right; **R. Todd Davis:** 22 top left, 85 top right, 106 bottom left; **John R. Dunmire:** 66 left, 74 middle; **Derek Fell:** 3 middle, 26 top right, 26 middle right, 32, 65 bottom, 86 middle; **Pamela Harper:** 61 bottom left; **Lynne Harrison:** 7 middle right, 17 middle top, 34 bottom right, 52 bottom, 62 bottom right, 69 bottom right, 77 bottom; **Saxon Holt:** 9 middle right, 9 bottom right, 19 top left, 34 top right, 44 top, 46 bottom, 53 top, 63 right, 76 top, 91 bottom, 99 bottom; **Phil Johnson:** 89 top left; **Dency Kane:** 8 top left; **Renee Lynn:** 107 bottom right; **Charles Mann:** 9 left, 9 top right, 16 bottom, 17 top, 18 middle top, 28 top left, 29 middle top, 41 middle left, 42 top right, 45 top right and bottom right, 48 left, 52 top, 64 middle, 65 top, 68 bottom right, 75 bottom, 76 bottom, 78 left, 80 right, 85 top left, 89 right, back cover top left; **Ells Marugg:** 67 bottom; **B. McCarthy/Woodlanders, Inc.:** 54 left; **David McDonald/PhotoGarden, Inc.:** 8 bottom right, 11 top, 14 top, 15 top left, 19 middle bottom, 22 middle right, 29 middle bottom, 38 bottom, 41 bottom right, 51 bottom right, 59 top, 61 top, 97 top right, 107 top; **Jerry Pavia:** 3 top, 4, 22 bottom, 23 top, 28 middle left, 36 middle, 40 middle right, 42 left, 47 top left, 48 bottom, 49 left, 53 bottom, 55 bottom right, 58 bottom, 59 bottom, 60 right, 63 top left, 64 top left, 64 bottom, 68 bottom left, 69 middle right, 72 bottom left, 72 bottom right, 73, 74 top left, 74 bottom right, 78 middle bottom, 79 top left, 80 top, 83 top left, 86 top right, 87 top right, 88 top, 90 top right, 90 bottom right, 91 left, 93 top, 94 bottom left, 94 bottom right, 94 top right, 95 top, 96 bottom, back cover right; **Joanne Pavia:** 55 top left; **Norman A. Plate:** 105 top right; **Susan A. Roth:** 18 middle bottom, 19 middle top, 23 bottom left, 35 middle left, 39 bottom, 40 middle left, 43 bottom, 45 top left, 48 right, 56 top, 57 bottom, 58 top right, 63 bottom, 67 top, 70 top, 75 top right, 81 top, 82 left, 84 top left, 90 left; **Richard Shiell:** 7 top right, 11 middle, 12 middle, 12 bottom, 13 top, 13 middle, 13 bottom, 14 center, 15 top right, 15 bottom, 16 top, 16 middle top, 17 bottom, 17 middle bottom, 18 top, 18 bottom, 19 bottom, 20 top right, 20 bottom right, 21 top, 21 middle right, 21 bottom, 24 top right, 24 middle right, 24 bottom right, 25 top, 25 middle, 25 bottom, 26 left, 26 bottom right, 27 top, 27 middle, 27 bottom, 30 top, 30 middle, 30 bottom, 31 top left, 31 middle left, 31 bottom left, 31 top right, 43 top left, 55 bottom left, 68 top right, 68 middle right, 69 bottom left, 77 top, 78 top, 83 top right, 86 bottom left, 87 bottom left, 88 bottom, 93 bottom left, 104, 106 top left; **Southern Living Archives:** 50 left; **J. G. Strauch, Jr.:** 16 middle bottom, 19 top right, 21 middle left, 39 left, 39 middle, 40 bottom left, 47 top right, 58 top left, 62 top left, 72 top middle, 81 bottom, 82 bottom, 97 bottom left, 107 middle left; **Michael S. Thompson:** 7 top left, 7 bottom right, 14 bottom, 23 bottom right, 24 left, 28 bottom right, 36 top, 37 top, 37 bottom left, 38 top, 50 bottom right, 54 right, 57 top, 60 top, 61 bottom right, 66 bottom, 69 top left, 71 right, 79 top right, 80 bottom, 84 bottom, 89 top middle, 89 bottom middle, 98 top left; **Deidra Walpole:** 11 bottom; **Martha Woodward:** 106 middle left; **Tom Woodward:** 2, 10 top, 10 bottom, 12 top, 20 left, 28 bottom left, 34 top left, 35 middle right, 36 bottom, 37 right, 40 top left, 41 middle right, 43 right, 45 bottom left, 46 left, 49 bottom right, 70 bottom left, 75 left, 78 bottom, 81 top, 85 bottom right, 89 bottom left, 92 middle left, 95 middle, 96 middle left.

# CONTENTS

Rambling, scrambling, clinging, colonizing…vines and ground covers are the garden's restless inhabitants, always seeking out new territory. It's this very mobility that accounts for much of their charm and many of their uses. While shrubs, trees, and even lawn are relatively static parts of the land-

## VINES AND GROUND COVERS

# ON STAGE

scape, vines and ground covers flow—whether you're looking at wisteria stretching out tentacles of new growth, star jasmine tumbling its perfumed blossoms over a low wall, or a patch of sweet woodruff creeping through a rhododendron glade.

In these pages, you'll find an alluring assortment of upwardly and outwardly mobile garden ornaments, both familiar and exotic. Their great variety suits them to a range of landscape styles, from ultra-structured to thoroughly natu-ralistic. Whether they're used as decorative details or given a more prominent role, these plants are vital components of a well-turned-out garden.

Artfully trained Japanese wisteria *(Wisteria floribunda)* adorns
a meandering path bordered by mixed perennials and ground cover plants.

# Anatomy of Vines and Ground Covers

*It is easy to recognize a vine: it climbs. Identifying a ground cover is equally simple—it's a plant that spreads over a patch of earth and obscures it. But these seemingly straightforward distinctions mask a more complex situation. Not all vines climb by the same means, not all ground covers do their covering in the same fashion—and to complicate the issue, some vines can double as ground covers. The differences among individual vines and ground covers are of more than botanical interest: the way each one climbs or spreads will in part determine its suitability for your needs.*

## TYPES OF VINES

Defined in the most basic terms, a vine is simply a flexible shrub that doesn't stop growing in height or length (depending on whether you train it vertically or horizontally). In fact, if unsupported, it won't climb at all but will, instead, form a sprawling mass; some vines have a parallel life as ground covers. And though many of us might automatically describe all vines as "clinging," these plants scale their supports in different ways. Five typical modes are discussed below.

TWINING. As new growth elongates, it twists or spirals—wrapping around around other growth (new or old) on the same plant, stems of nearby plants, or specially provided vertical guides. Nearly all twining vines make too tight a spiral to encircle a post, so cord or wire is the best vertical support.

COILING TENDRILS. These vines' stems grow straight, but specialized growths reach out and wrap around whatever is handy—wire, cord, another stem on the same vine, another plant. Some vines (grape, for example) produce tendrils directly from the stems, but often the tendril is part of a leaf—sometimes carried at the tip of a leaflet, sometimes growing as a separate part of a leaf (in place of a leaflet).

COILING LEAFSTALKS. Clematis offers the best example of this climbing mechanism. As a stem grows and puts out leaves, the leafstalks of young leaves encircle anything slender they encounter (cord, wire, plant stems), behaving more or less like tendrils.

CLINGING. Several kinds of specialized structures let some vines attach themselves to a variety of flat surfaces. Ivy *(Hedera)* and winter creeper *(Euonymus fortunei)* are two familiar examples: their stems are equipped with small roots that cling tenaciously to all but absolutely smooth and slick surfaces. Other well-known clingers, like Boston ivy and Virginia creeper *(Parthenocissus* species), have tendrils that terminate in discs tipped with suction cups; these vines climb with their tendrils and attach to vertical surfaces with their discs. A few others, represented by cat's claw *(Macfadyena unguis-cati),* have tendrils with hooklike claws or tips, letting them gain purchase in the smallest irregularity or crevice.

CLAMBERING. Some vines lack any specialized structures to assist upward growth. Instead, they simply thread their way through and over other plants, depending on this interweaving to hold their stems in place. A few, such as bougainvillea and climbing roses, have thorns or prickles on their stems and/or leaves; these help secure the stems as they scramble, but they offer no permanent grip. In the garden, you'll always need to tie clambering vines to their structural supports.

**VINE ATTACHMENTS**

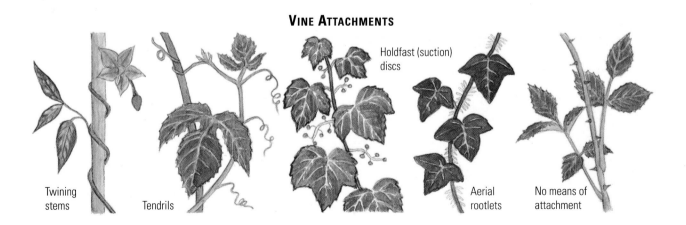

Twining stems

Tendrils

Holdfast (suction) discs

Aerial rootlets

No means of attachment

*Vinca minor* (spreading-rooting)

## TYPES OF GROUND COVERS

Unlike vines, which have in common a distinct growth habit (with various adaptations to facilitate it), ground covers comprise a variety of plant types that can be pressed into service for the purpose of covering bare earth. The group includes some vines, sprawling but rigid shrubs, and various perennials. By growth habit, these varied plants can be separated into the following groups.

TRAILING-SPREADING. Many ground cover plants have either lax, naturally sprawling stems or fairly rigid ones that spread horizontally rather than growing upright. All growth spreads from a single root system; the overlapping, interweaving stems of adjacent plants produce the coverage. Star jasmine *(Trachelospermum jasminoides)* is a vining example of this type; the junipers *(Juniperus)* are shrubby sorts.

SPREADING-ROOTING. Some ground covers spread not only by stems arising from a common root system, but also from roots that sprout wherever the stems contact moist soil. Each rooted point in essence becomes a new plant, which then sends out its own stems. In time, such ground covers become a dense mass of stems and foliage, their extensive root systems effectively binding the soil. Ivy *(Hedera)* and winter creeper *(Euonymus fortunei)* are classic examples among vines, rosemary *(Rosmarinus officinalis)* among shrubby plants, and periwinkle *(Vinca)* among perennials.

COLONIZING. In contrast to spreading-rooting ground covers, whose stems root as they spread, another ground cover type binds soil by producing underground stems that spread laterally and (usually) shallowly, producing roots and sending up stems as they grow. A single plant eventually develops into a colony of

growth that forms a tightly knit patch of stems and leaves. Bunchberry *(Cornus canadensis)* is a perennial of this sort; sarcococca is a woody-stemmed example.

CLUMP-FORMING. Among popular perennial ground covers are a number of plants that form dense clumps and achieve ground cover status only when planted close together, to form a solid foliage mass. Plantings can remain undisturbed for many years before needing division to improve performance. The best of these plants are featured on pages 22–23.

TOP TO BOTTOM: *Juniperus squamata* 'Blue Carpet' (trailing-spreading); *Cornus canadensis* (colonizing); *Hosta* varieties (clump-forming)

Planted to grow together, climbing roses and large-flowered hybrid clematis offer a lavish floral display.

# VINES AND GROUND COVERS IN THE GARDEN

*Enter the realm of vines and ground covers and you'll find a highly diverse assortment of plants. When you consider their garden functions, however, you'll realize that they have one trait in common: all are usually planted for adornment, be it understated or outspoken. In some situations, they provide decorative finishing touches in an already well-structured landscape. In others, they are used frankly to obscure, cloaking bare earth, bare walls, or a barely tolerable view. Understanding the varied roles these plants can fill will help you make your choices as you explore the plant encyclopedia on pages 33–99.*

## THE VIRTUES OF VINES

Some of the things vines do aren't exclusive to these plants alone. After all, trees can give shade, shrubs will make screens, lawn easily covers bare earth. But thanks to the pliant growth that produces interesting outlines and intricate, filigreelike traceries,

vines do all these things in a uniquely beautiful way. Used alone or with other plants, they bring something special to the garden. Here are four ways vines can shine.

**As decorations.** By itself, a wall is just a wall. Add a vine, though, and it becomes a sculpture that changes through the seasons and the years. Similarly, a bare window is both softened and accented when surrounded or swagged by a flowering vine like a climbing rose. Trained along eaves, a vine accents the architectural line while drawing attention to its own beauty. Even a utilitarian lamppost can double as a display pillar for a showy blossoming vine. And if you want vertical accents where support structures for them are lacking, you can grow your vines on freestanding tripods or pillars.

**As companions.** Some vines are perfect companions or complements for other plants. That "other plant" may well be a second vine: climbing roses and clematis, for example, are a classic duo. But think about mature shrubs or trees, as well; these can serve as both trellis and display vehicle. Take caution in this case to choose a vine that won't strangle or overwhelm its host; many climbing roses and clematis hybrids are good choices, but aggressive beauties like wisteria and many kinds of honeysuckles *(Lonicera)* pose a potential threat to smaller shrubs or trees.

**As space definers.** If it's given the right support, a dense-growing vine can become a wall of foliage. If you choose an openwork fence or freestanding trellis as support, you'll get a leafy screen that visually separates space. If you turn the foliage wall to the horizontal—by growing it atop a pergola, for example—you'll have a shade-casting roof.

**As ground covers.** Without support, vines tend to sprawl, and those that do so attractively can be used as ground covers. In fact, some vines—ivy *(Hedera)* and star jasmine *(Trachelospermum jasminoides)* come to mind—are more widely used in this unsupported mode.

Create a living fence with a dense-growing vine. This *Clematis montana* provides a traffic-stopping flower show, too.

# THE GENIUS OF GROUND COVERS

It would be easy to dismiss ground covers as purely utilitarian, nothing more than plants to be used for a fairly low, fairly even foliage cover in places where lawn (the best-known ground cover) won't serve. They do, of course, fill this role—but with imagination and a good knowledge of the many choices available, you can make such plantings beautiful as well as practical. And of course, you can also create purely artistic ground cover plantings, intended more for good looks than for usefulness. Below, we highlight a few of the roles ground covers can play.

**Covers for practicality.** Look at the plantings in institutional and municipal settings and you'll see ground covers at their most practical: they've been planted to blanket bare earth with greenery, providing dust control and weed suppression in the process. Such plantings typically contain just one kind of plant; the result is neat and uniform, but often monotonous if the area is large. On sloping land, any soil-binding ground cover will help control erosion.

**Covers for beauty.** In a home garden, ground cover plantings are often installed largely for attractive appearance or to complement a landscape design, though the practical role still applies. Plantings are often used as shapes that define open spaces; as carpets that provide settings for the shrubs, trees, and garden ornaments that rise above them; as streams of foliage to flow around boulders in naturalistic landscapes; or simply as ribbonlike or patch-shaped transition zones between paving or lawn and plantings of shrubs or perennials.

Combinations of more than one ground cover can produce striking plantings. Sometimes you can achieve a tapestry effect with different varieties of just one plant, such as heather *(Calluna vulgaris);* you can also create a distinctly varied composition by combining completely different plants that enjoy the same conditions.

**Traffic control.** Whatever else they may do, one point is true for nearly all ground covers: they function as barriers rather than as the green bridge between areas that a lawn provides. An expanse of ground cover implies "go around" rather than "walk across." (A few ground cover plants, however, also will withstand a bit of foot traffic; examples include *Arenaria montana, Chamaemelum nobile, Duchesnea indica, Hippocrepis comosa, Phyla nodiflora, Pratia angulata,* and *Sagina subulata.*

TOP RIGHT: A ground cover of *Vinca major* is a practical solution to stabilizing a drainage swale.

MIDDLE: *Helianthemum nummularium* (left) and lantana and gazania (right) are planted for the beauty of their blossoms.

BOTTOM: Carpet of English ivy *(Hedera helix)* keeps foot traffic directed to brick path.

*Lonicera japonica*

# FLOWER COLOR THROUGH THE YEAR

*What is a garden without color? Not too interesting, say most gardeners—and most gardens, no matter how small, are designed to feature color for as much of the year as possible. Listed on these four pages are all the vines and ground covers with decorative blossoms described in the encyclopedia (pages 33–99) and in the special features in this chapter (pages 22–23, 28–29). The chart indicates each plant's bloom period.*

*Lonicera sempervirens*

\* = can be used as a ground cover

| Vine Name (Encyclopedia Page Listing) | Bloom Season | | | | Zones |
|---|---|---|---|---|---|
| | SP | SU | F | W | |
| Akebia quinata (36) | ■ | | | | 3–24, 29–41 |
| Allamanda cathartica (36) | | ■ | | | 24–27 |
| Antigonon leptopus (37) | | ■ | | | 12, 13, 18–30 |
| Aristolochia macrophylla (39) | | ■ | | | 1–24, 29–43 |
| Asarina (40) | | ■ | | | All zones (annual) |
| Beaumontia grandiflora (42) | ■ | | | | 12, 13, 16, 17, 21–27 |
| Bignonia capreolata (43) | ■ | | | | 4–9, 14–24, 26–33 |
| Bougainvillea* (43) | | ■ | | | 12, 13, 15–17, 19, 22–28 |
| Campsis (45) | | ■ | | | Zones vary |
| Clematis (50) | | ■ | | | Zones vary |
| Clerodendrum thomsoniae (53) | | ■ | | | 22–28 |
| Clytostoma callistegioides (53) | | ■ | | | 9, 12–28 |
| Cobaea scandens (40) | | ■ | | | All zones (annual) |
| Distictis (56) | | ■ | | | Zones vary |
| Dolichos lablab (40) | | ■ | | | All zones (annual) |
| Gelsemium sempervirens* (63) | ■ | | | ■ | 8–24, 26–33 |
| Hardenbergia (63) | | | | ■ | Zones vary |
| Hibbertia scandens* (65) | | ■ | | | 16, 17, 21–24 |
| Hydrangea (67) | | ■ | | | 2–21, 31–41 |
| Ipomoea (40, 70) | | ■ | | | Zones vary (some are annual) |
| Jasminum* (70) | | ■ | | | Zones vary |
| Lapageria rosea (74) | | ■ | | | 5, 6, 15–17, 23, 24 |
| Lathyrus odoratus (41) | ■ | | | ■ | All zones (annual) |
| Lonicera* (75) | | ■ | | | Zones vary |
| Macfadyena unguis-cati* (76) | | ■ | | | 8–29, 31 |
| Mandevilla (77) | | ■ | | | Zones vary |
| Millettia reticulata (77) | ■ | | | | 20–24 |
| Pandorea (80) | | ■ | | | 16–27 |
| Passiflora* (81) | ■ | | | | Zones vary |

| Vine Name (Encyclopedia Page Listing) | Bloom Season | | | | Zones |
|---|---|---|---|---|---|
| | SP | SU | F | W | |
| Petrea volubilis (83) | | ■ | | | 19–25 |
| Podranea ricasoliana (84) | | ■ | | | 9, 12, 13, 19–27 |
| Polygonum* (84) | ■ | ■ | | | Zones vary |
| Pyrostegia venusta (86) | ■ | | ■ | ■ | 13, 16, 21–27 |
| Rosa* (87) | ■ | ■ | | | Zones vary |
| Schizophragma hydrangeoides (90) | | ■ | | | 4–9, 14–17, 31–34, 39 |
| Senecio confusus (90) | | ■ | | | 13, 16–28 |
| Solandra maxima (91) | ■ | | | ■ | 17, 21–25, 26 (southern), 27 |
| Solanum (91) | | ■ | | | Zones vary |
| Sollya heterophylla* (92) | | ■ | | | 8, 9, 14–28 |
| Stephanotis floribunda (92) | | ■ | | | 23–25 |
| Stigmaphyllon* (92) | | ■ | | | Zones vary |
| Tecomaria capensis* (93) | | ■ | ■ | | 12, 13, 16, 18–28; protected in 14, 15 |
| Thunbergia (41, 94) | | ■ | ■ | | Zones vary (some are annual) |
| Trachelospermum* (95) | ■ | ■ | | ■ | Zones vary |
| Tropaeolum* (41) | | ■ | | | All zones (annual) |
| Wisteria* (98) | ■ | | | ■ | Zones vary |

| Ground Cover Name (Encyclopedia Page Listing) | Bloom Season | | | | Zones |
|---|---|---|---|---|---|
| | SP | SU | F | W | |
| Agapanthus (22) | | ■ | | | Zones vary |
| Ajuga reptans (35) | ■ | | | | 1–24, 26–45 |
| Arenaria montana (28) | ■ | | | | 1–9, 14–24, 32–45 |
| Arctostaphylos (37) | ■ | | | ■ | Zones vary |
| Arctotheca calendula (38) | ■ | ■ | | | 8, 9, 13–24 |
| Armeria maritima (22) | ■ | | | | 1–9, 14–24, 33–43 |
| Bergenia (22) | | | | ■ | 1–9, 12–24, 30–45 |
| Calluna vulgaris (44) | | ■ | ■ | | 2–6, 15–17, 34, 36–41 |
| Campanula (45) | ■ | ■ | | | Zones vary |
| Carissa macrocarpa (46) | ■ | ■ | | | 22–27 |

TOP: *Clematis montana*
BOTTOM: *Jasminum polyanthum*

*Wisteria sinensis*

* = can be used as a ground cover

*Cistus salviifolius*

*Erica cinerea* 'Atropurpurea'

*Genista pilosa* 'Vancouver Gold'

| Ground Cover Name (Encyclopedia page listing) | Bloom Season | | | | Zones |
|---|---|---|---|---|---|
| | SP | SU | F | W | |
| Ceanothus (46) | ■ | | | | 4–9, 14–24 |
| Cerastium tomentosum (48) | ■ | | | | 1–24, 32–45 |
| Ceratostigma plumbaginoides (48) | | ■ | ■ | | 2–10, 14–24, 29–41 |
| Chamaemelum nobile (28) | | ■ | | | 1–24, 30–43 |
| Chrysogonum virginianum (48) | ■ | ■ | | | 3–6, 14–17, 28–32, 34–39 |
| Cistus (49) | ■ | ■ | | | 6–9, 14–24 |
| Convallaria majalis (54) | ■ | | | | 1–7, 14–20, 31–45 |
| Cornus canadensis (54) | ■ | | | | 1–7, 32–45 |
| Coronilla varia (55) | | ■ | ■ | | 1–24, 28–45 |
| Cotoneaster (55) | ■ | | | | Zones vary |
| Duchesnea indica (57) | ■ | | | | 1–24, 29–43 |
| Epimedium (57) | ■ | | | | 1–9, 14–17, 31–43 |
| Erica (58) | | | ■ | ■ | Zones vary |
| Erigeron karvinskianus (59) | ■ | ■ | | | 8, 9, 12–28 |
| Fragaria chiloensis (61) | ■ | | | | 4–24 |
| Galium odoratum (61) | ■ | ■ | | | 1–6, 15–17, 31–43 |
| Gaultheria (62) | ■ | | | | Zones vary |
| Gazania (62) | | ■ | | | 8–30 |
| Genista (63) | ■ | | | | Zones vary |
| Helianthemum nummularium (65) | | ■ | | | 3–9, 14–24, 32, 34 |
| Helleborus orientalis (23) | | | | ■ | 2–10, 14–24, 31–41 |
| Hemerocallis (23) | | ■ | | | All zones |
| Hippocrepis comosa (66) | ■ | | | | 8–26 |
| Hosta (23) | | ■ | | | 1–10, 12–21, 28, 31–45 |
| Hypericum calycinum (67) | | ■ | | | 3–24, 31–34 |
| Iberis sempervirens (23) | ■ | | | | 1–24, 31–45 |
| ICE PLANTS (68–69) | ■ | ■ | ■ | | Zones vary |

| Ground Cover Name (encyclopedia page listing) | Bloom Season | | | | Zones |
|---|---|---|---|---|---|
| | SP | SU | F | W | |
| Lamium maculatum (28) | ● | ● | | | 1–24, 32–43 |
| Lantana (73) | | ● | ● | ● | 8–10, 12–30 |
| Liriope spicata (74) | | ● | | | 2–41 |
| Mahonia (76) | ● | | | | Zones vary |
| Myosotis scorpioides (78) | ● | | | | 1–24, 32–45 |
| Nepeta × faassenii (28) | ● | ● | | | 1–24, 30, 32–43 |
| Oenothera speciosa (78) | ● | ● | | | 3–24, 29, 30, 33 |
| Ophiopogon japonicus (79) | | ● | | | 5–9, 14–31, 32 (warmer parts) |
| Osteospermum fruticosum (79) | ● | ● | | | 8, 9, 12–26 |
| Pachysandra terminalis (79) | ● | | | | 1–10, 14–21, 31–43 |
| Pelargonium peltatum (82) | ● | ● | | | 8, 9, 12–24 |
| Phyla nodiflora (83) | ● | ● | | | 8–29 |
| Polygonum (84) | ● | ● | | | Zones vary |
| Potentilla neumanniana (85) | ● | ● | | | 1–24, 31–43 |
| Pratia (29) | ● | ● | | | 4–9, 14–24 |
| Prunella (29) | | ● | | | 1–24, 29–43 |
| Pyracantha (85) | ● | | | | Zones vary |
| Ranunculus repens (86) | ● | | | | 1–11, 14–24, 28–43 |
| Rosa (87) | ● | ● | | | Zones vary |
| Rosmarinus officinalis (88) | ● | | ● | ● | 4–24, 26–32 |
| Rubus pentalobus (89) | ● | | | | 4–6, 14–17, 31, 32 |
| Santolina (89) | ● | ● | | | Zones vary |
| Stachys byzantina (29) | ● | ● | | | 1–24, 29–43 |
| Teucrium chamaedrys (94) | | ● | | | 3–24, 28–34, 39 |
| Vancouveria (95) | ● | | | | Zones vary |
| Vinca (96) | ● | | | | Zones vary |
| Viola (96) | ● | | | ● | Zones vary |

TOP: *Helianthemum nummularium*
BOTTOM: *Lampranthus spectabilis*

*Osteospermum fruticosum*
'African Queen'

# Selection Guide
## FOR VINES AND GROUND COVERS

*When you choose vines or ground covers, you often start with a mind's-eye picture of the plant you want, then sort through the possible choices for a reasonable match. We list selections with colorful blossoms on pages 10–13; for other desirable characteristics, such as shade tolerance or fast growth, look through the lists on the following pages. Many of the categories contain both vines and ground covers; a few deal specifically with one or the other.*

*You'll find descriptions of the plants on these lists in the encyclopedia (pages 33–99) and in the two special features in this chapter (pages 22–23 and 28–29). Before you make your choices, review the climate zone information on pages 108–111 to be sure the vines and ground covers you want to grow will succeed in your climate.*

## SELF-ATTACHING VINES

As described on page 6, these vines have special structures that let them cling unaided to a wide variety of surfaces. They may take a few years to begin their climb—but once they start, they'll go the distance on their own. Be aware, though, that their tight grip can, in time, lead to the deterioration of wood or mortar.

Bignonia capreolata

Campsis

Euonymus fortunei

Ficus pumila

Hedera

Hydrangea

Macfadyena unguis-cati

Parthenocissus

Schizophragma
    hydrangeoides

# FALL FOLIAGE COLOR

In climates with distinct seasons, plants providing autumn foliage color are especially welcome. The choices below include flaming reds, oranges, and yellows, as well as more subtle bronze and burgundy shades. While most of these plants are deciduous, a few evergreens assume a colorful mantle during the coldest months of the year.

*Hydrangea petiolaris*

## VINES

*Bignonia capreolata*  
*Celastrus*  
*Euonymus fortunei* (several)  
*Hydrangea*  
*Parthenocissus*  

*Rosa* (some)  
*Vitis*  
*Wisteria*  

## GROUND COVERS

*Bergenia*  
*Calluna vulgaris* (some)  
*Ceratostigma plumbaginoides*  
*Cornus canadensis*  
*Cotoneaster dammeri,*  
*C. salicifolius*  
*Epimedium*  

*Erica carnea* 'Vivellii'  
*Juniperus horizontalis* (several)  
*Mahonia aquifolium* 'Compacta', *M. repens*  
*Nandina domestica*  
*Polygonum vacciniifolium*  
*Rhus aromatica*  

THIS PAGE, FROM TOP TO BOTTOM: *Parthenocissus tricuspidata,* close up and scaling a wall; *Mahonia aquifolium* 'Compacta'

OPPOSITE PAGE, FROM TOP TO BOTTOM: *Hedera helix* 'Buttercup'; *Parthenocissus tricuspidata; Schizophragma hydrangeoides*

# DECORATIVE FRUITS

Where there are flowers, fruits may follow. Some of the plants below start by bearing showy blossoms, then follow up that display with conspicuous fruits or berries; others produce virtually invisible blooms, but surprise you with a show of fruit later on. The fruits of still others—clematis and hops *(Humulus lupulus),* for instance—forgo bright color for interesting form. Kiwi *(Actinidia deliciosa),* passion flower *(Passiflora),* and a few others give you fruits that are edible as well as decorative.

## VINES

| | |
|---|---|
| *Actinidia* | *Humulus lupulus* |
| *Akebia quinata* | *Kadsura japonica* |
| *Ampelopsis brevipedunculata* | *Lonicera* (some) |
| *Asparagus* | *Parthenocissus* |
| *Celastrus* | *Passiflora* (most) |
| *Clematis* | *Rosa* (some) |
| *Cocculus carolinus* | *Solanum* (some) |
| *Dolichos lablab* (annual) | *Vitis* (most) |
| *Euonymus fortunei* (some) | |

## GROUND COVERS

| | |
|---|---|
| *Arctostaphylos* | *Liriope muscari* |
| *Ardisia japonica* | *Mahonia* |
| *Carissa macrocarpa* | *Ophiopogon japonicus* |
| *Carpobrotus* (ice plant) | *Pachysandra terminalis* |
| *Cornus canadensis* | *Pyracantha* |
| *Cotoneaster* | *Rhus aromatica* |
| *Duchesnea indica* | *Rubus pentalobus* |
| *Fragaria chiloensis* | *Sarcococca hookerana* |
| *Gaultheria* | *humilis* |
| *Juniperus* (some) | *Taxus baccata* |

TOP TO BOTTOM: *Celastrus scandens; Vitis* hybrid; *Cotoneaster horizontalis; Arctostaphylos uva-ursi*

# DECORATIVE FOLIAGE

Flowers may be fleeting, but foliage is with you throughout the growing season—and that fact alone underscores the desirability of plants with leaves in colors other than plain green. The list below includes choices with foliage in gray, chartreuse, bronze, and plum, as well as those with green leaves variegated in colors including white, cream, yellow, pink, and red.

## VINES

*Actinidia kolomikta*

*Euonymus fortunei* (some)

× *Fatshedera lizei* 'Variegata'

*Ficus pumila* 'Variegata'

*Hedera* (some)

*Humulus lupulus* 'Aureus'

*Lonicera japonica* 'Aureoreticulata'

*Parthenocissus henryana*

*Trachelospermum jasminoides* 'Variegatum'

## GROUND COVERS

*Aegopodium podagraria* 'Variegatum'

*Ajuga reptans* (several)

*Ardisia japonica* (several)

*Asarum shuttleworthii*

*Calluna vulgaris* (some)

*Cerastium tomentosum*

*Convallaria majalis* 'Variegata'

*Cotoneaster horizontalis* 'Variegatus'

*Gazania* (some)

*Genista* (some)

*Helianthemum nummularium* (some)

*Hosta*

*Houttuynia cordata* 'Chameleon'

*Juniperus* (some)

*Lamium maculatum*

*Liriope spicata* 'Silver Dragon'

*Pachysandra terminalis* 'Silver Edge'

*Pelargonium peltatum* 'L'Elegante'

*Pleioblastus* (some)

*Polygonum capitatum*

*Sagina subulata* 'Aurea'

*Santolina chamaecyparissus*

*Stachys byzantina*

*Vinca* (some)

TOP TO BOTTOM: *Hedera colchica* 'Sulphur Heart'; *Parthenocissus henryana*; *Ajuga reptans* 'Variegata'; *Vinca major* 'Variegata'

# PLANTS THAT TOLERATE SHADE

Limited sunlight need not limit your plant choices: in nature, many vines and ground covers grow in dappled sun or light shade. The following plants thrive with less than full sunlight. Some must have shady conditions; others will accept shade but are happy in sun as well. For the specifics, check the encyclopedia listings.

## VINES

*Actinidia*

*Akebia quinata*

*Ampelopsis brevipedunculata*

*Aristolochia macrophylla*

*Asparagus*

*Beaumontia grandiflora*

*Bignonia capreolata*

*Bougainvillea*

*Campsis*

*Cissus*

*Clematis*

*Clerodendrum thomsoniae*

*Clytostoma callistegioides*

*Cocculus carolinus*

*Distictis*

*Euonymus fortunei*

× *Fatshedera lizei*

*Ficus pumila*

*Gelsemium sempervirens*

*Hardenbergia*

*Hedera*

*Hibbertia scandens*

*Humulus lupulus*

*Hydrangea*

*Jasminum*

*Kadsura japonica*

*Lapageria rosea*

*Lonicera*

*Macfadyena unguis-cati*

*Mandevilla*

*Pandorea*

*Parthenocissus*

*Passiflora*

*Petrea volubilis*

*Podranea ricasoliana*

*Rosa* (some)

*Schizophragma hydrangeoides*

*Senecio confusus*

*Solanum*

*Sollya heterophylla*

*Stephanotis floribunda*

*Thunbergia*

*Trachelospermum*

*Wisteria*

TOP TO BOTTOM: *Akebia quinata; Clematis montana; Epimedium × rubrum; Lonicera japonica* 'Halliana'

## GROUND COVERS

*Epimedium pinnatum*

*Aegopodium podagraria*

*Ajuga reptans*

*Arctostaphylos*

*Ardisia japonica*

*Asarum*

*Bergenia*

*Campanula*

*Carissa macrocarpa*

*Cerastium tomentosum*

*Ceratostigma*
  *plumbaginoides*

*Chamaemelum nobile*

*Chrysogonum virginianum*

*Convallaria majalis*

*Cornus canadensis*

*Duchesnea indica*

*Epimedium*

*Fragaria chiloensis*

*Galium odoratum*

*Gaultheria*

*Helleborus orientalis*

*Hemerocallis*

*Hosta*

*Houttuynia cordata*

*Hypericum calycinum*

*Juniperus*

*Lamium maculatum*

*Liriope spicata*

*Mahonia*

*Myosotis scorpioides*

*Nandina domestica*

*Ophiopogon japonicus*

*Pachysandra terminalis*

*Paxistima canbyi*

*Pleioblastus*

*Polygonum capitatum*

*Potentilla neumanniana*

*Pratia*

*Prunella*

*Ranunculus repens*

*Rhus aromatica*

*Rubus pentalobus*

*Sagina subulata*

*Sarcococca hookerana*
  *humilis*

*Taxus baccata*

*Vancouveria*

*Vinca*

*Viola*

TOP TO BOTTOM: *Hypericum calycinum; Pachysandra terminalis; Vinca minor; Juniperus scopulorum* 'Blue Creeper'

# PLANTS THAT TOLERATE DRYNESS

Tending a yardful of plants that need moisture all the time gives a gardener true appreciation for those individuals that can do with less. And where water is scarce or the dry season is long, less-thirsty plants move to the head of any list of desirable choices. The vines and ground covers noted here can all take less than regular water; some accept just a bit of dryness, while others are heroically drought tolerant. For the specifics, check the encyclopedia listings.

## VINES

*Clytostoma callistegioides*
*Euonymus fortunei*
*Hardenbergia*
*Lonicera*
*Macfadyena unguis-cati*
*Polygonum*
*Pyrostegia venusta*
*Senecio confusus*
*Solanum jasminoides*
*Tecomaria capensis*
*Vitis*
*Wisteria*

*Lonicera sempervirens*

TOP: *Wisteria sinensis* 'Cooke's Special'
BOTTOM: *Clytostoma callistegioides* framed by *Solanum jasminoides*

## GROUND COVERS

Aegopodium podagraria
Agapanthus
Arctostaphylos
Arctotheca calendula
Armeria maritima
Baccharis pilularis
Ceanothus
Cerastium tomentosum
Ceratostigma plumbaginoides
Chamaemelum nobile
Cistus
Coronilla varia
Cotoneaster
Duchesnea indica
Epimedium
Erigeron karvinskianus
Gazania
Genista
Helianthemum nummularium
Hypericum calycinum
Juniperus
Lantana
Liriope spicata
Mahonia
Nepeta × faassenii
Oenothera speciosa
Osteospermum fruticosum
Pelargonium peltatum
Phyla nodiflora
Polygonum capitatum
Potentilla neumanniana
Pyracantha
Rhus aromatica
Rosmarinus officinalis
Santolina
Stachys byzantina
Taxus baccata
Teucrium chamaedrys
Vancouveria
Vinca

COUNTERCLOCKWISE FROM TOP: *Erigeron karvin-skianus; Polygonum capitatum; Santolina chamaecyparissus; Phyla nodiflora*

Hemerocallis

# PERENNIALS FOR MASS PLANTINGS

*Here are seven favorite perennials that can also serve as ground covers; gazania (page 62) is another good choice. Set plants close enough so that foliage overlaps slightly to form a solid cover. Most can remain in place for many years; clumps will increase in size without losing vigor.*

AGAPANTHUS. Lily-of-the-Nile. Evergreen and deciduous. Zones vary. Full sun or light shade where summers are mild; needs light afternoon shade in hot-summer regions. In summer, fountainlike clumps of strap-shaped leaves send up flower stalks bearing blue or white blossoms in expanded clusters that look like bursts of fireworks. Several evergreen kinds thrive in Zones 7–9, 12–31. Of these, 'Peter Pan' has a foot-high foliage mass and blue flowers on 1½-foot stems; 'Rancho White' and blue-flowered 'Queen Anne' have foliage to 1½ feet, stems to 2 feet. Largest of the evergreen kinds (foliage to 2 feet, stems to 5 feet) is *A. orientalis,* bearing blue or white blooms. Deciduous kinds for Zones 3–9, 12–21, 28–31, and warmest parts of 32 are 4- to 5-foot *A. inapertus,* with clusters of drooping blue flowers, and the Headbourne Hybrids, with blue or white blossoms on 2½-foot stems.

Lily-of-the-Nile grows in soils ranging from light to heavy. It performs best with regular water but is quite drought tolerant. In shaded locations, stems will lean toward the source of light. Space plants 1 to 1½ feet apart, depending on ultimate size.

ARMERIA maritima. Common thrift. Evergreen. Zones 1–9, 14–24, 33–43. Full sun. At first glance, common thrift could pass for fancy chives: clumps of linear leaves send up thin, 6- to 10-inch stems topped by tight clusters of blossoms in pink shades varying from pale pink to deep raspberry. The main

*Agapanthus*

*Armeria maritima*

*Bergenia cordifolia* 'Purpurea'

bloom time comes in spring, but in mild-winter, cool-summer climates, plants flower on and off throughout the year.

Common thrift performs well even in poor, sandy soil, but it must have good drainage if it is to thrive. Only plants in well-drained soil can take regular watering; it's safer to water moderately in dry regions, only sparingly where summers are rainy. Space plants about 8 inches apart.

BERGENIA. Evergreen. Zones 1–9, 12–24, 30–45. Partial to full shade; will take full sun in cool-summer areas. These superb foliage plants just happen to have flowers as well. Paddle-shaped leaves up to 1 foot long are carried on short leafstalks. Leaves are thick, almost rubbery, with a deeply veined surface; in cold weather, the normal rich green color often takes on a bronzy cast. Each plant grows from a thick, creeping rootstock to form a foliage rosette; clumps of these rosettes expand slowly and eventually reach 1½ feet high. The bell-shaped flowers are borne in dense spikes. Winter-blooming bergenia, *B. crassifolia,* has pale to deep pink flowers carried above wavy-edged leaves; heartleaf bergenia, *B. cordifolia,* bears its dark pink spring blossoms tucked into the foliage mass. Named hybrids have flowers in white, pink shades, and magenta purple.

Good soil and regular watering give best results, but plants are tough and will get by with poorer soil and less attention to watering. Space 1½ feet apart.

**HELLEBORUS orientalis.** Lenten rose. Evergreen. Zones 2–10, 14–24, 31–41. Partial to full shade; takes morning sun in cool-summer regions. Ruggedly elegant, bold-textured foliage forms mounding clumps to 1½ feet high. Each leaf has up to seven leathery leaflets (to 9 inches long) carried like outstretched fingers at the end of a long stalk. In late winter and early spring, branched flower clusters rise above the leaves, bearing nodding blooms with the simplicity of wild roses. Blossoms come in white, pink, or brownish purple, often with dark speckling in the center.

*Helleborus orientalis*

Give Lenten rose good, organically enriched soil, regular moisture, and dappled sun or high shade. Set plants about 16 inches apart.

**HEMEROCALLIS.** Daylily. Evergreen, semievergreen, or deciduous, depending on variety. All zones. Full sun or partial shade. In large drifts—or even as a bank cover on sloping ground—daylilies' fountainlike clumps of narrow, linear leaves look almost like ornamental grass. But in late spring, plantings come alive with lilylike, single or double blooms in dazzling colors: yellow, orange, red, maroon, creamy white, lavender, pink, and various two- and three-color combinations. Individual flowers last just one day, but since each blossom stalk carries numerous buds, there's a prolonged display. Size varies; you'll find foot-tall small- and miniature-flowered varieties as well as standard sorts with 2-foot (or taller) foliage clumps and 3- to 5-foot flower stems.

Plants are quite tolerant of neglect, but perform best with good soil and regular water. In partial shade, all flowers will face the source of light. Space 1 to 1½ feet apart, depending on ultimate size.

**HOSTA.** Plantain lily. Deciduous. Zones 1–10, 12–21, 28, 31–45. Partial to full shade; will take considerable sun where summers are cool. All hostas have handsome leaves carried at the ends of elongated leafstalks that radiate from the center of a clump, forming a mound of leaves that overlap in shinglelike fashion. Leaf sizes, shapes, textures, colors, and markings are infinitely varied. Colors run through shades of green to nearly gold, gray, and blue, often with variegations in white, cream, or gold. Texture may be smooth, veined, puckered, or quilted; the surface is sometimes glossy, sometimes covered with a powdery bloom. Leaf shape ranges from nearly linear to nearly circular, leaf size from around 2 inches to well over a foot; total plant size varies from several inches to 3 feet high and wide. Bell-shaped summer flowers come in white, lilac, and violet; in some varieties they are held on slender stems well above the leaves, while in others they barely top the leaves and are somewhat lost among them.

Good soil, regular moisture, and a humid atmosphere (either cool or warm) are important for success with hostas. Where necessary, protect foliage from slugs and snails. Set plants 8 to 18 inches apart, depending on ultimate size.

**IBERIS sempervirens.** Evergreen candytuft. Zones 1–24, 31–45. Full sun; light afternoon shade where summers are hot. In full spring flower, a candytuft planting is a sheet of sparkling, detergent-clean white. Individual flowers are tiny, but they are packed into 2-inch, flattened clusters. Spreading plants reach 1 foot high and wide, densely clothed in narrow, dark green leaves to 1½ inches long. Numerous named selections are available. 'Alexander's White', 'Kingwood Compact', and 'Little Gem' grow no higher than 6 inches; 'Purity' and 'Snowflake' spread considerably wider than their 1-foot height; 'Autumn Snow' flowers again in fall.

Well-drained soil is crucial. In cool-summer regions, plants can get by on moderate watering; where summers are hot, regular watering is needed. To keep plantings tidy, remove spent flowers after bloom. When plantings start to decline, dig them out and begin again with new plants. Space plants about 1 foot apart.

*Hosta*

*Iberis sempervirens*

# FAST-GROWING PLANTS

When you want results *now*, choose the vines and ground covers below. Some grow so quickly they almost seem to climb or spread while you watch; others aren't quite so speedy, but will cover or fill in within a few years of planting.

## VINES

*Akebia quinata*
*Allamanda cathartica*
*Ampelopsis brevipedunculata*

*Rosa banksiae* 'Lutea'

Annual vines (pages 40 – 41)
*Antigonon leptopus*
*Aristolochia macrophylla*
*Asparagus*
*Bignonia capreolata*
*Bougainvillea*
*Campsis*
*Celastrus*
*Cissus*

*Clematis armandii,*
*  C. montana*
*Clytostoma callistegioides*
*Distictis*
*Hedera*
*Humulus lupulus*
*Ipomoea*
*Jasminum*
*Lonicera* (most)
*Macfadyena unguis-cati*
*Millettia reticulata*
*Parthenocissus* (most)
*Passiflora*
*Petrea volubilis*
*Polygonum*
*Pyrostegia venusta*
*Rosa*
*Senecio confusus*
*Solanum jasminoides*
*Stigmaphyllon*
*Tecomaria capensis*
*Thunbergia*
*Vitis*
*Wisteria*

## GROUND COVERS

*Aegopodium podagraria*
*Ajuga reptans*
*Arctotheca calendula*
*Asarum caudatum*
*Baccharis pilularis*
*Campanula poscharskyana*
*Ceanothus*
*Cerastium tomentosum*
*Ceratostigma plumbaginoides*
*Coronilla varia*
*Cotoneaster* (some)
*Duchesnea indica*
*Erigeron karvinskianus*
*Forsythia* 'Arnold Dwarf'
*Fragaria chiloensis*
*Galium odoratum*
*Gazania*
*Hippocrepis comosa*
*Houttuynia cordata*
*Lantana*
*Oenothera speciosa*
*Osteospermum fruticosum*
*Pelargonium peltatum*
*Phyla nodiflora*
*Polygonum*
*Potentilla neumanniana*
*Ranunculus repens*
*Vinca major*

COUNTERCLOCKWISE FROM TOP LEFT:
*Bougainvillea* 'Rosenka'; *Clematis armandii; Clytostoma callistegioides; Osteospermum fruticosum* 'African Queen'; *Gazania; Campanula poscharskyana*

# EVERGREEN FOLIAGE

Where winter chill is mild or lacking, evergreen plants (broad-leafed sorts in particular) dominate the landscape. In the warmest of these regions, in fact, anything that *isn't* evergreen looks out of place. The vines and ground covers listed here are guaranteed to maintain a presentable amount of foliage throughout the year.

## VINES

*Allamanda cathartica*

*Asparagus*

*Beaumontia grandiflora*

*Bignonia capreolata*

*Bougainvillea*

*Bougainvillea*

*Cissus*

*Clematis armandii*

*Clerodendrum thomsoniae*

*Clytostoma callistegioides*

*Cocculus carolinus*
 (in milder climates)

*Distictis*

*Euonymus fortunei*

× *Fatshedera lizei*

*Ficus pumila*

*Gelsemium sempervirens*

*Hardenbergia*

*Hedera*

*Hibbertia scandens*

*Ipomoea* (perennial kinds)

*Jasminum* (some)

*Kadsura japonica*

*Lapageria rosea*

*Lonicera* (some)

*Macfadyena unguis-cati*
 (in milder climates)

*Mandevilla* (most)

*Millettia reticulata*

*Pandorea*

*Passiflora* (some)

*Petrea volubilis*

*Podranea ricasoliana*
 (in milder climates)

*Polygonum*
 (in milder climates)

*Pyrostegia venusta*

*Senecio confusus*
 (in milder climates)

*Solandra maxima*

*Solanum* (most)

*Sollya heterophylla*

*Stephanotis floribunda*

*Stigmaphyllon*

*Tecomaria capensis*

*Thunbergia*, perennial kinds
 (in milder climates)

*Trachelospermum*

## GROUND COVERS

Agapanthus (some)

Ajuga reptans

Arctostaphylos

Arctotheca calendula

Ardisia japonica

Arenaria montana

Armeria maritima

Asarum (some)

Baccharis pilularis

Bergenia

Calluna vulgaris

Campanula

Carissa macrocarpa

Ceanothus

Cerastium tomentosum

Chamaemelum nobile

Chrysogonum virginianum
   (in milder climates)

Cistus

Cotoneaster (some)

Duchesnea indica

Epimedium (some)

Erica

Erigeron karvinskianus

Fragaria chiloensis

Galium odoratum

Gaultheria procumbens

Gazania

Genista lydia

Helianthemum
   nummularium

Helleborus orientalis

Hemerocallis (some)

Hippocrepis comosa

Hypericum calycinum

Iberis sempervirens

Juniperus

Lamium maculatum
   (in milder climates)

Lantana

Liriope spicata

Mahonia

Myosotis scorpioides

Nandina domestica

Nepeta × faassenii
   (in milder climates)

Ophiopogon japonicus

Osteospermum fruticosum

Pachysandra terminalis

Paxistima canbyi

Pelargonium peltatum

Phyla nodiflora

Pleioblastus

Polygonum
   (in milder climates)

Potentilla neumanniana

Pratia

Prunella

Pyracantha

Rosmarinus officinalis

Rubus pentalobus

Sagina subulata

Santolina

Sarcococca hookerana
   humilis

Stachys byzantina
   (in milder climates)

Taxus baccata

Teucrium chamaedrys

Vancouveria
   (in milder climates)

Vinca

Viola (most)

COUNTERCLOCKWISE FROM TOP LEFT: *Hardenbergia violacea; Distictis buccinatoria; Gelsemium sempervirens; Mahonia aquifolium* 'Compacta'; *Pachysandra terminalis* 'Green Sheen'; *Helianthemum nummularium*

# SMALL-SPACE GROUND COVERS

*Some inherently good ground covers don't work well in large spaces. Either they're too fine-textured to be effective, or they're impractical because they need periodic rejuvenation to remain dense. But in small patches, where they can be appreciated at close range, their beauty will stand out and maintenance will be easy to manage.*

*Stachys byzantina*

ARENARIA **montana.** Evergreen. Zones 1–9, 14–24, 32–45. Full sun; light afternoon shade where summers are hot. At bloom time (from mid- to late spring and into summer), plantings are sheets of glistening white, 1-inch blossoms. Lax, thread-thin stems bear gray-green, narrow, ¾-inch leaves that form a carpet about 4 inches high. Stems root as they spread.

Set plants 1 foot apart in well-drained soil. Give regular water, but be sure to avoid overwatering in heavy soil, in winter, and in humid-summer regions.

CHAMAEMELUM **nobile.** Chamomile. Evergreen. Zones 1–24, 30–43. Full sun or partial shade. Low, dense growth and finely cut bright green leaves make this one useful as a green carpet or even a small-scale lawn substitute. In summer, plants produce small, buttonlike yellow flowers like daisies without petals (some varieties bear small white daisies). Stems root as they spread, making a solid "turf" up to 1 foot high; mow or shear occasionally to maintain a uniformly low surface. 'Treneague', a nonblooming variety that grows only 3 inches high (and thus needs no mowing), makes a good "living mortar" between stepping-stones. Foliage of all varieties emits a pleasant, applelike scent when bruised or stepped on.

*Arenaria montana*

*Chamaemelum nobile*

Growth is best in well-drained, light to medium soil. Chamomile is deep rooted and needs only moderate water (even less where summers are cool). Set plants 1 foot apart.

LAMIUM **maculatum.** Dead nettle. Deciduous in all but mild-winter areas. Zones 1–24, 32–43. Partial to full shade in mild-summer areas; must have full shade where summers are warm to hot and dry. Sprawling stems root as they spread, forming a foliage mass to about 6 inches high; the furry, 2-inch-long leaves are heart shaped and distinctly veined. In late spring or summer, small, hooded, typically pink flowers bloom on short spikes above the foliage. Named varieties feature silver-variegated or chartreuse foliage, pink or white flowers.

*Lamium maculatum*

Set plants 1 to 1½ feet apart in good, well-drained soil, in a spot where they'll receive regular moisture during dry periods. Growth is best in cool regions, less satisfactory in hot, humid climates.

NEPETA × **faassenii.** Catmint. Evergreen to deciduous. Zones 1–24, 30, 32–43. Full sun. Throughout the growing season, plantings are dense, undulating, foot-tall carpets of gray-green foliage; oval, textured leaves to 1½ inches long are pleasantly aromatic and, as the name suggests, attractive to cats. From midspring into summer, spikes of small flowers envelop plantings in a lavender blue haze. Plants are evergreen in milder areas but die back where winters are cold.

Catmint needs only average, well-drained soil and moderate watering. Set plants 1½ feet apart. After bloom, you can shear off spent flower spikes for neatness; this can stimulate a second (but less lavish) flowering. Just as growth is beginning in late winter or early spring, cut out all of the last year's growth to make way for new stems.

PRATIA. Evergreen. Zones 4–9, 14–24. Full sun or partial shade where summers are mild; must have partial shade in hot-summer regions. Creeping plants hug the ground to make lush, dense carpets of tiny, rounded to oval, glossy leaves; stems root at leaf joints. Low, flowing growth and tolerance of the occasional footstep make them good choices for fillers between paving stones. Dark green, ½-inch leaves of *P. angulata* set off small, lobelialike, white to ice blue summer flowers. Blue star creeper, *P. pedunculata*, is generally sold under its former name, *Laurentia fluviatilis;* its bright green, ¼-inch-long leaves form a backdrop for equally tiny, star-shaped pale blue blossoms in late spring and summer.

Give good, well-drained soil, regular water, and periodic fertilizing. Set plants 8 to 12 inches apart.

PRUNELLA. Self-heal. Evergreen. Zones 1–24, 29–43. Full sun or light shade. Upright spikes of hooded summer flowers clearly show this plant's relationship to ajuga (page 35), but the foliage mass is higher and somewhat coarser. Clumps of pointed-oval, 2- to 4-inch, textured leaves spread by underground stems. The largest species is *P. grandiflora*, with 4-inch leaves and 1½-foot flower stems; purple is the standard color, but there are lilac, pink, and white varieties. Smaller *P. webbiana* (2-inch leaves, 1-foot flower stems) comes in the same color assortment. Purple-flowered *P. vulgaris* is similar in size and height to *P. webbiana;* its volunteer seedlings sometimes make it a garden pest.

Though rugged and deep rooted, the self-heals look their best with average to good soil and regular moisture. Set plants

*Nepeta × faassenii*

*Prunella grandiflora*

*Pratia angulata*

*Sagina subulata* 'Aurea'

1 foot apart. After bloom, shear off spent flower spikes to keep plantings neat and prevent seed formation.

SAGINA subulata. Irish moss, Scotch moss. Evergreen. Zones 1–11, 14–24, 32–43. Full sun or partial shade. Although undeniably mosslike, these "mosses" actually are two separate flowering plants (*Minuartia verna*—formerly *Arenaria verna*—and *Sagina subulata*) so similar that they are interchangeable in the garden. Both bear tiny white flowers, but those of the former come in small clusters, while those of the latter appear individually. Green-foliaged plants of both are sold as Irish moss; golden green *Sagina subulata* 'Aurea' is sold as Scotch moss. Both are often used between paving stones; in larger patches, plantings tend to become lumpy.

Unlike true mosses, these plants need good, well-drained soil. They're usually sold in flats; to plant, cut into 3-inch squares and plant the pieces 6 inches apart, with edges of squares level with or slightly lower than the soil surface. If a planting becomes unattractively lumpy, cut narrow strips out of it, then press the remaining "turf" flat.

STACHYS byzantina. Lamb's ears. Evergreen to deciduous. Zones 1–24, 29–43. Full sun; some afternoon shade in hot-summer areas. The thick, furry gray-green leaves explain the common name. These feltlike leaves grow to 6 inches long on plants that spread by creeping, rooting stems to form dense colonies; plants are evergreen in mild-winter areas but die back where winters are cold. In late spring to early summer, clumps send up 1- to 1½-foot stems bearing tiered whorls of lavender blossoms; cut flower stems off after bloom to maintain neatness. For ground cover use, flowerless 'Silver Carpet' is the best choice; plantings of this variety stay dense, whereas flowering forms tend to develop bare patches where plants bloomed.

Lamb's ears demands only well-drained soil and moderate watering. Set plants about 16 inches apart.

# PLANTS FOR HILLSIDES AND EROSION CONTROL

Growing a lawn on bare, sloping ground is a stiff challenge—yet such sites call out for some sort of foliage cover. Fortunately, a number of vines and ground covers fill the bill. Many vines can simply be planted at the top of a slope and allowed to drape their meandering stems downward to form a blanket of foliage. If you choose a shrubby or perennial ground cover, though, you'll need a higher-density planting to achieve good coverage. Plants marked with an asterisk (*) have root systems that can thoroughly infiltrate the soil to combat erosion.

## VINES

*Akebia quinata*

*Cissus*

*Euonymus fortunei**

*Gelsemium sempervirens*

*Hedera**

*Hibbertia scandens*

*Jasminum* (some)

*Lonicera japonica*

*Macfadyena unguis-cati**

*Parthenocissus henryana,*
   *P. quinquefolia*

*Passiflora mollissima*

*Polygonum*

*Rosa* (some)

*Senecio confusus*

*Sollya heterophylla*

*Stigmaphyllon littorale*

*Tecomaria capensis*

*Trachelospermum **

*Wisteria*

TOP TO BOTTOM: *Gelsemium sempervirens; Jasminum nitidum; Sollya heterophylla*

*Ceanothus griseus horizontalis* 'Yankee Point'

## GROUND COVERS

*Arctostaphylos\**

*Arctotheca calendula*

*Baccharis pilularis*

*Calluna vulgaris*

*Carissa macrocarpa*

*Ceanothus\**

*Cistus\**

*Coronilla varia\**

*Cotoneaster\**

*Duchesnea indica*

*Erica*

*Forsythia* 'Arnold Dwarf'

*Fragaria chiloensis*

*Genista*

*Hippocrepis comosa\**

*Hypericum calycinum\**

Ice plants (pages 68–69)

*Juniperus\**

*Lantana\**

*Mahonia*

*Oenothera speciosa*

*Osteospermum fruticosum*

*Pelargonium peltatum*

*Pleioblastus\**

*Polygonum capitatum\**

*Pyracantha*

*Rhus aromatica\**

*Rosmarinus officinalis\**

*Santolina*

*Vinca\**

TOP TO BOTTOM: *Baccharis pilularis* 'Twin Peaks'; *Oenothera speciosa;*
*Hypericum calycinum*

## VINES AND GROUND COVERS

# ENCYCLOPEDIA

*Enter the realm of vines and ground covers and you'll encounter a diverse group of garden ornaments and problem solvers—plants that can turn trouble spots into lovely cloaks or carpets of greenery and bloom. The following 66 pages introduce you to dozens of choices—some of them widely known, others deserving of broader recognition, and still others that are stellar performers within rather limited climate ranges. Working from these descriptions and the photos accompanying them, you'll be able to narrow your selections to the vines and ground covers that meet your needs.*

*Most of these plants are noted for ease of culture. But no matter how vigorous, tough, or abuse resistant a particular individual may be, it must suit the climate and its garden location if it is to achieve its full potential (or even survive). As you evaluate each plant, think about its adaptability and cultural needs as well as its beauty. Remember, too, that even properly chosen plants, no matter how carefree they are supposed to be, need at least a modicum of routine attention after planting until their roots are well established.*

Climbing roses and large-flowered hybrid clematis are a favorite vining duet.

*Actinidia kolomikta*

# VINES AND GROUND COVERS
## READING THE ENTRIES

*In the profiles that follow, you'll find a description of each plant as well as advice on its care. Each entry begins with the plant's botanical name, followed by its common name (if there is one). The next line tells you whether the plant is a vine (🌿), ground cover (🌿), or both, and if it is evergreen (its foliage is present all year), semievergreen (it loses some leaves in fall), or deciduous (it drops all leaves in fall). Plants described as "evergreen to deciduous" are typically evergreen in the warmer parts of their range, deciduous in cooler areas. This line also notes whether the plant is woody or perennial. Woody-stemmed plants form a more or less permanent structure; perennials have fleshy stems that may or may not die to the ground each year. The few plants described as "shrubby perennials" have longer-lived, fairly stiff stems but no true wood.*

*The next line, introduced with 🌿, indicates the climate zones where the plant will grow. For details, turn to the zone map and descriptions on pages 108–111.*

*Preferred exposure is noted in the next line. ☼ indicates bright, unshaded sun; ● means no direct sun at all. ◑ describes plants that do equally well in partial shade (a spot that's sunny in the morning, shaded in the afternoon), light shade (no direct sun but plenty of light), or dappled sun (mixed shafts of sun and shade, as under a canopy of lath or beneath a high-branching tree).*

*Finally, moisture needs are identified. ◐ indicates a preference for regular water: the plant always needs moisture, but soil shouldn't remain saturated. ◌ describes plants that must have some moisture, but soil can become somewhat dry to quite dry between waterings. ◐◐ means the plant needs ample water and will grow even in soggy soil.*

*Sollya heterophylla*

## ACTINIDIA

🌿 DECIDUOUS WOODY VINES

🌿 ZONES VARY BY SPECIES

☼ ◑ SUN OR PARTIAL SHADE

◐◐ REGULAR TO MODERATE WATER

Among *Actinidia* species, three large-leafed, bold-textured vines offer varied attractions: one has unusually colorful foliage, while the other two are noted for their delicious fruit. In all species, male and female flowers appear on separate plants—a fact to keep in mind if you want a crop of fruit. The twining vines develop fairly thick trunks and heavy limbs that require sturdy support or attachments.

Flamboyant foliage is the outstanding feature of *A. kolomikta*, suited to Zones 2–9, 15–17, 31–41. The 5-inch leaves, shaped like elongated hearts, may be solid green, white-splashed green, or green strikingly variegated in pink to red. Variegated forms show the best color variety and intensity in cool weather and, in warmer regions, when grown in partial shade. Because male plants are reputed to have better foliage than females, they are generally the kind sold. Reaching as high as 15 feet, the vines bear small, fragrant white flowers in early summer; if plants of both sexes grow near one another, the female vine may later produce inch-long, sweet-tasting yellow fruits.

*Actinidia deliciosa*

Kiwi (Chinese gooseberry), *A. deliciosa*, grows in Zones 4–9, 12, 14–24, 29–31. If you grow both male and female plants, you're assured a crop of fuzzy brown, egg-sized fruits with delicious green flesh that tastes something like a blend of strawberry, melon, and banana. Sizable vines can reach 30 feet, outfitted in broadly oval, 5- to 8-inch leaves that are dark green on the surface, furry white beneath; new growth is covered in reddish fuzz. Creamy beige, 1½-inch flowers come in summer; fruit ripens in mid- to late fall. 'Chico' and 'Hayward' both bear excellent fruit; in the mildest-winter zones, look for 'Vincent'.

Hardy kiwi, *A. arguta*, grows in Zones 2–10, 12, 14–24, 28, 31–41. Though its vines can grow as large as those of kiwi (above), this species has a finer-textured appearance. Leaves, flowers, and fruit are all smaller—leaves reach 3 to 6 inches long, fuzzless fruits just 1½ inches (they're borne in large clusters, though). Female varieties 'Ananasnaja' and 'Hood River' need a pollinator; 'Issai' (not always easy to locate) is self-fertile.

All the above species grow best in good, well-drained soil. They appreciate regular moisture during the growing season, though they can get by with moderate watering. Train vigorous new stems into place as they lengthen; prune and thin vines in winter while they are leafless. Fruit comes on shoots that are at least 1 year old; on dormant stems, fruiting buds appear knoblike, while foliage buds are flat.

# AEGOPODIUM podagraria
BISHOP'S WEED, GOUT WEED

- DECIDUOUS PERENNIAL GROUND COVER
- ZONES 1–9, 12, 14–24, 30–45
- SUN OR SHADE
- MODERATE WATER

Beauty, vigor, a strong constitution, and the ability to thrive in shade—bishop's weed offers them all. Plants spread by underground stems to form a lush, foothigh green carpet of three-leafleted leaves similar to those of box elder *(Acer negundo)*—hence another common name, "ground elder." More frequently planted than the species is 'Variegatum', with gray-green leaves irregularly margined in white. Flat-topped clusters of inconsequential flowers appear above the leaves on slender stems in summer. In well-watered gardens, self-sowing can lead to quantities of unwanted volunteer seedlings; if possible, cut or shear off flowering stems before they set seed.

Average soil, moderate watering, and a little winter chill are all bishop's weed needs for good growth. Set out plants from pots about 1 foot apart. In hot-summer regions, 'Variegatum' should receive light shade during the hottest part of the day,

*Aegopodium podagraria* 'Variegatum'

since the leaf margins may burn and look unattractive if plants are grown in full sun.

A planting of bishop's weed will expand limitlessly unless you curb it. To establish control, install wood, concrete, or metal barriers that extend 8 to 12 inches into the soil. If a planting appears uneven or shabby during the growing season, mow or shear it to stimulate new growth.

*Ajuga reptans*

# AJUGA reptans
CARPET BUGLE

- EVERGREEN PERENNIAL GROUND COVER
- ZONES 1–24, 26–45
- SUN OR PARTIAL SHADE
- REGULAR WATER

Carpet bugle is one of the best-loved low ground covers. It forms an even foliage carpet and spreads rapidly, and numerous varieties are available with different leaf colors, patterns, and sizes. As a beautiful bonus, showy flower spikes provide seasonal color.

The basic species has lustrous dark green leaves with a quilted appearance. Each oval to tongue-shaped leaf is 2 to 3 inches wide in sun, up to 4 inches wide in shade; the entire foliage mass tops out at around 4 inches high. Six-inch-tall spikes of blue flowers appear in spring and early summer. Each plant sends out runners that terminate in new plants, letting a planting advance to cover a considerable area.

Many named varieties are sold, some of them (unfortunately) under more than one name. The names usually give a clue to foliage or flower color. 'Alba' and 'Rosea' are, respectively, white- and pink-flowered forms. 'Purpurea' ('Atropurpurea') has bronze-tinted green leaves; leaves of 'Variegata' are splashed and margined with creamy yellow. 'Burgundy Lace' ('Burgundy Glow') features white and pink variegation on reddish purple leaves. Some varieties, such as 'Pink Silver' and 'Silver Carpet', present distinctly silver-sheened leaves. Sorts with the words "giant" and "jungle" in their names have larger leaves, higher foliage masses (some reaching 9 inches tall in shade), and taller flower spikes; both green- and purple-leafed forms are available.

Given regular watering to keep its shallow roots moist and an annual application of fertilizer at the start of the growing period, carpet bugle spreads rapidly. Set plants from pots or flats about 1 foot apart; full sun is acceptable where summers are cool, but in warmer climates, choose a spot in partial or light shade. Plant in well-drained soil, since root rots and fungus diseases can afflict plantings in heavy soils where roots can become waterlogged. After flowering is over, you can mow plantings to restore a tidy, even surface. When bare patches appear and vigor declines, dig plants, amend the soil, and replant healthy divisions.

# AKEBIA quinata
FIVELEAF AKEBIA

- Semievergreen to deciduous woody vine or ground cover
- Zones 3–24, 29–41
- Sun or shade
- Regular water

Distinctive, attractive flowers and fruit make this vine a certain conversation piece, but in the landscape it is valued chiefly for its lovely, fine-textured foliage. Even a large vine has a delicate look. Each leaf resembles a cloverleaf, with five oval leaflets up to 2 inches long radiating out from the end of a long leafstalk. Pendent clusters of vanilla-scented blossoms appear in spring. Female flowers (toward the cluster base) consist of three shell-like segments in an odd chocolate purple color; smaller male flowers in rosy

*Akebia quinata*

purple appear farther down. Purplish, sausage-shaped, 4-inch fruits—edible but insipid—may appear in summer. Both flowers and fruit are somewhat obscured by the foliage. White- and pink-flowered forms exist but are not widely available.

The vigorous stems easily twine to 30 feet if given some support; arbors, walls, and trees are all suitable. The plant also makes a fine ground cover (to about 1 foot high) for large spaces and (especially) for sloping ground. If you use it this way, try to locate it on its own, since it is likely to overwhelm any plants (other than trees) in its path. Set out plants from 1-gallon cans about 6 feet apart.

Fiveleaf akebia is semievergreen in the mildest areas; elsewhere, all leaves drop in fall. It grows readily in average, well-drained soil. Do major thinning and pruning during winter. Thin out superfluous and tangling stems while plants are growing actively.

*Akebia quinata*

# ALLAMANDA cathartica
GOLDEN TRUMPET

- Evergreen woody vine
- Zones 24–27
- Sun
- Regular water

In warm climates where winters are virtually frost-free, golden trumpet puts on a show second to none. The yellow-flowered vine's looks reveal its relationship to the familiar shrubby oleander: clusters of trumpet-shaped blossoms appear among whorls of glossy, leathery, narrow leaves to 6 inches long. Flowers

*Allamanda cathartica* 'Hendersonii'

(each up to 5 inches across) appear over much of the year. The vine is vigorous and far-reaching, achieving heights of over 50 feet; it can clamber through trees, but it must be tied to other supports. 'Hendersonii' has orange-yellow flowers opening from brown buds.

Golden trumpet is not fussy about soil, but it does need regular moisture. Frequent fertilizing stimulates vigorous growth and bloom.

*Note:* As is true for oleander, all parts of golden trumpet are poisonous if ingested.

## AMPELOPSIS
brevipedunculata
PORCELAIN BERRY

- DECIDUOUS WOODY VINE
  - ZONES 2–24, 28–41
  - SUN OR SHADE
  - REGULAR TO MODERATE WATER

A close relative of *Parthenocissus* (page 80), this vine bears similar grapelike leaves and fruits on plants of great vigor. What's missing is the flaming fall foliage display—but in exchange, you get a late summer-to-autumn show of clustered, pealike fruits that ripen from greenish ivory to lavender to striking metallic blue. Broad, three-lobed leaves reach 5 inches wide; foliage cover is just open enough to show off the fruit. Vines climb 20 to 30 feet by stem tendrils, but mature plants are heavy and need the strong support of an arbor or pergola (or strong attachments to walls). The fruits are a favorite among some birds, which can result in numerous volunteer seedlings. Japanese beetles may cause damage to foliage.

Porcelain berry isn't fussy about soil type. It prefers regular moisture, but established plants do quite well with only moderate watering during the growing period. Do any significant pruning and thinning to shape during the leafless winter months. During the growing season, thin out excess growth as needed.

*Ampelopsis brevipedunculata*

*Antigonon leptopus*

## ANTIGONON leptopus
CORAL VINE, QUEEN'S WREATH

- DECIDUOUS PERENNIAL VINE
  - ZONES 12, 13, 18–30
  - SUN
  - REGULAR TO MODERATE WATER

Where summers are hot and long, coral vine builds into a mammoth froth (to 40 feet tall) of foliage and flowers. Light green, arrowhead-shaped leaves to 5 inches long make a coarse-textured, pleasantly airy cover. From summer into early fall, small, papery, hot pink flowers bloom in long, branched sprays that terminate in tendrils. With some nursery searching, you can find white-blossomed 'Album' and nearly red 'Baja Red'. Only in frostless regions is coral vine evergreen; elsewhere, stems are killed completely at some point during winter.

Coral vine needs no more than average, well-drained soil for good growth. Greatest vigor and bloom come in warm to hot areas; bloom is poor where summers are cool. In the desert, vines need regular water to stay in best condition. On a fence or wall, provide wire mesh or netting for support. Or train a vine onto an arbor to create shade over an outdoor-living area. Where vines are killed to the ground by frost, remove dead stems from their support before new growth emerges from the ground in spring.

APTENIA. See page 68

## ARCTOSTAPHYLOS
MANZANITA

- EVERGREEN WOODY GROUND COVERS
  - ZONES VARY BY SPECIES
  - SUN OR PARTIAL SHADE
  - MODERATE TO LITTLE WATER

The manzanitas forgo showiness in favor of a year-round neat appearance. The small, thick, leathery leaves are glossy and fresh looking at all times; many species have smooth, red to purple bark on main stems. Stems typically root all along their length as they grow. Clusters of small (less than ½-inch), urn-shaped, white or pink flowers bloom in late winter to early spring; later in the year, these may be followed by small, round fruits.

The most widely grown species is *A. uva-ursi*, bearberry or kinnikinnick. Native to northern latitudes in North America, Asia, and Europe, it will grow in Zones 1–9, 14–24, 34, 36–45. Plants form a dense foot-high mat that spreads at a moderate rate, ultimately covering a wide area.

*Arctostaphylos uva-ursi* 'Wood's Red'

Inch-long, bright green leaves can turn red in fall and winter; white or pink flowers are followed by pealike, pink to bright red fruits.

Some nurseries offer named selections of *A. uva-ursi* with special attributes. 'Alaska' and 'Massachusetts' are especially flat growers with small leaves; 'Vancouver Jade' is similarly low but less wide spreading, with jade green leaves that turn bronzy red in winter. 'Point Reyes' has plentiful dark foliage and is the most tolerant of heat and dryness. 'Radiant', with lighter green, more widely spaced leaves, and 'Wood's Red', with small deep green leaves, both produce reliable crops of large bright red fruits. >

*Arctostaphylos uva-ursi*

Western North America is home to a number of other species that are good ground covers within their native territory.

Similar to bearberry (and a hybrid of it) is *A. × media,* which grows in Zones 4–9, 14–24. It is faster growing and taller than its parent (to 2 feet high), with darker foliage and brighter red stems. Monterey manzanita, *A. hookeri,* also grows in Zones 4–9, 14–24. The basic species is a mounding-spreading shrub, but its selection 'Monterey Carpet' hugs the ground to about 1 foot high, growing at a moderate rate and spreading widely as branches take root. Glossy leaves are slightly less than an inch long; white to pink-tinted blossoms are followed by bright red fruits.

Little Sur manzanita, *A. edmundsii,* is a foot-tall species adapted to Zones 6–9, 14–24. Several named selections are good ground covers. 'Indian Hill' thrives in light shade; pink-flowered 'Parviflora' has bronze new growth and notably glossy foliage. Fast-growing 'Carmel Sur', with gray-green leaves and pink flowers, is more tolerant of moist soil than most other forms. 'Little Sur' is a low, slow grower with red-tinted leaves and pink flowers in early spring.

Also growing in Zones 6–9, 14–24 is the appropriately named *A.* 'Emerald Carpet'. Uniformity is its hallmark: ½-inch leaves in shiny bright green adorn a spreading plant that grows at a moderate rate, presenting a virtually flat

surface 8 to 14 inches high. Pale pink flowers bloom in early spring, but they aren't especially showy.

Set out young manzanita plants from pots or 1-gallon containers about 2 feet apart, then mulch thoroughly to suppress weeds and encourage rooting along stems. Well-drained, acid to neutral, sandy to loamy soil is best for all manzanitas. As a group, they have a low tolerance for waterlogged soil, which can rot roots and kill plants. In heavier soils where drainage is less than ideal, pay special attention to the timing of waterings. In all soils, water newly set plants often enough to keep soil moist while roots are establishing; thereafter, you can water just once or twice a month, adjusting for summer heat and dryness.

*Arctotheca calendula*

## ARCTOTHECA calendula
CAPE WEED

- ☀ EVERGREEN PERENNIAL GROUND COVER
- ✿ ZONES 8, 9, 13–24
- ☀ SUN
- ○ MODERATE TO LITTLE WATER

Supremely easy to grow and tough enough to be called indestructible, cape weed excels in sunny locations—even on hillsides and in poor soil—where you need a low, fast-growing cover. Elongated gray-green leaves are deeply cleft; plants are clumping but spread by runners to make a thick cover no higher than 1 foot. Yellow, 2-inch, gazanialike

flowers are most profuse in spring but can appear throughout the year.

Cape weed is not for small spaces, since the rapidly spreading plants soon invade surrounding territory (though they are easy to remove). Unfussy about soil, plants are similarly casual about water. Give new plantings regular water until they are established; moderate to little water (depending on heat and dryness) is sufficient thereafter. Set out plants from pots about 1½ feet apart. Mow shaggy plantings to tidy them up.

## ARDISIA japonica
MARLBERRY

- ☀ EVERGREEN WOODY GROUND COVER
- ✿ ZONES 5, 6, 15–17, 28–31
- ◑ ● PARTIAL TO FULL SHADE
- ♦ REGULAR WATER

Elegant foliage and seasonal color recommend marlberry for small, shaded areas. Leathery oval leaves to 4 inches long are bright green and glossy, clustered toward the tips of upright, 6- to 18-inch-tall stems. Small clusters of tiny white flowers appear among the leaves in mid- to late summer; these are followed by pea-size bright red fruits that sparkle throughout winter, untouched by birds. Plants spread by underground stems at a

*Ardisia japonica*

moderate to rapid rate, forming ever-expanding colonies. Several variegated forms exist, usually bearing Japanese names; most of these feature cream to white leaf margins, but leaves of 'Hinode' are green with a central yellow stripe.

This is a woodland plant, naturally preferring regular moisture and well-drained, organically enriched, acid to neutral soil. Set out plants from 1-gallon containers about 2 feet apart, in a location receiving partial to full shade.

*Aristolochia macrophylla*

*Aristolochia macrophylla*

# ARISTOLOCHIA
macrophylla
DUTCHMAN'S PIPE

- DECIDUOUS WOODY VINE
- ZONES 1–24, 29–43
- SUN OR SHADE
- AMPLE WATER

In bygone days, this was a favorite for screening a porch or other summertime outdoor living area. Fast growth (to 20 to 30 feet) and a dense, attractive foliage cover still make it an ideal "living wall," and the truly odd flowers are a certain conversation piece. Twining stems bear glossy dark green, kidney-shaped leaves that may reach 14 inches long; as the vine climbs, the leaves overlap one another like shingles to form a visually impenetrable surface. The early summer flowers are not profuse and are sequestered among the leaves—but they're well worth seeking out. Borne on a threadlike stalk is a yellowish green tube that curves upward, then flares out into three brownish purple lobes about an inch wide; in profile, the blossom looks like an old-fashioned pipe.

Average to good soil and plentiful water produce the fastest growth and largest leaves. For the best-looking foliage, avoid planting in windy locations. When vines become too tangled, thin out superfluous growth during winter.

*Note*: This plant was once known as *Aristolochia durior* and may still be sold under that name.

## ASARINA. See page 40

## ASARUM
WILD GINGER

- EVERGREEN AND DECIDUOUS PERENNIAL GROUND COVERS
- ZONES VARY BY SPECIES
- PARTIAL TO FULL SHADE
- AMPLE WATER

Given the shade and moisture they need, the wild gingers are among the lushest and most handsome of low ground covers. Leaves of all are carried atop long leafstalks and overlap to form a ground-concealing carpet. Unusual bell-shaped flowers, usually brownish purple in color, appear in spring but are largely hidden beneath the foliage. All species spread by creeping rhizomes; they expand their territory at a moderate rate unless otherwise noted.

Hailing from northeastern to central North America, *A. canadense* grows in Zones 1–6, 31–45. The deciduous dark green leaves are kidney shaped and up to 6 inches wide, making a foliage cover about 6 inches high. Almost as cold tolerant is evergreen *A. europaeum*, which grows in Zones 2–6, 32–43. It too has kidney-shaped, glossy dark green leaves, but they reach only about 3 inches across and make a cover about 5 inches high.

Native to western North America is *A. caudatum*, adapted to Zones 4–6, 14–24, 31, 32. It's a quickly spreading plant with heart-shaped, almost rubbery, dark green leaves about 6 inches across on 7-inch leafstalks. Foliage is evergreen where winters are mild, deciduous elsewhere.

Appalachian native *A. shuttleworthii* grows in Zones 4–6, 31–37, 39. Its evergreen, heart-shaped to rounded leaves, pleasingly mottled in silvery gray, are 4 inches across and carried about 8 inches above the ground. The species spreads rather slowly; its selection 'Callaway', with more elaborately marked leaves, is a faster grower.

All wild gingers need ample moisture for good growth. They do best in rich, organically amended, moisture-retentive soil, though they can thrive in well-drained (and well-amended) soil if given plenty of water and periodic applications of fertilizer. Set out plants from pots about 1 foot apart. For best appearance, protect from slugs and snails.

*Asarum europaeum* with narcissus

# ANNUAL VINES

*A number of all-time favorite vines are annuals—and no wonder. Starting from seeds planted early in the year, these plants grow quickly to flowering size, giving you both color and bountiful foliage from spring into autumn (except for cool-season* Lathyrus odoratus *and* Tropaeolum majus*). They succeed in all zones—and in the mildest regions, some will live from year to year as perennials. Grow them on trellises, posts, walls, and fences; the largest growers make a nice display on arbors. A few are even suited to ground cover use. Unless otherwise noted, all do best in a sunny location.*

*Lathyrus odoratus*

ASARINA (Climbing snapdragon, chickabiddy). You wouldn't mistake this for the traditional snapdragon (*Antirrhinum majus*) growing as a vine, but the spring-to-summer flowers do resemble the "snapless" (bell-shaped) sort of snapdragon bloom. The twining stems will climb string, wire, or sticks, clamber over the ground,

*Asarina scandens*

or spill over a retaining wall. Largest is *A. barclayana,* growing to 12 feet and bearing 2- to 3-inch flowers in white, pink, or purple. The same colors are available in somewhat smaller-flowered *A. scandens,* which reaches just 4 to 8 feet. *A. antirrhinifolia* may reach 6 feet, bearing 1-inch, yellow-throated flowers in lavender, violet, blue, and red. Best garden location for these plants is one that provides shade for their roots, sun for their tops. In Zones 17–27, plants are perennial.

COBAEA scandens (Cup-and-saucer vine). The actual petals are a broad-based, 2-inch, chalicelike cup; this rests on a circular, saucerlike green calyx. The cup is green at first, turning purple as it expands and ages; 'Alba' has white cups. Leaves are composed of two or three pairs of oval, 4-inch leaflets and a terminal tendril by which the vigorous vine will climb 20 to 25 feet, clinging not only to string or wire but even to rough surfaces.

Cup-and-saucer vine needs a long growing season for its midsummer-to-fall bloom, but seeds are likely to rot if planted outdoors in cool, damp soil. For best success, start seeds

*Cobaea scandens*

indoors in pots while weather is still cool; then plant out seedlings when conditions are warmer. In cool-summer regions, flowering won't begin until late summer. Vines are perennial in Zones 24–27; they bloom in midsummer the first year, from spring into fall in subsequent years.

DOLICHOS lablab (Hyacinth bean). This vine offers both colorful blooms and edible beans. Like the familiar vining snap beans, it's a twining climber (to about 10 feet) with leaves composed of three broadly oval, 3- to 6-inch-long leaflets. In spring and summer, loose clusters of purple, sweet pea–like flowers stand out from the vine on long stems; these are followed by 2½-inch-long beans in velvety magenta purple. A white-flowered form is available.

*Dolichos lablab*

IPOMOEA (Morning glory). Prominent among these annual relatives of perennial morning glories (see page 70) is the old-fashioned favorite *I. tricolor,* a vigorous twiner to 10 to 15 feet bearing heart-shaped leaves and the familiar funnel-shaped flowers 3 to 4 inches across. The traditional blue-flowered variety is 'Heavenly Blue', but there are other color choices, among them white 'Pearly Gates' and mixed-color strains including pink, crimson, purple, and lavender in addition to blue and white. Flowers open in the morning and close by afternoon (though they'll remain open all day when weather is overcast). *I. nil* looks much like *I. tricolor* in plant and blossom, and it too bears the common name "morning glory." The large-flowered (up to 6-inch-wide) Imperial Japanese strain belongs to this species; other selections include rosy red 'Scarlett O'Hara', the odd pinkish tan 'Chocolate', and the mixed-color Early Call strain.

*Ipomoea* Early Call

Cypress vine, *I. quamoclit,* is a complete departure from the preceding two species. The 20-foot vine has leaves up to 4 inches long, finely divided into threadlike segments; the scarlet, 1½-inch flowers are tubes that flare into five starlike points.

Seeds of all these vines have hard coats. For best germination, soak them in warm water overnight before planting. Where the growing season is short, start plants indoors, then set seedlings outside after danger of frost is past.

LATHYRUS odoratus (Sweet pea). Climbing to 5 feet or taller, this long-time charmer offers a winning combination of beauty, color, and fragrance. The silky, ruffled blossoms have the typical pea-flower form: an upright, rounded petal (the *standard*), two narrow side petals *(wings),* and two lower petals that form a boat-shaped *keel.* Borne in long-stemmed, upright clusters, the flow-

*Lathyrus odoratus*

ers come in cream, white, blue, purple, violet, red, pink, lavender, and in bicolor combinations of single colors with white or cream. Seed companies offer a number of strains and varieties.

Unlike many other annual vines, sweet peas are at their best in cool to mild weather; hot temperatures end their productivity. The planting time and variety best for you depend on your climate. In mild-winter, hot-summer areas, the early-flowering strains will bloom in winter from seed sown in late summer; spring-flowering strains planted from October to early January will bloom from spring until hot weather arrives. In regions with cool winters and warm to hot summers, plant seeds of spring-flowering strains as soon as soil is workable. Summer-flowering strains are best for regions with cold winters and warm (but not hot) and/or short summers.

To enhance germination, soak seeds in warm water for 24 hours before planting. Plant in good, well-amended soil; keep soil moist but not saturated. To prolong bloom, remove all spent flower clusters to keep seedpods from forming.

THUNBERGIA alata (Black-eyed Susan vine). Twining, 10-foot vines with triangular, 3-inch leaves stage a summer-

long show of Halloween colors. Bright orange flowers with black throats are slender, 1-inch tubes that flare out into five indented lobes. Yellow- and white-flowered varieties sometimes are available; if you prefer solid orange flowers, look for *T. gregorii,* known as orange clock vine. In all but the mildest-winter zones, start seeds indoors so plants will be ready to set out when frost danger is past. In Zones 23–27, vines may live from year to year as perennials.

*Thunbergia* also includes perennial vines; see page 94.

*Thunbergia alata* 'Aurantiaca'

TROPAEOLUM (Nasturtium). The garden nasturtium, *T. majus,* is a timeless favorite, so easy to grow that it's often used to introduce children to the joys of gardening. Vines climb to about 6 feet by coiling leafstalks; without support, they serve as colorful ground covers. Thick stems bear almost rubbery, virtually circular leaves that look rather like waterlily pads; the long leafstalk connects off-center. Foliage is edible and adds a tangy, watercresslike flavor to salads. Shallow-throated flowers reach nearly 3 inches across; each has five spreading lobes and a spur projecting from behind. Orange is the traditional color, but choices also include creamy white, yellow, red, red brown, and maroon. Best performance is in cool and mild weather; heat stops growth. In the mildest-winter regions, plant the pealike seeds in fall for bloom in winter and spring (and into summer, in cool coastal gardens). Elsewhere, plant seeds in late winter or early spring.

*Tropaeolum majus*

Canary bird flower, *T. peregrinum,* will climb or scramble to 15 feet if given its preferred location in light shade. Leaves are a deeply lobed version of garden nasturtium foliage; they look something like small fig

*Tropaeolum peregrinum*

leaves. Yellow, 1-inch flowers are oddly constructed, with two deeply fringed lobes the most conspicuous feature. Sow seeds in early spring. Plants flower through summer until stopped by frost, and may be perennial in Zones 24–27.

## ASPARAGUS

🌿 EVERGREEN PERENNIAL VINES

✂ ZONES 12–28

☀ ◑ SUN OR PARTIAL SHADE

💧 REGULAR WATER

If the only asparagus you know is the edible kind, these clambering plants will hardly seem like members of the same group! But if you've seen edible asparagus plantings in the months after harvest, the ultra-fine-textured foliage may have a familiar look. In fact, the true leaves are so minute as to be absent; what look like leaves (and are referred to as such in the descriptions) are flattened branches *(cladodes)* which take on the

*Asparagus setaceus*

appearance and function of leaves. Both the species described here are used for cut greenery in floral arrangements; both bear tiny white flowers followed by pea-like, dark blue to black fruits.

Smilax asparagus, *A. asparagoides*, sends up slender, branched stems that can climb to 20 feet. Stiff, inch-long, sharp-pointed leaves are broadly ovate, with a lacquerlike sheen. 'Myrtifolius' is a smaller-growing variety with smaller leaves. Stems must be tied to a support or threaded through the openwork of wire mesh or trellis. Established vines need

periodic thinning to relieve the accumulated tangle of stems and branches.

Its common name—fern asparagus—well describes *A. setaceus* (formerly *A. plumosus*). Dark green sprays reminiscent of elaborate fern fronds contain countless truly tiny leaves. Wiry, spiny stems climb 10 to 20 feet if supported by (and initially tied to) wire or trellis.

Both smilax and fern asparagus grow from clumps of fleshy, tenacious roots. For best results, plant in good, organically enriched soil and provide regular moisture. (Though the plants will endure erratic watering and periods of drought thanks to their fleshy roots, they won't look particularly good.) In cool-summer regions, the vines are attractive in sun as well as light or partial shade; in warmer-summer locations, some shade is best. Avoid heavy shade, though: leaves will turn yellow. Fertilize plants in early spring and thin out old, ratty stems before new growth begins. Use either species to decorate a post or pillar or to create a foliage screen.

## BACCHARIS pilularis
### DWARF COYOTE BRUSH

🪴 EVERGREEN WOODY GROUND COVER

✂ ZONES 5–11, 14–24

☀ SUN

💧💧 💧 REGULAR TO LITTLE WATER

Although native to coastal locations in California, this tough ground cover thrives in a wide range of soils and climates—from sandy soil and coastal fog to heavy or alkaline soil and desert heat. Toothed, glossy bright green, ½-inch leaves densely clothe the branches of stiff, mounding plants that reach 8 to 24 inches high and spread rapidly to 6 feet or wider. Male and female flowers are carried on separate plants; male plants are better garden subjects, since they don't produce the cottony seed heads that can be messy when blown about by wind. The most widely available male (seedless) selections are 'Pigeon Point', with larger,

*Baccharis pilularis 'Twin Peaks'*

lighter leaves than the species on a faster-growing, wider-spreading plant, and 'Twin Peaks', a slightly slower grower with small dark green leaves.

Set out plants from 1-gallon containers about 3 feet apart. Dwarf coyote brush will accept—but does not require—regular garden watering in all soils. In coastal and inland areas, plants may get through the dry months with no supplemental watering; where summers are extremely hot, occasional watering will be needed. Before growth begins each year, prune out any upright or arching stems that disrupt the evenness of a planting's surface; also thin out old, woody, sparse branches as needed.

## BEAUMONTIA grandiflora
### EASTER LILY VINE, HERALD'S TRUMPET

🌿 EVERGREEN WOODY VINE

✂ ZONES 12, 13, 16, 17, 21–27

☀ ◑ SUN OR PARTIAL SHADE

💧 REGULAR WATER

The blossoms may be plain white, but this vine makes a dramatic statement nonetheless. For starters, it's *big:* a 30-foot height and spread is not unusual. Foliage is equally imposing: 6- to 9-inch, broadly oval, glossy leaves that, in spring and summer, provide the perfect backdrop for intoxicatingly fragrant flowers the shape (and nearly the size) of Easter lilies. On close inspection, the blossoms aren't wholly white; they show pink shad-

*Beaumontia grandiflora*

ings on their outermost segments, green tinting at the base and in the throat.

Easter lily vine grows best in well-drained, average to good soil enriched with organic matter. Plants need regular moisture during the growing season but prefer just moderate water during the cooler months. For the most lavish leaves and flowers, fertilize when the growing period begins, then once or twice more before autumn. Do any pruning to shape after flowering has finished. Flowers are produced on wood 2 years old or older, so heavy pruning of old wood will temporarily decrease flowering. Stems climb by twining, but they may need some additional attachment as they grow. The heavy growth and eventually stout branches require strong support, so use these vines on arbors and pergolas, along eaves, or on fences or walls.

## BIGNONIA capreolata
### CROSSVINE

- Evergreen to semievergreen woody vine
- Zones 4–9, 14–24, 26–33
- Sun or partial shade
- Regular to moderate water

Here is a vine that merits the word "trouble-free"—and it's attractive, too. In midspring, small clusters of trumpet-shaped, 2-inch, brownish orange blossoms with yellow centers appear against a background of glossy dark green foliage. Each leaf has two oval leaflets to 6 inches long and a central, branching tendril with small holdfast discs. As the vine rapidly ascends to 30 feet or more, the tendrils do the climbing; the discs let stems adhere to wood, stone, brick, and concrete surfaces. Foliage cover is fairly dense in sun, more open in shaded locations; leaves turn purplish in cold weather. In the coldest zones, vines lose some leaves in winter. The selection 'Tangerine Beauty' offers blossoms of bright apricot orange.

Although crossvine prefers average, well-drained soil and regular water, it puts up with a variety of less-than-ideal conditions: heavy soil, deep shade, capricious watering. Do any necessary thinning or pruning in winter, before the year's growth begins.

## BOUGAINVILLEA

- Evergreen woody vines or ground covers
- Zones 12, 13, 15–17, 19, 22–28
- Sun or partial shade
- Regular to moderate water

A bougainvillea in bloom is impossible to overlook. "Flamboyant" certainly describes the neon brightness of the purple, red, and orange varieties, and even the more pastel colors have a brilliant clarity. This dazzling show comes not from the inconspicuous true flowers, but rather from the papery, petal-like bracts that surround them in a vibrant frame of purple, magenta, crimson, brick red, orange, bronze, yellow, pink, or white. Bloom reaches its peak in summer, but in the mildest-winter regions flowers may appear from spring through fall, and even into winter. Both single- and double-flowered types are sold; double kinds can look messy, since they hold faded blooms for a long time.

All vining bougainvilleas (there are also shrubby varieties) are fast and vigorous growers, reaching 15 to 30 feet depending on the variety. Long, needle-like thorns arm stiff stems that are moderately to densely clothed in medium green, 2½-inch, heart-shaped leaves. Plants perform superbly on walls and fences, on trellises as living screens, and on arbors and pergolas as shade-casters. Since the vines have no means of attachment (though the thorns help them scramble through shrubs and trees), you'll need to tie stems to the support while the basic structure is establishing.

You also can use bougainvillea vines as an impenetrable ground cover. They're especially good for bank and hillside plantings, where plants at the top of the bank can spill down to cover the slope.

Old favorite *B. spectabilis*, with grape purple bracts, is the most frost-

*Bignonia capreolata*

*Bougainvillea 'San Diego Red'*

tolerant bougainvillea, an ultra-vigorous plant that flowers heavily even where summers are cool. Multitudinous named varieties also exist. Some of the more widely sold ones are listed below, grouped by color; all are single flowered unless otherwise noted.

*Pink:* 'Cherry Blossom' (double), 'Pink Tiara', 'Southern Rose', 'Tahitian Maid' (double), 'Texas Dawn' (purplish pink). *Purple:* 'Don Mario', 'James Walker', 'Lavender Queen'. *Red:* 'Barbara Karst', 'Betty Hendry' (with yellow and purple touches—also sold as 'Indian Maid'), 'Manila Red' (double), 'Mrs. Butt' (also sold as 'Crimson Lake'), 'Rosea' (rosy red), 'San Diego Red' (also sold as 'San Diego', 'Scarlett O'Hara'). *Yellow, orange, bronze:* 'Afterglow' (yellow orange), 'California Gold' (deep yellow; also sold as 'Sunset'), 'Isabel Greensmith' (orange red), 'Orange King'. *Multicolor:* 'Camarillo Festival' (pink and gold), 'Rosenka' (gold fading to pink), 'Tahitian Dawn' (gold fading to rosy purple). *White:* 'Jamaica White', 'Mary Palmer's Enchantment', 'White Madonna'.

Bougainvillea grows best in regions that are virtually frost-free. Even in slightly colder zones, however, established vines quickly recover from light frosts (though sometimes at the expense of the last season's more tender growth).

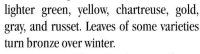

*Bougainvillea*

Where light frosts are routine, locate bougainvillea in the garden's warmest spot; an ideal place is against a sheltered, sunny wall. In desert zones, where sun is intense and summers are long, vines appreciate light shade during the hottest hours of the day.

Bougainvillea grows well in a range of soils, from light to heavy. Set out plants from containers in spring; be very careful to keep the rootball intact, since too much root disturbance can be fatal. A foolproof planting method is to dig an extra-broad hole to just the depth of the rootball, then set the container in the hole. With sharp, needle-nosed shears, cut around the base of the container—starting from a drainage hole—to separate it from the sides. Slide the detached base from beneath the container; then lift off the container, filling in around the plant with soil as you go. (You won't damage the plant; bougainvillea is flexible, with little horizontal growth.) For ground cover use, set gallon-size plants 6 to 8 feet apart.

Water plants regularly during their first year. In the following years, water regularly in spring, then moderately during the flowering period. Fertilize plants when the growing season begins and again in early summer. Do any major pruning to shape after flowering has ceased (in frost-free regions) or as early as possible in spring after danger of frost is past. During the growing period, don't hesitate to head back or pinch errant stems to direct growth.

# CALLUNA vulgaris
## HEATHER, SCOTCH HEATHER

- ❀ EVERGREEN WOODY GROUND COVER
- ☈ ZONES 2–6, 15–17, 34, 36–41
- ☀ SUN
- ◖ REGULAR WATER

Were it not for its insistence on certain cultural conditions, heather would be much more widely grown as a ground cover. The plants are mannerly (noninvasive), fine-textured, and always attractive, offering a variety of flower and foliage colors. The typical form is a dense, mounded to spreading plant that can reach 3 feet high, with branches clothed in tiny, scalelike, dark green leaves. Spikes of ½-inch, urn-shaped, rosy purple flowers appear at branch tips—usually in mid- to late summer, though some varieties bloom in fall. Many named selections exist, with flowers in white, pink, lavender, and purple shades; foliage variants include

lighter green, yellow, chartreuse, gold, gray, and russet. Leaves of some varieties turn bronze over winter.

For ground cover planting, choose varieties with low, spreading growth. You can make a mass planting of one kind if you want an entirely uniform appearance, but some gardeners enjoy creating "tapestry plantings" including different flower and foliage colors. Here is a sample of suitable ground cover types, all under 1 foot tall: 'Aurea' (purple blooms, gold foliage turning rust in winter); 'David Eason' (red-purple blooms in fall, light green foliage); 'J. H. Hamilton' (pink double flowers); 'Minima Prostrata' (light rosy purple blooms, bronze winter foliage); 'Mrs. Ronald Gray' (red-purple flowers), 'Nana' (purple blooms).

Heather has an absolute requirement for very well-drained, acid soil, and it actually thrives in sandy and gravelly soils considered too poor for most preferred garden plants. It also demands cool to mild summer weather with moist rather than dry air. Where summers are dry, heather will survive only with regular watering to keep soil moist; under these conditions, apply an acid fertilizer in late winter and in late spring. To tidy up a heather planting, shear off faded flowers and branch tips just after flowers fade (for summer-blooming varieties) or in late winter (for fall bloomers).

*Calluna vulgaris* varieties

## CAMPANULA

BELLFLOWER

🌿 EVERGREEN PERENNIAL
   GROUND COVERS

◢ ZONES VARY BY SPECIES

☀ ◑ SUN OR PARTIAL SHADE

💧 REGULAR WATER

Of the many *Campanula* species, two are excellent flowering ground covers for moderate-size areas. Despite their somewhat delicate looks, these natives of Balkan mountains are rugged and easy to grow; both spread by rooting runners to form solid foliage carpets.

Serbian bellflower, *C. poscharsky-ana*, is adapted to Zones 1–9, 14–24, 31–45. It grows to about a foot tall, its long, trailing, many-branched stems bearing long-stalked, heart-shaped, 1- to 3½-inch-long leaves of a

lettucelike green. From spring to early summer, blue to lavender, star-shaped blossoms up to an inch across dapple the foliage carpet; specialty nurseries sometimes offer a white-flowered form. Plants spread at a moderate to rapid rate.

A lower-growing species is Dalmatian bellflower, *C. portenschlagiana* (often sold as *C. muralis*), suited to Zones 2–9, 14–24, 31–41. Its dark green foliage mass reaches 4 to 7 inches high; the long-stalked leaves to 1½ inches across are nearly round, with deeply toothed and wavy margins. From midspring well into summer, the leaves are nearly obscured by inch-long, bell-shaped flowers of bright violet blue. 'Resholt' offers larger blossoms. The plants spread moderately quickly but are never invasive.

Set out plants from pots about 1 foot apart. Both the above species perform best if given good, well-drained soil and regular watering (Serbian bellflower can survive on moderate or even infrequent watering, but it won't look good). Light or partial shade suits both species, though in cool-summer regions they will also thrive in sunny spots. For best appearance, protect from slugs and snails.

ABOVE: *Campanula poscharskyana*
LEFT: *Campanula portenschlagiana*

*Campsis radicans*

## CAMPSIS

TRUMPET CREEPER,
TRUMPET VINE

🌿 SEMIEVERGREEN TO DECIDUOUS
   WOODY VINES

◢ ZONES VARY BY SPECIES

☀ ◑ SUN OR PARTIAL SHADE

💧 ◖ REGULAR TO MODERATE WATER

These exuberant vines capture the essence of summer, bearing radiant orange-toned blossoms from midsummer to fall. All have leaves consisting of glossy, 2½-inch, ovate leaflets arranged along a leafstalk; the flowers, carried in clusters at branch tips, are widely flaring trumpets to 3 inches long and 2 inches across. Stems cling to surfaces with aerial rootlets.

Common trumpet creeper, *C. radicans* (formerly *Bignonia radicans*) is the most widely adapted species, growing in Zones 2–21, 26–41. It is found wild in the southeastern United States and is hardy to severe cold, though in hard-freeze territory its stems die to the ground and roots produce new growth each year. Leaves contain up to 11 leaflets each. Fast growth carries the vine as high as 40 feet; it often scales tree trunks in the wild. The species bears flowers with orange tubes and red lobes; 'Flava' has lovely yellow blooms and somewhat lighter green leaves.                    >

Chinese trumpet creeper, *C. grandiflora* (formerly *Bignonia chinensis*), grows in Zones 4–12, 14–21, 28–32. Although certainly no slouch in the vigor department, it is less aggressive and far-reaching than common trumpet creeper, attaining about 30 feet under ideal conditions. Flowers are slightly larger and redder than those of common trumpet creeper, and leaves have fewer leaflets (up to nine). For a softer color, look for the peach-colored selection 'Morning Charm'.

A hybrid between the American and Chinese species, *C.* × *tagliabuana*, grows in Zones 3–24, 26–34. In plant and flower size, it takes after the Chinese parent, but individual leaflets are a bit smaller. Salmon red 'Mme. Galen' is the most widely sold selection; 'Crimson Trumpet' has flowers of pure red.

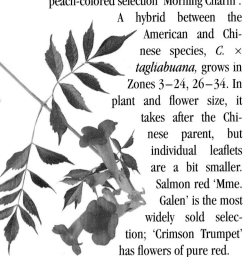

*Campsis radicans*

Good, well-drained soil, full sun, and regular water spur these colorful climbers on to their showy best. Thanks to their inherent toughness, however, they'll perform adequately in a range of soils (from heavy to light), in partial shade, and with just moderate watering.

Use trumpet vines on walls or fences, as living screens, trained up onto overhead structures, or simply as decoration for the trunks of mature, tall trees. Don't depend entirely on aerial roots to hold older stems firmly to vertical surfaces; give some sort of tie-in attachments to prevent heavy mature vines from pulling away from their support.

Branches may root where they touch soil, and roots may send up new plants far from the parent, particularly if they are cut or injured. Prune vines as needed (preferably after flowering has ended) to thin out excess or errant growth.

*Carissa macrocarpa*

# CARISSA macrocarpa
NATAL PLUM
- EVERGREEN WOODY GROUND COVER
- ZONES 22–27
- SUN OR PARTIAL SHADE
- REGULAR TO LITTLE WATER

Where winters are frost-free (or almost always so), Natal plum is known as one of the handsomest and most rugged of shrubby ground covers. Seacoast gardeners appreciate its ability to thrive in salty ocean winds, even in sea spray.

The entire plant is the picture of polished good health. Rich green, glossy, oval leaves to 3 inches long clothe stems armed in needlelike forked spines. Highly fragrant, star-shaped white flowers to 2 inches wide appear throughout the year. Blossoms are followed by 1- to 2-inch, plum-shaped fruits that turn from green to red as they ripen; they have a cranberrylike flavor and can be eaten fresh or used in preserves. The spiny branches make Natal plum a good choice for barrier plantings. It's particularly attractive spilling over the edges of raised beds or retaining walls.

Several named selections make good ground covers. 'Green Carpet' has smaller leaves on a plant that may reach 1½ feet high, 4 or more feet wide. 'Horizontalis', with trailing, more vinelike stems, can build to about 2 feet high. 'Prostrata', despite its name, forms a branch mass to 2 feet high; it occasionally produces upright stems that must be cut out to maintain uniformity. 'Tuttle' (sometimes sold as 'Nana Compacta

Tuttlei') is more of a mounding, spreading shrub, reaching 3 feet high and 5 feet across; it offers especially profuse flower and fruit production. All varieties grow slowly until established, then spread at a moderate rate.

Set out plants from 1-gallon cans about 3 feet apart. They'll grow in a wide range of soils, from heavy to sandy and even slightly saline. Near the coast, Natal plum is fairly drought tolerant; farther inland, away from moist coastal air, it needs moderate to regular watering, depending on the soil. Prune at any time to remove erratic growth.

# CARPOBROTUS. See page 68

# CEANOTHUS
CEANOTHUS, WILD LILAC
- EVERGREEN WOODY GROUND COVERS
- ZONES 4–9, 14–24
- SUN
- MODERATE TO LITTLE WATER

The wild lilacs of western North America (no relation to true lilac, *Syringa*) are cherished for their standout contribution of blue to the early spring landscape. Though most of these plants are fairly sizable shrubs, a few are naturally prostrate growers that make excellent large-scale ground covers for the Pacific Coast region.

Point Reyes ceanothus, *C. gloriosus*, grows quickly and easily in coastal and cool-summer areas but suffers where summers are hot. The species has oval, dark green, inch-long leaves with spiny margins; small light blue blossoms come in inch-wide, rounded clusters. The plant reaches just 1 to 1½ feet high but spreads

*Ceanothus griseus horizontalis*

*Ceanothus griseus horizontalis* 'Yankee Point'

Heat and poorly drained soil spell trouble for ceanothus: if the two conditions occur together, they can rot roots and kill plants. Though the ground cover types are more tolerant of normal garden conditions than many of their large, shrubby relatives, the safest course is still to plant in well-drained soil and water sparingly over summer. Set out plants from 1-gallon containers; space the smaller growers 3 feet apart, the more wide-spreading individuals 6 feet apart.

## CELASTRUS
BITTERSWEET

- DECIDUOUS WOODY VINES
- ZONES VARY BY SPECIES
- SUN
- REGULAR WATER

With its colorful fruits and bright fall foliage, bittersweet is a well-loved symbol of autumn in eastern North America. Native to that region is American bittersweet, *C. scandens;* it grows in Zones 1–7, 10, 29–44. During spring and summer, the twining vine is outfitted in pale green, 4-inch, oval leaves. Elongated clusters of small whitish flowers in late spring go largely unnoticed, but the seed

capsules that follow are impossible to overlook: held up above the bright gold fall foliage, they split open to display red fruits against a yellow collar. The one drawback is that male and female flowers occur on separate plants—and you need

*Celastrus orbiculatus*

two vines, one of each sex, for a fall fruit bonanza on the female. Nurseries sometimes offer plants with the sexes labeled, but usually you just take your chances. The vine is vigorous and far reaching, climbing readily to 20 feet or more; give it a tall, mature tree to scale and it will do the job completely. Don't let it infiltrate small trees or shrubs, though; the twining stems can girdle the host plant's limbs.

Chinese bittersweet, *C. orbiculatus,* grows in Zones 2–7, 10, 29–41. It's similar to its American relation but less showy, since the fruits are partially hidden among the leaves. This species is even more aggressive than *C. scandens,* reaching 30 to 40 feet; in parts of the Northeast, it has naturalized and become a roadside weed. Self-fertile forms are sometimes available.

Set out young vines in average soil of any type. (Be aware that good soil promotes really rank growth, while poorer soils help keep vines to a more manageable size). Plants will grow in some shade, but at the expense of fruit production. Freely cut fruiting branches for autumn decoration. Prune tangled, intertwined branches in winter or early spring, before growth begins; prune as needed during summer to guide or regulate growth.

widely—up to 16 feet. Its variety 'Anchor Bay', with especially dense foliage and somewhat darker blue blossoms, spreads only about half as wide. For deep violet-blue flowers on a plant to 3 feet high and 12 feet wide, choose *C. g. exaltatus* 'Emily Brown'; this one will take heavy soil and routine garden watering in its preferred coastal climates.

Carmel creeper, *C. griseus horizontalis,* is a fast grower that offers a different look in foliage: its glossy, 2-inch, oval leaves have a slightly quilted appearance. Spreading from 5 to 15 feet and reaching 2½ feet tall, it bears light blue blossoms in 1-inch clusters. Among available varieties, light blue–flowered 'Hurricane Point' is a 2- to 3-footer that can rapidly cover an area up to 36 feet across; 'Yankee Point', with medium blue flowers and darker green leaves, forms a dense, even cover 2 to 3 feet tall and 10 feet wide. Deer are notably fond of Carmel creeper. Where summers are warm, this species and its varieties are more successful than *C. gloriosus*—but the best choice for warm-summer regions is the hybrid *C.* 'Centennial'. It grows at a moderate to fast rate, reaching 2 feet high, 10 feet across; the small leaves are glossy dark green, the blossoms deep blue.

*Celastrus scandens*

## CEPHALOPHYLLUM. See page 68

## CERASTIUM tomentosum
SNOW-IN-SUMMER

🌱 EVERGREEN PERENNIAL GROUND COVER

✂ ZONES 1–24, 32–45

☼ ◑ SUN OR PARTIAL SHADE

💧 ⬤ REGULAR TO MODERATE WATER

Small, snowy white blossoms nearly obscure this plant's foliage from late spring into summer—hence the common name. After the "snow" is gone, you're left with an attractive, silvery gray, 4- to 6-inch-high mat formed from tufts of narrow leaves under an inch long. Plants spread by creeping rhizomes, growing so fast that just one plant may cover 2 to 3 feet in a single year.

*Cerastium tomentosum*

Snow-in-summer succeeds almost anywhere; only extreme heat and humidity will defeat it. It does, however, need light shade in hot-summer regions and well-drained soil everywhere (to avoid root rot). It grows fastest with regular watering but is quite drought tolerant. Set out plants from pots 1 to 1½ feet apart for a quick, even cover. You can also start from seed, if it's available; sow it on prepared ground in spring. After flowers have faded, tidy up the planting by shearing off the flower stems or mowing the entire area.

Snow-in-summer is not long lived as a ground cover, so use it where you can

easily rejuvenate plantings. Bare patches will begin to show in several years, at which time you should divide (in fall or early spring) and replant.

## CERATOSTIGMA
plumbaginoides
DWARF PLUMBAGO

🌱 DECIDUOUS PERENNIAL GROUND COVER

✂ ZONES 2–10, 14–24, 29–41

☼ ◑ SUN OR PARTIAL SHADE

⬤ MODERATE WATER

Dwarf plumbago provides a patch of vivid blue in the garden from midsummer to midautumn, when cool tones are especially welcome. Its leaves are 3-inch, bronzy green ovals that ascend wiry, 6- to 12-inch stems; they turn to bronzy red when frosty weather begins. At bloom time, loose clusters of phloxlike flowers in an intense bluebird blue appear at the stem ends. Bloom is heaviest and longest lasting where the growing season is long.

Dwarf plumbago spreads fairly rapidly by underground stems to form a dense, soil-knitting cover. It grows well in a range of soils (from clayey to sandy types) but spreads fastest in light soils. Because it will overwhelm smaller annuals and perennials, it is best used by itself or beneath shrubs or trees. Set out plants from pots about 1 foot apart, those from 1-gallon containers 1½ feet apart.

At some point in fall, plants begin to look shabby as stems die to the ground;

*Ceratostigma plumbaginoides*

shear or mow the planting to remove dead stems and foliage before new growth resumes the next spring. In time, plantings will become overcrowded and begin to show sparse or dead patches. At that time, dig and replant rooted divisions at the start of the growing season.

*Chrysogonum virginianum*

## CHRYSOGONUM
virginianum
GOLDEN STAR, GREEN AND GOLD

🌱 SEMIEVERGREEN PERENNIAL GROUND COVER

✂ ZONES 3–6, 14–17, 28–32, 34–39

☼ ◑ SUN OR PARTIAL SHADE

⬤ REGULAR WATER

Imagine a blanket of carpet bugle (*Ajuga reptans,* page 35) or mint foliage scattered with single yellow marigolds, and you'll have a good picture of golden star, a charming, long-flowering woodland ground cover that grows wild in many states east of the Mississippi. The plant spreads at a moderate rate, advancing by underground stems; scallop-edged, oval, 1- to 3-inch leaves form a foliage carpet to 8 inches high. The bright, 2½-inch-wide blossoms are plentiful in spring and fall, sporadic but noticeable over summer.

Good, somewhat acid soil liberally amended with organic matter gives golden star its preferred woodland conditions. A location in dappled sun or light shade—under deciduous trees, for example—is appreciated in all areas, but plants will tolerate more sun where summers are cool. Set out small plants from pots about 1 foot apart.

# CISSUS

- 🌿 ⬛ EVERGREEN WOODY VINES OR GROUND COVERS
- ✂ ZONES VARY BY SPECIES
- ☼ ◑ ● SUN OR SHADE
- 💧 MODERATE TO LITTLE WATER

Where frost is rare, these warm-climate relatives of Virginia creeper and Boston ivy (*Parthenocissus,* page 80) make handsome ground covers or cloaks for walls or fences. Flowers are insignificant, and the small fruits (like tiny grapes, when produced) are not decorative. All the species below climb by tendrils.

Grape ivy, *C. rhombifolia,* is native to South America. Well known as a houseplant, it's adapted to outdoor life in Zones 13, 15, 16, 21–27, where it can climb to 20 feet high. Each glossy dark green leaf has three diamond-shaped, tooth-edged leaflets to 4 inches long. Variety 'Ellen Danica' is smaller growing, with lobed leaflets.

Another South American, *C. striata,* grows in Zones 13–27. Reaching about 20 feet, it resembles a more delicate version of Virginia creeper, with each leaf divided into three to five 3-inch leaflets. The leathery dark green foliage offers a pleasing contrast to the reddish stems.

Kangaroo treebine, *C. antarctica,* grows in Zones 16–25, 27. Its glossy, spear-shaped leaves reach 3½ inches long, their toothed edges and prominent veins providing a subtle decorative element. Plants reach about 10 feet and pro-

*Cissus rhombifolia* 'Ellen Danica'

vide a dense foliage cover. Another dense grower is rampant *C. hypoglauca,* successful in Zones 13–25, 27. Established vines can reach 30 feet or more. The highly polished, bronze-tinted leaves are divided into five rounded, leathery leaflets, each to about 3 inches long; new growth is covered with rust-colored fuzz.

None of the above species is particular about soil. Once established, *C. antarctica* and *C. hypoglauca* can get by with little water; *C. rhombifolia* and *C. striata* need at least moderate watering. Prune vines to thin during winter, before new growth begins; during the growing season, cut out unneeded and tangling stems as they appear. As vines, these plants make handsome green "walls"; you can train them on supports against walls or fences, or grow them on wire screens to provide freestanding partitions in outdoor-living areas. As ground covers, they spread rapidly to carpet sizable areas thoroughly and are particularly fine on hillsides. For ground cover use, set out plants from 1-gallon containers about 5 feet apart.

# CISTUS
ROCKROSE

- 🌿 EVERGREEN WOODY GROUND COVERS
- ✂ ZONES 6–9, 12–24
- ☼ SUN
- 💧 MODERATE TO LITTLE WATER

The rockroses evoke images of their Mediterranean homeland in spring: dry, sunny days, rocky hillsides, air filled with spicy foliage scents. They grow best in regions with the dry summers and cool, moist winters of their native climate—but as long as those general conditions are met, they'll thrive in areas as diverse as seacoast and desert.

*Cistus salviifolius*

Though flower size and color vary, all rockroses have blossoms with five broad petals that open out flat, like fine single roses. Each flower lasts just one day, but a seemingly endless supply of buds keeps the show going for a month or more in spring to early summer. Foliage is coarse textured, often wrinkled, and pleasantly aromatic on warm days.

Sageleaf rockrose, *C. salviifolius,* is one of several good ground cover types. The densely foliaged plants grow quickly, reaching up to 2 feet high and about 6 feet across; stems root here and there where they contact soil. Wrinkled, wavy-edged leaves to an inch long are a light, gray-tinted green; masses of 1½-inch, yellow-centered white flowers form a cloud over the foliage at bloom time.

For pink flowers, you can choose from two fast-spreading hybrids. The paler blossomed of the two is *C.* 'Warley Rose', with 1-inch, light purplish pink blooms on a dark-leafed plant to about 1 foot high and 4 feet across. *C.* 'Sunset', a spreader to about 2 feet high and 8 feet across, bears 2-inch magenta flowers against a backdrop of gray-green leaves.

Rockroses thrive in sun, heat, and dryness. Soil is not an issue: they'll take it good or poor, claylike or sandy. Set out plants from 1-gallon containers 2½ to 3 feet apart. >

*Cistus salviifolius*

Young plants need fairly regular watering until their roots are established; thereafter, plantings will thrive with moderate to little supplemental moisture in hot regions, little or none in coastal and cool areas. Only if soil is decidedly well-drained will plants accept regular garden watering. No fertilizer is needed. Cut out errant growth whenever it occurs; pinch tips of vigorous stems, if needed, to encourage branching.

## CLEMATIS

🌿 DECIDUOUS (WITH ONE EXCEPTION) WOODY VINES

✿ ZONES VARY BY SPECIES

☀ ☽ SUN OR PARTIAL SHADE

💧 REGULAR WATER

*Clematis*

Clematis is among the most beloved of vines, but its members are so diverse they defy a blanket description. It's true that all climb by coiling their leafstalks around a support—but beyond that, the variation is enormous. In size, species and hybrids range from modest vines (reaching 8 feet or so) to tree-consuming colossi like *C. armandii* and *C. montana*. Flowers may be small and delicate, like the bell-shaped blooms of *C. texensis,* or flat and saucer sized, as in many of the widely sold hybrids. The color range (widest in the large-flowered hybrids) runs from white, cream, and pastel shades to vibrant blue, lavender, violet, purple, pink, and red. The true flowers of clematis are tiny and inconspicuous; what look like petals (and are referred to as such in the descriptions that follow) are really petal-like sepals surrounding the clustered true flowers.

Depending on the species or hybrid, the plants will flower in spring, in summer, or once in spring and a second time in summer or fall; in mild-winter climates, some begin blooming in late win-ter. Many produce decorative heads of silky seed tassels after bloom.

In keeping with the great variety it offers, clematis is a versatile vine. The largest growers make striking statements as cloaks for walls, fences, pergolas, and arbors; given the chance, they will happily festoon mature trees. The smaller-growing types, including species as well as the popular large-flowered hybrids, are at home as solo acts or used with other plants—the combination of clematis and climbing roses, for example, is a classic partnership that always bears repeating. For individual display, nothing is showier than a pillar, a post, or even a tree trunk converted into a tower of clematis flowers (outfit the support with string or mesh to give the vines a grip). Displayed against garden walls, scrambling over arched arbors, or covering trellises, these plants are guaranteed focal points. Or take a cue from nature and let them clamber over and through shrubbery or intertwine with other flowering vines.

### CLEMATIS CULTURE AND PRUNING

Once established, these aren't demanding plants. However, particular attention to planting and initial care will pay dividends in the long run. Vines like the sun (give them some shade in hot-summer regions), but their roots prefer cool soil. To keep the soil temperature down, cover the surface with a mulch or a shallow-rooted ground cover; even a large rock placed over the root area will help. Another trick is to use low shrubs (with noncompetitive root systems) to shade the ground near the vine.

Clematis revel in good soil—the sort you'd give your best vegetables—but the drainage must be good. Dig plenty of organic matter into the soil before planting. Somewhat acid to slightly alkaline soils are all acceptable, but if soil tests show a calcium deficiency, add lime when you dig in the organic matter. Set out plants so that the top of the root-

TOP: *Clematis* 'Belle of Woking'
BOTTOM: *Clematis* 'Nelly Moser'

ball is slightly below the soil surface. When planting a dormant, leafless plant, cut back stems to about 1 foot long (make cuts just above a node, easily identified as a distinct bump in the stem where leaves have been attached). Stems and new growth are easily broken, so it's a good idea to protect plants from accidental damage by surrounding them with wire cylinders or the like.

Clematis and fertilizer were made for each another. Young plants will produce the fastest, most luxuriant growth if

TOP: *Clematis* 'Comtesse de Bouchard'
BOTTOM: *Clematis* 'Lasurstern'

fertilized monthly during the growing season. Once vines are established, make at least one application yearly, at the start of the growing season.

Young vines are likely to need some pruning simply to guide development and remove superfluous growth. Established vines (especially the large-growing types) can be pruned and thinned as needed, usually when they become too tangled to look attractive. Pruning a clematis isn't tricky, but timing is important: when you prune depends on the particular plant's

bloom time. There are three sets of basic instructions, designated below by numbers; these numbers also appear with the individual descriptions to indicate the appropriate pruning schedule for each species or hybrid.

**Clematis that bloom once annually in spring (1).** These vines flower in spring directly from wood (stems) produced in the previous year. The best time to do any significant thinning and cutting back is after bloom; pruning before bloom simply discards potential flowers.

**Clematis that bloom once in spring, then again in summer or fall (2).** These twice-blooming kinds flower in spring on old growth (as do the Group 1 types, above). In summer or fall, more flowers come on growth produced during the growing season. Prune lightly in late fall or in early spring (before buds swell) as needed to thin out and untangle stems, but leave as much growth as possible to bear the initial flower crop. After spring flowers fade, prune more heavily so that plenty of healthy new stems will develop for the second round of bloom.

**Clematis that bloom once annually in summer (3).** This group (which includes many of the large-flowered hybrids) blooms only at the ends of new stems produced in spring. When pruning seems necessary, do it at some point from late fall to early spring, before new growth begins.

## CLEMATIS CHOICES

The average retail nursery is likely to stock a modest selection of large-flowered clematis hybrids and, possibly, a few popular species (*C. montana*, for example). Catalogs from mail-order clematis specialists offer a greater assortment of hybrids and a much wider range of species. Below, we list the most widely grown species and hybrids; some of these will be sold at nurseries, some only by mail-order.

SPECIES. Two rugged species will thrive even where winters are very cold. *C. alpina* (1), suited to Zones 1–6, 15–17,

31–43, climbs to about 12 feet; in spring, it's adorned with flowers that dangle from long stalks. Each 1- to 1½-inch bloom has four pointed, spreading petals (like a flared skirt) with a central cup of modified stamens. Among the many named varieties are 'Helsingborg' (dark blue purple), 'Pamela Jackman' (intense blue), 'Ruby' (red purple), and 'Willy' (pale pink). Downy clematis, *C. macropetala* (1), grows in Zones 1–9, 14–17, 31–43. It too is of modest size (6 to 12 feet). Bloom time comes in early spring; each 3½- to 4-inch blossom has four petals and enough modified stamens to make the flower look double. Lavender to blue is the standard color, but named varieties include popular 'Markham's Pink' (lilac pink) and choices in deep pink and white. Silvered bronzy pink seed heads follow the flowers.

Only slightly less cold tolerant are four other species. Scarlet clematis, *C. texensis* (3), grows in Zones 2–9, 14–17, 29–41. It's a fast-growing, somewhat drought-tolerant vine to about 10 feet; the blue-green foliage provides a

*Clematis alpina*

*Clematis montana*

backdrop for 1-inch, scarlet, chalice- or lily-shaped flowers that bloom from early summer until the onset of chilly fall weather. A number of *C. texensis* hybrids show the same floral style, among them widely sold 'Duchess of Albany' (deep pink) and 'Lady Bird Johnson' (dark red). Two species grow in Zones 2–9, 14–17, 31–41. Golden clematis, *C. tangutica* (3), with gray-green foliage, clambers to 15 feet; its pendent yellow flowers, lantern shaped and 2 to 4 inches long, are profuse from midsummer into fall. Silvery seed clusters follow. *C. viti-cella* (3) reaches a vigorous 18 feet and bears 2-inch, rosy purple, four-petaled flowers in summer. You'll usually find its named selections and hybrids, such as 'Lady Betty Balfour' (violet), 'Mme. Julia Correvon' (wine red), and 'Polish Spirit' (blue purple). Sweet autumn clematis, *C. terniflora* (3), grows in Zones 3–9, 14–24, 26, 28–41; many nurseries offer it under its former names *C. dioscorei-folia, C. maximowicziana,* or *C. panic-ulata.* The creamy white, late summer to fall flowers are just an inch wide, but they are borne in such large, profuse clusters that the rampant, 30-foot vine is trans-

formed into a scented froth. Silvery, plumed seed heads come later.

Two other popular species thrive in regions where winters are moderately cold: Zones 3–9, 14–17, 31–39. Anemone clematis, *C. montana* (1), delivers a stunning early spring display of 2½-inch flowers like those of Japanese anemone. The basic species is a strong-growing vine to 20 feet or more, bearing white flowers that age to pink. Nurseries offer named selections, including 'Eliza-beth' (pale pink, with a vanilla scent), 'Grandiflora' (white, on a 40-foot vine), 'Mayleen' (3-inch pink blooms, bronze-tinted leaves), and 'Tetrarose' (4-inch mauve pink flowers, bronze new leaves). *C. m. rubens* has crimson new growth that matures to bronzy green; its flowers are pink to rosy red. Blossoms of its vari-ety 'Odorata' have a vanilla fragrance.

*C. florida* (3) is only moderately vigorous—8 to 10 feet tall, just the right size to keep the striking summer flowers within easy view. Its variety 'Sieboldii' has 3-inch, six-petaled white flowers with a showy, pompon-like purple center; both 'Alba Plena' and 'Duchess of Edin-burgh' bear double blooms in greenish white.

Evergreen clematis, *C. armandii* (1), grows in Zones 4–9, 12–24, 28, 31, and warmer parts of 32. A good word for this species is "overwhelming." Rapid growth takes the vine to 20 to 35 feet; it easily invades large trees, where it makes quite a show. The foliage is distinctive. Each leaf is composed of three dark green, lance-shaped leaflets to 5 inches long; these droop strongly, adding a graceful air to an other-wise coarse-textured vine. Large, branched flower clusters smother the plant in 2½-inch, glistening white,

*Clematis 'Will Goodwin'*

scented blossoms in early spring; 'Hen-dersonii Rubra' makes the same statement in light pink. Where it is adapted, this is the best clematis for large arbors and per-golas, house eaves, and large fences or walls. When you prune, don't be shy: thin and train relentlessly.

In contrast to the above hyperthyroid individual is delicate *C. chrysocoma* (2), which grows in Zones 4–9, 14–24, 28, 31, 32. This notably shade-tolerant, 6- to 10-foot vine creates a fairly open, filigree-like pattern as it climbs; a distinctive yel-low down covers all young growth. The 2-inch, four-petaled flowers are a pink-tinted white. Bloom comes in spring, then again in summer on new growth.

Large-flowered *C. lanuginosa* (2) grows in Zones 3–9, 14–17, 31–39. It is best known for its genetic contribution to many of the large-flowered hybrids. Its variety 'Candida' has breathtaking 8-inch white blooms on vigorous but modest (6- to 10-foot) vine. Flowers come in both spring and summer.

LARGE-FLOWERED HYBRIDS. These hybrids flaunt the show-stopping, 5- to 10-inch blossoms that put clema-tis in the top ranks of favorite flowering plants. Ancestries are varied and not always precisely known; prominent among par-ent species are *C. lanuginosa, C. patens,* and *C. viti-cella.* Most of these hybrids will grow in Zones 2–9, 14–17, 31–41. They are gen-erally mid-size (8- to 15-foot) plants; prune them as directed for Group 2 or 3 (page 51), depending on the particular hybrid's bloom times.

The choices most often sold are listed below by color. The double-flowered sorts have a profu-sion of pointed petals that almost gives them the look of small dahlias; most of these produce double flowers in the first spring bloom flush, but later blossoms on new growth are likely to be single.

**Blue.** You'll find a range of blues from light to dark, including 'Blue Ravine' (mauve blue), 'Edo Murasaki' (deep blue), 'General Sikorski' (medium blue lavender), 'Lasurstern' (deep lavender blue), 'Mrs. Cholmondeley' (light blue), 'Mrs. P. T. James' (double; dark blue), 'Prince Philip' (dark purplish blue), 'Prins Hendrik' (azure blue), 'Ramona' (sky blue), 'Vyvyan Pennell' (double; deep blue violet), and 'William Kennett' (lavender blue).

**Purple.** The original large-flowered hybrid was summer-blooming *C. × jackmanii,* with 5-inch, four-petaled, rich purple flowers on a vigorous vine to 15 feet. A superior version of this hybrid is 'Purpurea Superba' ('Jackmanii Superba'), still sold today. More recent varieties in deep shades are 'Gypsy Queen', 'Mrs. N. Thompson', 'Richard Pennell', 'Royalty' (semidouble), 'Royal Velvet', and 'The President'. Paler choices include 'Belle of Woking' (double; silvery lilac), 'Teshio' (double; lavender), and 'Will Goodwin' (light lavender).

**Red.** In all varieties, the red contains a bit of blue. The deepest in color is 'Niobe', which opens blackish red. Others include 'Allanah', 'Ernest Markham', 'Mme. Edouard André', 'Red Cardinal', and 'Ville de Lyon' (light red).

**Pink.** The pinks run the gamut from pale mauve and rose to deep rosy cerise, sometimes with contrasting bars of color running the length of petals. Possibilities include 'Comtesse de Bouchard' (rose pink), 'Dr. Ruppel' (deep pink, darker bars), 'Hagley Hybrid' (shell pink; also known as 'Pink Chiffon'), 'Nelly Moser' (lilac pink, carmine bars), 'Sugar Candy' (lilac pink, cerise bars).

**White.** Spectacular *C. lanuginosa* 'Candida' (facing page) fits in this company. Hybrids include 'Gillian Blades', 'Henryi', 'Marie Boisselot' ('Mme. Le Coultre'; opens palest pink), and 'Snow Queen' (blushed pink).

**Yellow.** No strong yellow exists in the large-flowered hybrids, but 'Guernsey Cream', with 5-inch flowers of light creamy yellow, comes the closest.

*Clerodendrum thomsoniae*

# CLERODENDRUM
## thomsoniae
### BLEEDING HEART GLORYBOWER

🌿 EVERGREEN WOODY VINE

🌡 ZONES 22–28

◐ PARTIAL SHADE

💧 REGULAR WATER

Tropical West Africa is home to this twining, handsome but frost-tender vine. The broadly ovate, 7-inch, glossy dark green leaves make a refined setting for the flattish, 5-inch flower clusters that appear in late summer and fall. Each cluster holds up to 20 white buds reminiscent of Japanese paper lanterns; these open into showy, three-lobed red flowers with prominent stamens. Restrained and mannerly, the vine reaches about 12 feet at most. Use it to decorate sheltered patio walls or fences, train it on arbor posts, or try it as a screen on a freestanding trellis. Because it also grows well in large containers, you can enjoy it in zones beyond its hardiness limits: just move it to a frost-free shelter over winter.

Plant bleeding heart glorybower in spring after all danger of frost is past, choosing a spot in light or partial shade. Give it good, organically enriched soil, regular water, and one or two annual fertilizer applications. Where light frost is possible or likely (in all but Zones 24 and 25), locate plants in the most sheltered garden areas and try to protect stems on potentially frosty nights.

# CLYTOSTOMA
## callistegioides
### VIOLET TRUMPET VINE

🌿 EVERGREEN WOODY VINE

🌡 ZONES 9, 12–28

☀◐ SUN OR PARTIAL SHADE

💧 MODERATE WATER

You may find this lovely vine going by various *noms-de-jardin:* Argentine or orchid trumpet vine, love charm, painted trumpet. It's also sold under its former botanical names, *Bignonia violacea* and *B. speciosa.* By any name, though, it's sure to win favor for its vitality, beauty, and long bloom period. Each leaf consists of two opposite leaflets—wavy-edged, dark green oblongs to 3 inches long—and a central tendril by which

*Clytostoma callistegioides*

the stems climb. Trumpet-shaped violet, lavender, or pale purple flowers appear in small clusters; each blossom is about 3 inches long and flares open to about 3 inches across. The heaviest bloom comes from mid- or late spring (depending on climate) through the first month or so of summer, but flowering continues sporadically into fall.

Violet trumpet vine's boundless vigor can carry its dense foliage canopy to heights of 30 feet or so, but timely pruning easily curbs growth. Where it is adapted, it makes a first-rate cover for arbors and pergolas, from which streamers of stems will spill like a living curtain. It can also conquer and beautify wire fences; and if the tendrils have something to coil around, it is a spectacular cover for walls or solid fences as well.

Violet trumpet vine grows well in a variety of soils, from sandy to claylike, but it does need reasonably good drainage. Plant in spring as soon as all danger of frost is past. Water regularly until plants are established; thereafter, moderate watering is sufficient except, perhaps, during prolonged hot periods. Thin or prune at any time to guide, shorten, or untangle stems.

## COBAEA scandens. See page 40

![Cocculus carolinus photograph]

*Cocculus carolinus*

## COCCULUS carolinus
### CAROLINA MOONSEED

- Evergreen to deciduous woody vine
- Zones 28, 30–35
- Sun or partial shade
- Regular water

In its native southeastern United States, this twining vine clambers through shrubs and trees, decorating them every fall with clusters of pea-size scarlet fruits. Move it to the garden, and you have a dense-growing vine of modest size (to about 15 feet) for training on wire or string supports. The 4-inch, glossy green leaves, sometimes shallowly lobed, vary in form from ovate to triangular or heart-shaped. Greenish-white male and female flowers come in separate 3- to 5-inch clusters, but neither kind is showy; only the fall fruits provide conspicuous proof that the plant did indeed flower earlier in the year! Leaves are deciduous in colder zones, evergreen or nearly so in coastal regions and the lower South.

Carolina moonseed grows in a wide range of soils, even in those that are somewhat alkaline, but fertile, well-drained soil and regular moisture through the growing season will yield the most luxuriant growth. Remove superfluous and dead stems during winter.

## CONVALLARIA majalis
### LILY-OF-THE-VALLEY

- Deciduous perennial ground cover
- Zones 1–7, 14–20, 31–45
- Partial shade
- Regular water

This old-fashioned favorite has been cherished by generations of gardeners for its sublime scent and elegantly simple blossoms. In early spring, waxy white bells suspended on 6- to 8-inch stems appear above and among the rich green, broadly lance-shaped leaves; each stem carries 12 to 20 blossoms. In time, plants spread by a network of creeping rhi-

zomes to create a thick cover. They'll form an increasingly attractive carpet beneath deciduous trees and shrubs (where they'll endure competition from roots) or simply make ever-enlarging patches in open shade. Bulb specialists sometimes offer forms with variegated leaves or with double or pink flowers.

Plant lily-of-the-valley from individual rootstocks (called "pips"), setting them 1 to 2 inches deep, 6 inches apart; or set out small clumps from containers about 1 foot apart. Plant in good soil liberally amended with organic matter. After foliage dies in fall (but before new growth emerges in spring), apply a top-dressing of leaf mold, compost, or other organic material.

*Convallaria majalis*

## CORNUS canadensis
### BUNCHBERRY

- Deciduous perennial ground cover
- Zones 1–7, 32–45
- Partial to full shade
- Regular water

Gardeners familiar only with the glorious flowering dogwood trees may be unwilling to believe that bunchberry, too, is a dogwood—until they see the flowers, that is. In spring, the plant's 4- to 6-inch stems carry typical dogwood blossoms about 1½ inches across: tiny true flowers framed by four white, petal-like bracts. Leaves, carried in whorls atop the stems,

*Cornus canadensis*

are pointed, deep green ovals 1 to 2 inches long, with distinctive veining that parallels the leaf margins. Small, edible bright red fruits appear in late summer to early fall; as fall progresses, the foliage turns yellow and the entire plant dies back to the ground.

Bunchberry has fairly exacting cultural needs, but under ideal conditions it will spread at a moderate rate by underground stems to form a dense, even carpet over a considerable area. This is a woodland plant, at its best in moist, acid, well-drained soil with plenty of organic matter. Set out small plants from pots about 1 foot apart. Small rooted pieces gathered from the woods may not establish easily.

# CORONILLA varia
CROWN VETCH

- 🌿 DECIDUOUS PERENNIAL GROUND COVER
- ✂ ZONES 1–24, 28–45
- ☼ SUN
- 💧 MODERATE WATER

*Coronilla varia*

No one would put crown vetch on the list of best ground covers for general garden use. But if you want to cover a large patch of sloping land with something indestructible that looks reasonably attractive and knits the soil to control erosion, look no further. Despite this plant's perpetual resemblance to a not-quite-tamed weed, its vigor and tenacity are unmistakable virtues under conditions that would defeat more refined ground covers.

Spreading rapidly from underground roots, crown vetch sends up a thick, rich green cover of sprawling 2-foot stems bearing complex leaves, each with 11 to 25 oval, ½-inch leaflets. From summer into fall, the foliage mass is decorated with clusters of small pinkish lavender flowers that look like miniature sweet pea blossoms; these are followed by fingerlike brown seed capsules. The entire plant dies back to its roots over winter. The selection 'Emerald' has foliage of a particularly rich green; 'Penngift' is even more vigorous than the species and grows well in shade.

Crown vetch is indifferent to soil type and quality—but because its roots contain nitrogen-fixing bacteria that convert gaseous nitrogen to a form usable by plants, it is especially useful in lighter soils lacking in fertility. Set out small plants from pots about 1 foot apart. For best appearance, mow crown vetch in early spring to clear away the remains of the last year's growth; then apply fertilizer and water well.

# COTONEASTER

- 🌿 EVERGREEN AND DECIDUOUS WOODY GROUND COVERS
- ✂ ZONES VARY BY SPECIES
- ☼ SUN
- 💧💧 REGULAR TO MODERATE WATER

Rugged and undemanding, the cotoneasters are always tidy and presentable, and in spring and fall their green neatness is punctuated with color. Springtime brings forth flattened clusters of small, wild

rose–like blossoms in white or pale pink; the fruits that follow grow to pea size (or sometimes larger) and turn brilliant red in fall, then hang on to decorate the branches well into winter. With the exception of *C. salicifolius,* the species discussed here have small (½- to 1-inch), oval leaves that range from bright to dark green on their upper surfaces, gray to white beneath. Foliage of the deciduous species turns red in autumn. Stems of all typically root as they spread.

Creeping cotoneaster, *C. adpressus,* grows in Zones 1–24, 29–43. Its branches hug the contours of the ground, growing slowly and remaining under 1 foot high while spreading to 4 to 6 feet. Faster growing and taller (to 2½ feet), with larger leaves and fruits, is *C. a. praecox.* Both the species and its selection are deciduous, with dark, glossy, wavy-edged leaves.

Rock cotoneaster, *C. horizontalis,* is a briefly deciduous species suited to Zones 2–11, 14–24, 31–41. Its branching habit is unique among cotoneasters: the main limbs grow horizontally, while secondary branches form a flat herring-

*Cotoneaster horizontalis*

bone pattern. The plant spreads moderately quickly, reaching 2 to 3 feet high and 15 feet across. 'Variegatus' has white-margined leaves, while *C. h. perpusillus*

*Cotoneaster dammeri* 'Coral Beauty'

is a smaller-leafed plant that is lower growing and not as wide spreading.

Evergreen and semievergreen species offer a greater number of ground cover choices; several are described below.

Bearberry cotoneaster, *C. dammeri* (sometimes sold as *C. humifusus*), grows in Zones 2–24, 29–41. It spreads rapidly to about 10 feet but rises no higher than 6 inches. Foliage typically takes on bronzy or purple tints in fall and winter. Among this species' varieties are 'Eichholz', about twice as tall as the species, with a scattering of orange-red leaves in fall; 'Coral Beauty' ('Royal Beauty'), with coral red fruits on plants that top out at 1 to 2 feet; 'Lowfast', a rapid grower with branches rising to 1 foot high; and 'Skogholm', another fast grower that reaches 1½ to 3 feet high and bears only sparse crops of fruit.

Rockspray cotoneaster, *C. microphyllus*, grows in Zones 2–9, 14–24, 31–41. The principal stems hug the ground, spreading at a moderate rate to around 6 feet, but the secondary branches grow upright to 2 to 3 feet. Rosy red fruits are just a bit larger than the leaves. 'Emerald Spray' has a mounding-arching

appearance; *C. m. thymifolius* has especially tiny leaves on a plant smaller than the species.

A heavily fruiting choice is willowleaf cotoneaster, *C. salicifolius*, adapted to Zones 3–24, 31–34, 39. As the common name suggests, its leaves are narrow and willowlike. The species is a tall shrub, but it has a number of fast-growing spreading selections. The lowest of these is ground-hugging 'Repens', followed by 15-inch-tall 'Emerald Carpet'. 'Autumn Fire' ('Herbstfeuer') and 'Scarlet Leader' can reach 2 to 3 feet high and about 8 feet across; 'Parkteppich' is a bit taller. Foliage of most willowleaf varieties takes on purple tints in winter.

Necklace cotoneaster, *C. conspicuus* 'Decorus', is suited to Zones 3–24, 31–33. Tiny leaves densely cover plants that grow at a moderate rate to 1½ feet high, at least twice as wide. The rich red fruits are particularly plentiful.

Although cotoneasters grow well in good soil with regular watering, they don't need such fine conditions. Poor soil—be it sandy or claylike—and moderate watering are entirely satisfactory and, in fact, promote a larger fruit crop. You should, however, provide regular water during the first year to get roots well established. Set out plants from 1-gallon containers; space smaller spreaders about 3 feet apart, more widely spreading kinds about 5 feet apart.

All cotoneasters are best located where they won't need frequent restrictive pruning. Part of these plants' beauty lies in their naturally irregular contours, and stubbed-off branch ends and abrupt, cut edges on plantings spoil the picture. When you prune to limit spread, cut back to branch junctures within the foliage mass to preserve the normal raggedness. If vertical branches disrupt the desired height or horizontal plane, cut them back to their points of origin or to horizontal branches within the foliage. Fireblight may cause sudden wilting and blackening of leaves and stems in spring; for controls, see *Pyracantha* (page 85).

**DELOSPERMA.** See page 68

## DISTICTIS

- EVERGREEN WOODY VINES
- ZONES VARY BY SPECIES
- SUN OR PARTIAL SHADE
- REGULAR WATER

Bursting with robust good health, these vines put on a spectacular and long-lasting floral show in their favored mild-winter climates. All have glossy foliage and trumpetlike flowers on vigorous vines that can reach 20 to 30 feet. Each leaf has two opposite leaflets and a central, three-part tendril that does the climbing.

Blood-red trumpet vine, *D. buccinatoria*, is the most widely adapted of the group, growing in Zones 8, 9, 14–28. Bursts of bloom come during warm periods, when the oval, 4-inch leaflets provide a backdrop for 4-inch-long, yellow-throated trumpets which open red orange, then age to rosy red. A less rampant species is vanilla trumpet vine, *D. laxi-*

*Distictis buccinatoria*

*flora*, adapted to Zones 16, 22–27. Deep green, oblong leaflets reach 2½ inches long; vanilla-scented, 3½-inch trumpets open violet, then age to lavender and finally fade to white. Flowering comes throughout the warmer months, and can cover 8 months or more in the mildest zones. A hybrid between the previous two species is royal trumpet vine, *D.* 'Rivers', suitable for Zones 16, 22–27. In vigor and foliage, it is nearly a match for *D. buccinatoria,* and its orange-throated trumpets are larger overall.

Plant these handsome vines in good, well-drained soil and provide regular moisture during growth and bloom; during winter, they'll get by with just moderate watering. All are fine candidates for arbors and pergolas. Given support, they also look lovely on eaves and any wall that needs a showy, touch-of-the-tropics adornment; be sure supports are sturdy, since growth is dense and heavy. Prune during winter to thin out stems and control size.

# DOLICHOS lablab. See page 40
# DROSANTHEMUM. See page 69

# DUCHESNEA indica
INDIAN MOCK STRAWBERRY

* EVERGREEN PERENNIAL GROUND COVER
* ZONES 1–24, 29–43
* ☼ ◐ ● SUN OR SHADE
* ◐ ◑ REGULAR TO MODERATE WATER

At first glance, this ground-hugging plant looks like the edible strawberry. Leaves are strawberrylike; plants spread by runners, rooting as they spread; and the red, ½-inch fruits beg to be tasted. But several details make the difference. The ½-inch flowers that bloom in spring and summer are yellow rather than strawberry-blossom white; the fruits are, unfortunately, bland to downright flavorless; and both flowers and fruits are carried above the foliage, whereas those of strawberry nestle among or beneath the leaves. In shade, the foliage mass may reach 6 inches high; in sun, it is lower growing. Plants grow rapidly and can be somewhat invasive (especially if given regular watering), but they are easy to control.

Indian mock strawberry takes any exposure. It does nicely as an underplanting for shrubs and trees; it also

*Duchesnea indica*

excels as a low cover on sloping land. It is not fussy about soil type, but it does need good drainage. Set out small plants from flats or pots, spacing them about 1½ feet apart. Given partial or full shade, plantings need only moderate watering and can tolerate extended dry periods. If the location is sunny, though, water frequently enough to prevent wilting. For neatness, mow annually in early spring.

# EPIMEDIUM

* EVERGREEN, SEMIEVERGREEN, AND DECIDUOUS PERENNIAL GROUND COVERS
* ZONES 1–9, 14–17, 31–43
* ◐ ● PARTIAL TO FULL SHADE
* ◑ MODERATE WATER

A delicate tracery of handsome leaves and a pleasant display of spring flowers recommend the epimediums for shaded or woodland gardens, where they spread at a slow to moderate rate to form a carpet beneath plants that enjoy the same conditions, such as camellias and pieris.

A number of species and hybrids are available; they differ in details of foliage and flower, but all conform to the same general design. Growing from a dense network of underground stems, wiry leaf-stalks bear heart-shaped, 3-inch-long leaflets that overlap to form handsome clumps of foliage. New growth emerges bronzy pink, turns green by summer, then changes to reddish bronze in fall. In spring, wiry flower stems appear, holding

airy blossom sprays either well above or just over the leaves, depending on the species. The waxy-textured flowers may look like a cup and saucer or a saucer alone; in some species, flowers have spurs like those of columbine *(Aquilegia).*

Among deciduous epimediums, *E. grandiflorum* bears the largest blooms (to 2 inches). The species has red-and-violet flowers with white spurs, but named selections are available with blossoms of pink, lavender, or white. The foliage mass reaches 1 foot high. The hybrid *E. × youngianum* is lower growing (averaging about 8 inches), with pale green leaves and blossoms in white or pink, depending on the selection.

*Epimedium × versicolor* 'Sulphureum'

Three semievergreen epimediums make good low foliage mats. *E. × cantabrigiense* forms 8- to 12-inch clumps of olive-tinted foliage; two-tone flowers of red and yellow are held above the leaves. Another hybrid, foot-tall *E. × rubrum,* is red in both foliage and flower: its spiny-edged leaves have red veins and margins, while the showy blossoms are red with white to cream spurs. The *E. grandiflorum* hybrid *E. × versicolor* offers bronze-tinted leaves on a plant 12 to 15 inches tall; its vigorous yellow-flowered variety 'Sulphureum' is widely grown.

Evergreen *E. alpinum* spreads faster than other epimediums, making a carpet of leaves to about 9 inches high. Its small cup-and-saucer flowers are red

*Epimedium × youngianum* 'Roseum'

and yellow. Glossy foliage of nearly evergreen Persian epimedium, *E. pinnatum*, rises to 12 to 15 inches; clouds of brown-spurred yellow blossoms float above it.

All epimediums need slightly acid soil liberally amended with organic matter. Set out plants from pots or 1-gallon containers 1 foot apart. To keep deciduous and semievergreen plantings neat, shear off old growth in late winter or in spring before new growth begins.

# ERICA
HEATH

🌿 EVERGREEN WOODY GROUND COVERS
✂ ZONES VARY BY SPECIES
☀ SUN
💧 REGULAR WATER

The heaths resemble their close relative heather (*Calluna vulgaris*, page 44) in both looks and cultural needs—and in fact, they are often called "heather" by home gardeners. The dense, mounding-spreading plants have small, needlelike leaves and small, bell- to urn-shaped flowers borne in large clusters or spikes; flower colors include lilac, purple, pink shades, rosy red, bright red, and white. Bloom season varies depending on the species or variety; if you make your choices carefully, you can have blooming

heath throughout the year. Some gardeners create patchwork plantings by mixing heaths of different colors and bloom seasons. Unless otherwise noted, the heaths described below spread at a slow to moderate rate.

The most widely adapted species, *E. carnea* (sometimes sold as *E. herbacea*), grows in Zones 2–10, 14–24, 31, 32, 34, 36–39. Flowering usually starts in early winter and may last until early summer. The basic species is a prostrate plant with upright-growing branches that reach 6 to 16 inches; its flowers are rosy red. Lower-growing (8- to 12-inch) selections include 'Springwood' ('Springwood White'), a fast grower with light green foliage and white flowers; pure pink 'Springwood Pink'; and carmine red 'Vivelli', with foliage that turns to bronzy red in winter.

*E.* 'Dawn' is an easy-to-grow hybrid for Zones 4–9, 14–24, 31, 32, 34, 39. Deep pink flowers bloom from early summer into fall on a spreading, mounding plant to 1 foot high. New growth is golden yellow.

Two Northern European species grow well in Zones 4–6, 15–17, 31, 32, 34, 39. Dorset heath, *E. ciliaris*, bears rosy red flowers from midsummer into fall on 6- to 12-inch plants with light green foliage; two selections with darker

*Erica carnea*

green leaves are foot-tall 'Mrs. C. H. Gill', with dark red blooms, and 1½-foot-high, white-flowered 'Stoborough'. Purple-blossomed twisted heath, *E. cinerea*, and its scarlet-flowered form 'Atrosanguinea' bloom from early summer into fall; both are mounding-spreading plants that reach no higher than 1 foot.

Cross-leafed heath, *E. tetralix*, grows in Zones 4–6, 15–17, 32, 34, 39. The species and most of its varieties are upright growing, but 'Darleyensis' is a spreading plant to 8 inches high, bearing salmon pink blossoms from early summer into fall against a backdrop of gray-green foliage.

Like heather, the heaths will succeed only if certain cultural needs are met.

*Erica* varieties

Soil must be both well-drained (well-aerated, really) and moist. The best soils, therefore, are well-drained sandy to loamy types liberally amended with organic matter. Root systems are dense and matted (good for erosion control) but shallow and intolerant of drought. Most heaths need acid soil; exceptions are *E. carnea* and its varieties, which also grow well in soil that is neutral to slightly alkaline. Plants seldom need fertilizer; only those in the poorest of sandy soils may benefit from an occasional feeding.

The best heath climates have moist, cool air. The ocean-influenced areas of the Pacific Northwest and Northern California are ideal, as is the maritime Northeast. In drier and hotter inland climates, plants are more likely to succeed if given light or partial shade during summer.

Set out plants from pots or 1-gallon containers about 1½ feet apart. Heaths are neat and fairly dense by nature, so annual maintenance consists of no more than shearing off flowering stems after blossoms have faded.

## ERIGERON karvinskianus
MEXICAN DAISY,
SANTA BARBARA DAISY

- 🌿 EVERGREEN PERENNIAL GROUND COVER
- 🌱 ZONES 8, 9, 12–28
- ☀ SUN
- 💧💧 REGULAR TO LITTLE WATER

Fine texture and a graceful appearance belie the ruggedness of this fast-growing, nearly ever-blooming daisy. Slender, wiry, branching stems bear inch-long, narrow, irregularly toothed leaves; ¾-inch, pinkish white daisies appear above the foliage from spring into fall. Each plant is a spreading mound with stems that root here and there as they grow.

Few plants are less particular than Mexican daisy. It will grow in heavy or light soils and those that are saline or alkaline; it accepts competition from tree and shrub roots. Established plants do nicely with just moderate watering, but

*Erigeron karvinskianus*

they also thrive on regular moisture and tolerate drought. Set out plants from pots or 1-gallon containers about 1½ feet apart. After a year, plants will reach 10 to 20 inches high and may start to look a bit lumpy or straggly. When this happens, simply shear or mow plantings at some point between the last flowering in fall and the onset of new growth in winter or early spring. After plants are established, volunteer seedlings are likely to pop up around the garden—even between paving stones or in the chinks in dry-laid walls.

## EUONYMUS fortunei
WINTER CREEPER

- 🌿 EVERGREEN WOODY VINE OR GROUND COVER
- 🌱 ZONES 3–17, 28–41
- ☀ ☼ ● SUN OR SHADE
- 💧💧 REGULAR TO MODERATE WATER

Winter creeper shares its growth habit with another popular vining ground cover, ivy *(Hedera,* page 64). Its juvenile growth is trailing and vinelike and will cover the ground, rooting as it spreads; when it encounters a vertical surface, it heads upward, attaching itself by stem rootlets. In time, these vertical-growing stems send out mature growth—shrubby stems that bear inconspicuous flowers and fairly showy orange fruits. Plants rooted from juvenile growth are vines; those rooted from mature growth

are shrubs (though some will grow as vines if given vertical support). Thus, the named varieties of this one species include both vines and shrubs.

Mutations are common with *E. fortunei*. Many selections have been named and sold over the years, and new ones continue to be marketed. Those described below are among the most widely available vining forms; all are dense and neat, and most have polished-looking oval leaves. In general, all grow at a moderate to rapid rate.

Common winter creeper, *E. f. radicans,* has thick, oval dark green leaves to about an inch long. Plants make a spreading, sometimes undulating ground cover; if they are grown as vines, some branches produce mature growth that bears flowers and fruits. Purple-leaf winter creeper, *E. f.* 'Coloratus', forms a more even-surfaced ground cover and has leaves that turn purple during fall and winter; the similar-looking 'Dart's Blanket' is reputed to withstand seashore conditions well. As ascending vines, these two will eventually climb as high as their support; as ground covers, they make foliage carpets 6 to 12 inches high.

For especially small foliage on plants that will climb or spread, you can choose from several named selections. 'Minimus' has the smallest leaves (just ½ inch long), followed by 'Kewensis' (to

*Euonymus fortunei* 'Emerald 'n Gold'

⅝ inch) and 'Longwood' (under 1 inch). All three of these are green foliaged, and all are very low as ground covers—just 2 to 4 inches tall. 'Gracilis' shows white or cream variegation that turns pinkish in cold weather. 'Azusa' has green leaves with lighter-colored veins; leaf undersides turn maroon in winter.

Several more or less shrubby forms will grow as vines if given support. 'Emerald Gaiety' is the finest textured of the group, with leaves ¾ to 1½ inches long; irregular white margins border each leaf, with the white becoming decidedly purplish pink in cold weather. 'Emerald 'n Gold' is similar, but with gold-edged leaves. 'Carrieri' has glossy, 2-inch leaves on a vine that freely produces fruiting mature growth. For the greatest production of fruiting branches, though, 'Vegetus' is your best choice: one of its common names is "evergreen bittersweet." Its matte leaves are thick and leathery, up to 1½ inches long. 'Dart's Cardinal' is a notably heavy-fruiting 'Vegetus' selection.

The various winter creepers tolerate a wide range of conditions: sandy to claylike soil, sun to shade, regular to moderate watering. For ground cover use, set out plants from 1-gallon containers; space the larger growers about 5 feet apart, the smaller types about 3 feet apart.

## × FATSHEDERA lizei

🌿 🌺 EVERGREEN WOODY VINE
    OR GROUND COVER

  ✎ ZONES 4–10, 12–31, WARMER
    PARTS OF 32

  ◑ ● PARTIAL TO FULL SHADE

  💧 REGULAR WATER

In times past, this plant was known as "botanical wonder"—and no wonder: its parents are vining English ivy (*Hedera helix*, page 64) and shrubby Japanese aralia (*Fatsia japonica*). Its appearance reflects about equal parts of each parent. Its 6- to 8-inch leaves, each with five (or sometimes only three) pointed lobes, resemble those of Japanese aralia—but

× *Fatshedera lizei*

the thick leaf stems are lax and trailing, like those of ivy (although, unlike ivy stems, they have no means of attachment). The usual form has rich green leaves with a highly polished look, but the less-vigorous 'Variegata' offers striking white leaf margins.

Like its parents, this is a plant without strict cultural demands. It will grow in virtually any soil, though it does best if soil (whatever the type) is kept moist but not saturated. Grown as a vine, it may reach 10 feet, forming a striking freeform sculpture on a wall or trellis; remember that you'll need to tie stems in place. Stems tend to grow in a straight line. To stimulate branching, pinch out tip growth or cut stems back to the point where you want them to branch.

To use fatshedera as a bold-textured ground cover, set plants from gallon containers 1½ feet apart. Let stems sprawl on the ground; branches that attempt to grow upright can be bent to horizontal and pegged down, or simply cut out.

## FICUS pumila
### CREEPING FIG

🌿 🌺 EVERGREEN WOODY VINE
    OR GROUND COVER

  ✎ ZONES 8–28

  ☼ ◑ ● SUN OR SHADE

  💧 REGULAR WATER

Some gardeners insist that creeping fig should be sold with a warning label: innocent and dainty in its youth, this vine can

grow up to be a coarse, aggressive individual with invasive tendencies. There's certainly no denying that young plants are the picture of charm. Their closely set, 1-inch leaves are heart shaped to oval, with a crinkly texture. When plants are set against a wall, the stems attach firmly by rootlets to form a flat, dense cover that extends its territory with a delicate tracery of new growth; as ground covers, they make the same statement horizontally.

However, like ivy (*Hedera*, page 64) and winter creeper (*Euonymus fortunei*, page 59), creeping fig has mature (fruiting) growth that is larger than and noticeably different from the more delicate juvenile growth. In time, a wall-grown vine will produce thick stems that stand well

*Ficus pumila*

out from the surface and bear leathery leaves 2 to 4 inches long; if conditions are favorable, large oblong fruits develop as well. And not only does the total aspect of the plant change with maturity, but its vigor seems to accelerate. There is really no limit to a vine's coverage—which translates to a maintenance issue when a plant reaches your desired limit but wants to continue its territorial conquest. Mature growth is less likely to develop on creeping fig grown as a ground cover, but its stems will briskly ascend any shrub or tree in their path. Roots are invasive and put up stiff competition for plantings located near a vine or growing within a ground cover.

Three named selections offer interesting foliage variations. 'Minima' has shorter, narrower leaves than the species, while 'Quercifolia' has foliage lobed in the manner of oak leaves. 'Variegata' shows white markings on leaves of the usual size and shape.

Plant creeping fig in average, well-drained soil; for ground cover, set out 1-gallon plants about 6 feet apart. Although vines will grow in full sun, avoid placing them against hot south- and west-facing walls in areas where summers are warm to hot. As vines, young plants may be a bit slow to form attachments to the vertical surface. Maintenance consists of control: cut back, shear, or remove any stems that overstep their bounds.

# FORSYTHIA

🌿 DECIDUOUS WOODY GROUND COVERS
🌡 ZONES 2–16, 18, 19, 30–41
☀ SUN
💧 REGULAR TO MODERATE WATER

Brilliant yellow forsythia blossoms are one of the glories of early spring. Unfortunately, that's the one thing these two ground cover types don't provide! The hybrid 'Arnold Dwarf' grows fairly rapidly to 3 feet high and 6 to 7 feet across, with stems rooting where they touch soil; what few flowers it produces are small and greenish yellow. *F. viridissima* 'Bronxensis' offers only a modest display of yellow flowers, on a low, spreading plant that

*Forsythia viridissima* 'Bronxensis'

grows fairly slowly to 12 to 16 inches high and just 3 feet across.

These plants adapt to a wide range of soils. Use 'Arnold Dwarf' to cover expanses of sloping ground (the multiple root systems knit the soil well), setting out plants from gallon containers about 5 feet apart. *F. v.* 'Bronxensis' is best in smaller areas on level ground; space gallon-size plants 2 feet apart. Prune wayward growth of both in the leafless winter period.

*Fragaria chiloensis*

# FRAGARIA chiloensis
WILD STRAWBERRY

🌿 EVERGREEN PERENNIAL GROUND COVER
🌡 ZONES 4–24
☀☽ SUN OR PARTIAL SHADE
💧 REGULAR WATER

This is indeed a wild strawberry, an ancestor of the succulent crimson fruits sold in markets. The familiar-looking leaves—glossy dark green, with three tooth-edged leaflets—betray the kinship. In winter, they take on red tints. White, inch-wide spring flowers are occasionally followed by small red fruits—edible, but far from commercial quality. Plants spread rapidly by runners, making a foliage mass 6 to 12 inches high.

In its native climates along the Pacific coastline of North and South America, wild strawberry thrives in full sun. In hotter and drier regions, however, it needs some shade. Provide reasonably good, well-

drained soil; set out rooted segments or young plants from pots or flats, spacing them 1 to 1½ feet apart. To keep plantings renewed and prevent buildup of stems, mow annually in early spring before growth begins. Later in spring, apply fertilizer to ensure vigorous, lush growth.

# GALIUM odoratum
SWEET WOODRUFF

🌿 EVERGREEN PERENNIAL GROUND COVER
🌡 ZONES 1–6, 15–17, 31–43
☀● PARTIAL TO FULL SHADE
💧 REGULAR WATER

A patch of sweet woodruff always suggests the coolness of a shady woodland. Closely set whorls of narrow bright green leaves clothe slender, 6- to 12-inch stems, forming a dense carpet. From late spring into summer, this lush mat is dotted with tiny, four-petaled white flowers. Dried sweet woodruff leaves are the traditional flavoring for May wine.

Like many other woodland natives, sweet woodruff needs reasonably good, organically enriched soil and a steady supply of moisture. Given these conditions, it will spread rapidly by rooting stems, even becoming somewhat invasive. Its shallow, noncompetitive root system makes it easy to contain, though—and also makes it a fine underplanting for shade-loving trees, shrubs, and larger perennials. Set out young plants from pots about 1 foot apart.

*Galium odoratum*

*Gaultheria procumbens*

# GAULTHERIA

- 🌿 EVERGREEN WOODY GROUND COVERS
- 🌡 ZONES VARY BY SPECIES
- ◑ PARTIAL SHADE
- 💧 REGULAR WATER

These unassuming woodland plants are neat without being institutionally tidy. The more widely adapted of two ground cover species is the plant known as wintergreen, teaberry, or checkerberry— *G. procumbens,* suited to Zones 1–7, 14–17, 32–45. Its creeping, rooting stems send up branches to about 6 inches high, with oval, 2-inch leaves clustered near the tips. Foliage is light green when new, maturing to glossy dark green and then taking on reddish tints with the onset of cold weather in fall. The small, pinkish white, urn-shaped flowers that bloom in late spring are followed by small, edible scarlet berries in autumn. Both the leaves and the berries have a wintergreen flavor.

Similar to *G. procumbens* but slightly taller (to 8 inches) is the Western native *G. ovatifolia,* which grows successfully in Zones 1–7, 14–17.

Given their preferred woodland conditions—organically enriched, constantly moist, acid soil with good drainage—these plants spread slowly but steadily. They make a perfect underplanting for acid-loving trees and shrubs such as rhododendron, mountain laurel *(Kalmia latifolia),* camellia, and pieris. Set out plants from pots about 1 foot apart.

# GAZANIA

- 🌿 EVERGREEN PERENNIAL GROUND COVERS
- 🌡 ZONES 8–30
- ☀ SUN
- 💧 💧 REGULAR TO MODERATE WATER

The sunny colors of summer come down to earth in gazanias: 3- to 4-inch daisies of yellow, orange, red, copper, pink, cream, or white, often with a contrasting dark central eye or a dark ring around a yellow center. Plants bloom most lavishly from late spring into midsummer, but they'll flower sporadically throughout the year in regions with moderate summers and mild winters. Flowers open on sunny days, close when evening approaches, and (with few exceptions) remain closed during cloudy or overcast weather.

You have a choice of two growth habits: clumping and trailing.

**Clumping types** form ever-thickening clumps; plants grow at a slow to moderate pace and must be spaced 8 to 12 inches apart to make a solid cover. Their leaves are usually long and narrow, with green upper surfaces and gray, furry undersides; some hybrids have narrow leaves with deeply lobed or cleft margins. Flowers come on 6- to 10-inch stems, putting them a few inches above the leaves. Both single-color and mixed-color choices are available. Among the mixed-color sorts are named strains such as Carnival, with silver leaves; early-blooming Chansonette; and Daybreak, with flowers that open at dawn. The Harlequin and Sundance strains feature striped or banded petals; Mini-Star is a compact and free-flowering group that's also available in single-color selections such as 'Mini-Star Yellow' and 'Mini-Star Tangerine'. Several named hybrids are widely sold, among them 'Aztec Queen' (a yellow-and-bronze multicolor), 'Burgundy', 'Copper King',

*Gazania 'Burgundy'*

and 'Fiesta Red'. 'Moonglow' has bright yellow double flowers that open even on sunless days.

**Trailing gazanias** spread rapidly by long, trailing stems and, when spaced 1 to 1½ feet apart, can thoroughly cover a sizable area (they're particularly good on sloping ground). Their foliage is typically silvery gray; flower stems are 6 to 10 inches high. The color range is more limited than that of clumping gazanias, including only yellow, orange, bronze, and white. Named varieties include black-centered orange 'Sunburst', solid yellow 'Sunglow', and 'Sunrise Yellow', with black-centered yellow blooms and green leaves.

Gazanias are not particular about soil type. They perform well with moderate watering everywhere but in the desert zones, where regular watering is needed. Fertilize in early spring, using a slow-release fertilizer. After several years, plantings may decline in vigor or become patchy (this is particularly likely with clumping gazanias). To rejuvenate them, you can dig, divide, and replant healthy rooted pieces in early spring.

*Gazania* (trailing)

*Gelsemium sempervirens*

## GELSEMIUM sempervirens
CAROLINA JESSAMINE

- ❧ ⚜ EVERGREEN WOODY VINE
  OR GROUND COVER
- ✀ ZONES 8–24, 26–33
- ☼ ◑ SUN OR PARTIAL SHADE
- ◌ REGULAR WATER

In late winter and early spring, when not much is happening in the garden, Carolina jessamine is a brilliant presence: the vine covers itself in bright yellow, sweet-scented, funnel-shaped blooms about 1½ inches long. It's attractive during the rest of the year as well, thanks to its dense cloak of glossy bright green, 1- to 4-inch, oval leaves. For double flowers, look for 'Pride of Augusta' (sometimes sold as 'Plena').

Carolina jessamine grows at a moderate rate. As a vine, it twines to about 20 feet; if it is trained where branch ends can trail from eaves or an overhead, you'll get a delicate curtain of foliage and stems that will sway in the breeze. As a ground cover, it excels on sloping ground, though you should keep in mind that the stems will climb any vertical support they encounter, be it shrub, tree, or fence. Grown this way, the plant builds up to about 3 feet high.

For best performance, plant Carolina jessamine in good, well-drained, slightly acid soil. It takes sun or partial shade but blooms most profusely in full-sun locations. Train vines and thin out tangling stems after bloom has finished.

For ground cover use, set out plants from 1-gallon containers 4 to 6 feet apart.

*Note:* All parts of Carolina jessamine are toxic if ingested.

## GENISTA
BROOM

- ⚜ EVERGREEN AND DECIDUOUS
  WOODY GROUND COVERS
- ✀ ZONES VARY BY SPECIES
- ☼ SUN
- ◌ MODERATE TO LITTLE WATER

For masses of brilliant yellow in late spring, the brooms are the ground covers to choose—the small, sweet pea–shaped blooms encrust the branches so heavily that foliage and stems are virtually obscured. The tiny, oval or needlelike leaves may not last through the growing season, but the green stems give even deciduous or sparsely foliaged brooms an evergreen appearance. Plants spread at a slow to moderate rate.

Most widely adapted of the ground cover brooms is *G. sagittalis,* suited to Zones 2–22, 32, 34, 37. This one can't really be called evergreen or deciduous, since it's entirely leafless! The slender green branches have winged appendages that give them a jointed look. The plant may remain as low as 6 inches, but it spreads to 3 feet or more.

*Genista lydia*

Deciduous *G. pilosa,* successful in Zones 3–22, 32, 34, 37, is an intricate tangle of gray-green twigs with matching grayish leaves to ½ inch long; it reaches about 1½ feet tall, 7 feet across. 'Vancouver Gold' is a superior selection to about 1 foot high and 3 to 4 feet wide.

Evergreen (but nearly leafless) *G. lydia* grows in Zones 4–6, 14–17, 32, 34. It's a much-branched, mounding plant to about 2 feet high and 4 feet wide.

Brooms prefer poor soil: sandy, well drained, and fairly dry. Giving them good soil and frequent watering can actually prove fatal. Set out plants from 1-gallon containers 2 feet apart. Little maintenance is needed; prune out any stems that depart from the general contour as they arise.

*Hardenbergia violacea* 'Happy Wanderer'

## HARDENBERGIA

- ❧ EVERGREEN WOODY VINES
- ✀ ZONES VARY BY SPECIES
- ☼ ◑ SUN OR PARTIAL SHADE
- ◌ MODERATE WATER

A flowering hardenbergia gives wisteria some stiff competition. Like wisteria, it's a twining vine that blooms during late winter and early spring, bearing long, slender clusters of sweet pea–shaped flowers in violet shades. Unlike wisteria, it is a modest grower, unlikely to overreach its allotted space. Two species are available, differing in hardiness and overall texture. Both reach about 10 feet tall.

The more adaptable plant is *H. violacea,* suited to Zones 8–24. Lance-

*Hardenbergia comptoniana*

shaped, deep green leaves to 4 inches long adorn a rather bushy vine. The 5-inch sprays of flowers may be violet, lilac, pink, or white; named varieties include pink-flowered 'Rosea' and ruggedly vigorous 'Happy Wanderer', with pinkish purple blossoms.

Lilac vine, *H. comptoniana*, grows in Zones 15–24. Its foliage has a more delicate look than that of *H. violacea*, since the dark green leaves are divided into three leaflets (each to 3 inches long). Vivid violet-blue blossoms come in narrow sprays to 6 inches or longer.

Well-drained sandy to sandy loam soil, enriched with organic matter before planting, is best for these vines. Because they are relatively short, they are fine choices for decorating pillars, trellises, and low fences or walls. Do any necessary thinning and untangling of stems after bloom finishes.

# HEDERA
IVY

🌿 🌺 EVERGREEN WOODY VINES OR
      GROUND COVERS

   ✂ ZONES VARY BY SPECIES

   ☀ ◑ ● SUN OR SHADE

   ◐ ◔ REGULAR TO MODERATE WATER

Some gardeners swear by ivy; others swear *at* it! Depending on whom you ask, it's either the perfect vine and ground cover or one of the most troublesome. Once established, ivy is relentless and seemingly immortal. Ground cover plant-

ings will head upward if given the chance, clinging tightly by aerial rootlets to climb any vertical surface—fences, walls, tree trunks, shrub stems, flower pots, even garden furniture. And vertical-growing vining plants, if not curbed periodically, will embark on ground-level conquests, spreading out over the soil and rooting as they go. In short, ivy requires vigilance and management.

The plant's very aggression and tenacity, however, can offer a distinct advantage in certain situations. Ivy ground covers root densely and deeply, providing an ideal erosion-control blanket. Vining ivy transforms any wire fence into a solid wall of handsome foliage. Solid walls, too, can be beautified by a dense cloak of ivy leaves, though wood surfaces and masonry joints will eventually suffer from the plant's aerial rootlets and the moist atmosphere created by its thick foliage.

*Hedera helix*
'Buttercup'

All ivies have two growth phases. Juvenile plants are vining, with distinctly lobed leaves; the number of lobes and degree of lobing vary from one species to another. Growth will remain in this juvenile phase on ivies grown as ground covers, but if plants are allowed to grow upward, they will eventually send out mature growth—shrubby, branching

stems with unlobed foliage, bearing clusters of tiny greenish flowers followed by berrylike black fruits. Plants grown from cuttings of mature growth are shrubby, not vining, and retain the more simple leaves. Once a vine begins fruiting, volunteer seedlings may pop up here and there as birds consume berries and scatter seeds.

English ivy, *H. helix*, is the best-known and most adaptable species. It grows easily in Zones 3–34 and 39; the hardiest varieties extend the range into Zones 35, 37, and the warmer parts of 38 and 41. The most typical form has matte dark green leaves with conspicuous paler veins; each leaf has three to five pointed lobes and can reach 2 to 4 inches wide and long. Specialty growers offer many named selections that vary widely in vigor and in foliage shape, size, and color. Leaves may be deeply lobed and cleft, ruffle edged, narrow and elongated, arrow shaped, or divided into distinct leaflets; colors range from deepest green through chartreuse to gold, and foliage may be solid colored or variegated in yellow, cream, or white. Many such selections are less aggressive than the species, making them good choices for modest-growing vines or smaller-scale ground covers. Gardeners in cold-

*Hedera canariensis*

winter areas may want to grow 'Baltica', with whitish-veined leaves just half the usual size; it's acknowledged to be the hardiest to cold. Other especially cold-tolerant varieties are 'Bulgarica', 'Hebron', 'Rochester', 'Thorndale', and '238ᵗʰ Street'.

The plant commonly known as Atlantic ivy may be offered as *H. helix* 'Hibernica' or as a separate species, *H. hibernica;* it has large leaves (to 3½ inches across, 5½ inches long) with five lobes.

Persian ivy, *H. colchica,* grows in Zones 3–34. It is the giant of the genus, with heart-shaped to oval, glossy dark green leaves that can reach up to 7 inches across and 10 inches long. Varieties include 'Dentata', with lightly toothed leaf margins; 'Dentata Variegata', with foliage in a marbled blend of deep green, gray green, and creamy white; and 'Sulphur Heart' ('Paddy's Pride'), with gold variegation in the leaf centers.

Algerian ivy, *H. canariensis,* is a familiar sight in Zones 8, 9, 12–28: great swaths of it are used for freeway and industrial plantings. Its shiny dark green leaves have three to five shallow lobes and can reach 8 inches wide and long. Widely planted 'Variegata' ('Gloire de Marengo') has dark leaves marbled with gray green and irregularly margined in creamy white.

Ivy is not particular about soil. For ground cover plantings, though, a bit of preparation ensures a good start. Begin by digging or tilling the soil deeply (to 8 to 12 inches, if possible) and incorporating a generous quantity of organic matter. Set out rooted cuttings or plants from flats or pots, spacing them 1½ feet apart; to decrease the mortality rate, thoroughly moisten roots and stems—and the soil —before planting. Give any ivy, whether ground cover or individual vine, regular watering during its first year to get roots established. Thereafter, Algerian and Persian ivies prefer regular watering; English ivy can manage with moderate watering in cool-summer regions but needs regular moisture in warm to hot climates. After several years, ground cover plant-ings will build up a deep thatch of stems with foliage riding on the surface—a haven for snails, slugs, and even rodents. At that point, shear the planting back to ground level or mow it with a heavy-duty power mower. Do this job in early spring, so new growth will quickly cover the scalped stems.

## HELIANTHEMUM
### nummularium
SUNROSE

- 🌱 EVERGREEN WOODY GROUND COVER
- ✿ ZONES 3–9, 14–24, 32, 34
- ☼ SUN
- ◖ MODERATE TO LITTLE WATER

In fairly small, sunny spaces, the sunroses shine. From midspring to midsummer, their spreading mat of fine-textured foliage is spangled with warm-colored flowers that resemble small single roses —or miniature versions of their rockrose relatives (*Cistus,* page 49). Many named varieties are sold in shades of pink, red, orange, copper, yellow, and white; some are double flowered. Each inch-wide blossom lasts only a single day, but countless buds produce a good show over a long (at least 2-month) bloom period. Narrow leaves to an inch long may be glossy dark green or nearly gray. Individual plants reach 6 to 8 inches high, about 3 feet across; they grow slowly until established, then begin to spread at a moderate rate.

Sunroses grow readily on level or sloping ground. Plant them in welldrained soil. They need moderate watering in hot-summer regions, but they'll get by with very little where summers are cool. Set out plants from pots or 1-gallon containers, spacing them about 2 feet apart. After bloom, lightly shear plants to keep them dense and to encourage a second round of flowering in late summer or early fall. In cold-winter Zones 3, 32, and 34, lightly cover plants with evergreen boughs over winter to keep the foliage from dehydrating.

*Helianthemum nummularium*

## HIBBERTIA scandens
GUINEA GOLD VINE

- 🌱 EVERGREEN WOODY VINE OR GROUND COVER
- ✿ ZONES 16, 17, 21–24
- ☼ ◑ SUN OR PARTIAL SHADE
- ◖ REGULAR WATER

Within its rather limited range, this handsome Australian native is one of the best multipurpose vines. Unless damaged by light frost (from which it easily recovers), it is attractive throughout the year. The twining, red-brown stems are well clothed in oval, glossy dark green leaves. From late spring through summer and on into fall, the polished foliage provides a backdrop for 3-inch, lemon yellow blossoms that look like single roses or, perhaps, like the blooms of Aaron's beard (*Hypericum calycinum,* page 67). Guinea gold vine is a modest grower, climbing only about 10 feet—a trait that

*Hibbertia scandens*

recommends it for pillars, trellises, and low fences. It can be used as a ground cover, too, and is especially suited for gently sloping areas.

Set out plants in good, well-drained soil. Choose a spot in full sun where summers are cool to mild, a partial-shade location in warmer regions. Avoid planting against hot south- or west-facing walls. For ground cover use, set out plants from 1-gallon containers about 6 feet apart. Do any significant thinning or pruning in late fall or winter, when plants are not in flower; during bloom time, remove errant stems as needed.

*Hippocrepis comosa*

## HIPPOCREPIS comosa

🌿 EVERGREEN PERENNIAL GROUND COVER

✂ ZONES 8–26

☼ SUN

💧💧 REGULAR TO MODERATE WATER

Like the similar crown vetch (*Coronilla varia*, page 55), hippocrepis is a useful ground cover for less-than-ideal situations where other, more tailored-looking choices would suffer or fail. It's tough enough to serve as a lawn substitute, even tolerating a bit of foot traffic; when it's grown on sloping land, its roots will bind soil to prevent erosion.

Despite its rugged constitution, hippocrepis has a fine texture and a soft appearance: each leaf is composed of seven to 15 tiny bright green leaflets, and the multibranched stems form a dense,

3-inch-tall mat that spreads and roots at a moderate to fast pace, eventually covering a wide area. In spring, plants bear small clusters of ½-inch flowers that look like yellow sweet peas.

Though it tolerates adversity, hippocrepis looks best when planted in average to good soil and given regular watering during dry spells. Set out plants from flats or pots about 1 foot apart. To keep plantings neat, mow them annually after the flowering season is over.

## HOUTTUYNIA cordata

🌿 DECIDUOUS PERENNIAL GROUND COVER

✂ ZONES 2–9, 14–24, 31–41

☼ ◑ ● SUN OR SHADE

💧💧 💧 AMPLE TO REGULAR WATER

From a bit of a distance, this plant (which desperately needs a common name) could be mistaken for English ivy (*Hedera helix*, page 64). Semiglossy, heart-shaped leaves to 3 inches long, carried on leafstalks that rise from spreading underground stems, form a blanket of foliage about 9 inches high. The species has medium green leaves, but nobody bothers to grow it—a decision that's easy to understand when you see the variety 'Chameleon' (also sold as 'Variegata' and 'Tricolor'). Its foliage is strikingly splashed with cream, yellow, pink, and red; the colors are most intense on plants growing in sun. Hout-

*Houttuynia cordata*

*Houttuynia cordata* 'Chameleon'

tuynia bears flowers reminiscent of tiny dogwood blossoms, but they're hardly noticeable. Gardeners who value understatement and eschew 'Chameleon' as gaudy and common may prefer 'Plena', which offers somewhat showier double blossoms on a green-leafed plant.

Houttuynia revels in good soil and as much moisture as you can supply, even thriving in the boggy areas at pond margins. In the garden, regular watering and soil on the clayey side yield the best results. Set out plants from pots or 1-gallon containers, spacing them 1½ to 2 feet apart. One caution, though: this plant can become an aggressive pest once it is growing well. To curb its spread, install wood, concrete, or metal barriers that extend 8 to 12 inches into the soil.

## HUMULUS lupulus
### COMMON HOP

🌿 DECIDUOUS PERENNIAL VINE

✂ ZONES 11–24, 28–45

☼ ◑ SUN OR PARTIAL SHADE

💧 REGULAR WATER

Although common hop is more widely planted as a commercial crop (its flowers are a traditional flavoring for beer), it is an asset in the home garden as well. Each year, rough-textured, twining stems spring from perennial roots and grow rapidly to 15 to 25 feet; the young shoots can be cooked and eaten as a vegetable. The hand-size leaves, usually three lobed and tooth edged, overlap like shingles as the vine gains height. Leaves of the species are a refreshing bright green; the more ornamental 'Aureus' has chartreuse to golden yellow foliage. Plants bloom in late summer. The actual flowers are tiny, but they're enclosed in conspicuous clusters of bracts that resemble pale green, soft, 1- to 2-inch pine cones and even have a piny fragrance.

Common hop does best in good, organically enriched soil, the sort you would use for vegetables or annual flowers. In hot-summer regions, 'Aureus' needs light shade during the heat of the day to keep its color from bleaching. Plants are sold as dormant roots; plant them just beneath the soil surface, with the thick end pointing up. Provide string, wire, or a trellis for support. At the onset of frosty weather in fall or early winter, leaves and stems will turn brown and die; remove them from their supports before new growth starts in spring.

*Humulus lupulus*

# HYDRANGEA
## CLIMBING HYDRANGEA
🌿 DECIDUOUS WOODY VINES
🌡 ZONES 2–21, 31–41
◐ ● PARTIAL TO FULL SHADE
💧 REGULAR WATER

If you know the shrubby hydrangeas with lace cap–type flower heads, you already know how their climbing relatives look: just visualize those familiar flowers and leaves ascending a wall or tree trunk.

*Hydrangea anomala*

Though botanists recognize two similar species of climbing hydrangea, the plants are often mislabeled in the nursery trade. The chief difference between the two lies in their ultimate size: *H. anomala* is the shorter grower (to about 35 feet), while *H. petiolaris* (often sold as *H. anomala petiolaris*) can reach 60 feet or more if not restrained. Both species have tooth-edged, glossy-surfaced, roundish to heart-shaped leaves to 4 inches long. The summer flowers come in heads to 10 inches across, with small, starlike fertile blossoms clustered in the center and showy, 1½- to 2-inch-wide white sterile blossoms surrounding them. Flower heads of *H. anomala* are slightly domed, while those of *H. petiolaris* are flat.

Plants climb like ivy (*Hedera*, page 64), their stems attaching firmly to vertical surfaces by aerial rootlets. In summer, shrubby flowering branches spring from these vining stems. Autumn brings no dramatic foliage display, but the peeling, cinnamon-colored bark on mature vines looks quite decorative in winter.

Given good, reasonably well-drained soil and regular moisture, climbing hydrangeas are vigorous and productive. They are among the best flowering vines for shade and partial shade; only where summers are cool do they thrive in sunny locations, and even there they should not be given a south- or west-facing exposure. Young plants must be tied to their supports at first, but in time the new growth will develop aerial rootlets and provide its own attachments. Prune vines only as needed to contain growth.

# HYPERICUM calycinum
## AARON'S BEARD,
## CREEPING ST. JOHNSWORT
👑 EVERGREEN TO SEMIEVERGREEN WOODY GROUND COVER
🌡 ZONES 3–24, 31–34
☀ ◐ ● SUN OR SHADE
💧 MODERATE WATER

Good looks and indestructibility combine in Aaron's beard. Thin, arching stems bearing paired 4-inch oval leaves arise from rapidly spreading underground stems to make a dense, even cover to 1 foot high. Foliage is rich green in sun, lighter green in shade. From late spring through summer, stems are adorned with 3-inch yellow blossoms that look rather like single roses centered with exaggerated powder-puffs of stamens. Plants spread aggressively and constantly enlarge their territory unless contained by a barrier like that suggested for *Houttuynia* (facing page). On the positive side, the dense mat of roots and underground stems competes easily with surface-rooted trees and helps prevent erosion on sloping ground.

Aaron's beard grows in virtually all soils. It is quite drought tolerant but looks much better with at least moderate watering. Set out plants from flats or pots about 1½ feet apart. To renew growth and maintain an even surface, mow plantings every 3 years in late winter or early spring. In the coldest zones, Aaron's beard may be killed to the ground in winter, but it regrows from the roots in spring. In such climates, shear or mow off dead material before new growth gets underway.

*Hypericum calycinum*

# ICE PLANTS

The ice plants are a group of low-growing perennial ground covers that earn their collective name by virtue of of the powdery gray or crystalline coating often found on their thick, succulent leaves. Most offer showy, bee-attracting flowers—some almost blindingly brilliant in color—that resemble silky-petaled daisies. All like sun and are unparticular about soil (some will grow in nearly pure beach sand). Water just often enough to keep foliage from wilting or shriveling, since overwatering can produce root rot or dieback, especially in heavy soil during hot weather. Set out plants from flats or pots, spacing them as directed for each entry. Fertilize lightly in midfall or after flowering has finished.

Though all ice plants were once grouped together as Mesembryanthemum, botanists have reclassified them into separate genera. Unless otherwise noted, plants spread at a moderate rate.

*Drosanthemum floribundum*

*Aptenia cordifolia*

APTENIA cordifolia. Zones 15–17, 21–27. Inch-long, bright green leaves are heart shaped to oval, borne on lax stems that grow at a moderate to fast rate, spreading to about 2 feet and reaching a height of several inches. 'Variegata' has white-edged foliage. Inch-wide blossoms in vivid purplish red bloom in spring and summer. Space plants 1 to 1½ feet apart.

CARPOBROTUS. Zones 12–27. These coarse-textured, trailing plants have fingerlike leaves and 2-inch, pastel blossoms in summer. Plants reach up to about a foot tall; they are fast growers and will cover a considerable area on level or gently sloping ground, but avoid planting them on steep banks, where the weight of a rain-soaked planting could cause the ground to slide. Set 2 feet apart.

*Carpobrotus chilensis*

West Coast native *C. chilensis* has soft rosy purple flowers on plants with three-sided, 2-inch-long leaves. South African *C. edulis* has pale yellow to rose pink blossoms and curved leaves to 5 inches long; edible but insipid fruits follow the flowers.

CEPHALOPHYLLUM 'Red Spike'. Zones 8, 9, 11–24. Individual plants reach 3 to 5 inches high and spread to 15 inches, their spiky, bronzy red leaves pointing upward like slender fingers. The 2-inch, cerise red flowers come mainly in winter, though scattered blossoms can appear throughout the year. Set plants 1 foot apart. In desert zones, water carefully and sparingly to avoid root rot.

DELOSPERMA. Zones vary by species. Set out all three of the following choices 1 to 1½ feet apart.

Two *Delosperma* species take ice plants into truly cold-winter regions. Hardiest is *D. nubigenum*, which grows in

*Cephalophyllum 'Red Spike'*

*Delosperma cooperi*

Zones 2–24, 28–41. Plants hug the ground, forming a thick, 3-foot-wide carpet of cylindrical, bright green leaves that turn glowing red in fall and remain that color until spring. Later in spring, bright yellow flowers to 1½ inches across blanket the planting for about a month. *D. cooperi* will grow in Zones 3–24, 28–31, and warmer parts of 32 (with winter protection of snow or mulch in the coldest areas). It spreads to about 2 feet wide and 5 inches high, bearing nearly cylindrical, fingerlike leaves; glistening purple, 2-inch flowers appear throughout summer.

The hybrid *D.* 'Alba', also known as white trailing ice plant, grows in Zones 12–24. Bright green, rounded leaves cover a low, trailing plant that roots as it spreads, eventually advancing to about 2 feet across. The small white summer flowers are noticeable but not really showy.

**DROSANTHEMUM.** Zones 14–27. Foliage covered with crystalline dots makes these fast spreaders the "iciest" of ice plants. Rosea ice plant, *D. floribundum*, covers large areas with a 6-inch-high mat of tiny leaves; in late spring, blossoms turn the planting into a solid sheet of cool, shimmering pale pink. Of all ice plants, this is the best choice for erosion control on steep banks. Shrubbier *D. hispidum* grows 1½ to 2 feet high and spreads to just 3 feet; inch-wide, bright purple flowers in summer make a fine display against the 1-inch-long, cylindrical leaves. Set out plants of both species 1½ feet apart.

LAMPRANTHUS. Zones 14–26. These take the prize for brilliance—a tapestry planting of mixed colors actually hurts the eyes! Plants are typically spreading and semishrubby, with gray-green, fingerlike, three-sided or cylindrical leaves; the

arresting floral show runs from mid- to late winter into spring. Space plants 1 to 1½ feet apart. After flowering, cut back lightly to prevent fruit set and encourage new growth.

The 2-inch flowers of *L. aurantiacus* are brilliant orange, produced on compact, bushy plants to 15 inches high and about 2 feet wide. Named color selections include 'Glaucus' (clear yellow) and 'Sunman' (golden yellow). Just as tall but more spreading in habit is *L. productus*, with inch-wide purple flowers and bronze-tipped foliage. Trailing ice plant, *L. spectabilis*, offers a range of colors—lilac pink, rose pink, red, purple—in 2½-inch flowers on spreading plants to 1 foot high, 2 feet wide. Redondo creeper, *L. filicaulis*, differs in size and texture from the preceding three species. Its slender, creeping stems and tiny leaves slowly form a pink-flowered mat with a height of about 3 inches and indefinite spread.

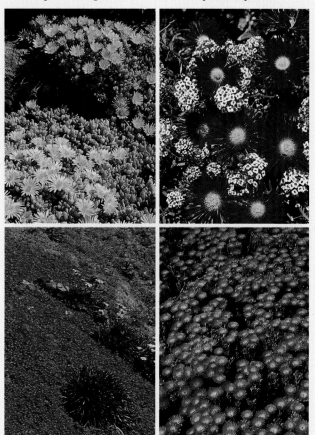

*Delosperma nubigenum*

*Lampranthus spectabilis*

*Drosanthemum floribundum*

*Lampranthus aurantiacus*

*Lampranthus aurantiacus*

*Ipomoea alba*

# IPOMOEA
## MORNING GLORY

- EVERGREEN PERENNIAL VINES
- ZONES VARY BY SPECIES
- SUN
- REGULAR TO MODERATE WATER

The old-fashioned favorite annual morning glory *(I. tricolor)* is profiled on page 40. Described here are its equally charming and vigorous kin—perennials in the zones listed for each, but so fast growing that they too can be treated as annuals in colder-winter regions. All feature the typical broad, funnel-shaped flowers borne on twining stems.

Blue dawn flower, *I. indica* (formerly *I. acuminata*), grows in Zones 8, 9, 12–28. Clustered, 3- to 4-inch blossoms bloom from spring into fall; they open an intense bright blue in early morning, then fade to pinkish purple by the time they fold at day's end. Outfitted in dark green, heart-shaped to three-lobed leaves to 6 inches long, the stems grow rapidly: the vine can become a smothering blanket of greenery to 30 feet high and wide, easily concealing an unsightly fence or other structure.

Moonflower, *I. alba,* succeeds in Zones 15–17, 23–27. As its name suggests, this summer-flowering, 30-foot vine is a night bloomer, showing off its fragrant, 6-inch white blossoms after sundown and into the night (and on cloudy days, too, when the overcast tricks it into remaining open). With its thick cover of 8-inch, heart-shaped leaves, moonflower is lovely as a shade caster on an arbor or as decoration for a trellis or fence.

In mild-winter Zones 25–28, *I. horsfalliae* provides vibrant color during midwinter. It differs notably from the previous two species in more than bloom time: its growth is more restrained (to about 20 feet), its glossy dark green leaves are deeply separated into five lobes, and its flowers are smaller (to just 2 inches wide) and more trumpet shaped, with distinct lobes. The usual color is maroon purple, though 'Briggsii' has brighter blooms in magenta-tinged crimson.

Morning glories are supremely easy to grow. Give them good, organically enriched soil and regular water during the growing season—and stand back! For support, provide wire netting or fencing; sturdy string is not strong enough, though it can initially guide the stems where you want them to go. Thin, prune, or cut back plants as needed to control rampancy. Do major pruning when vines are not in flower; prune and thin as needed throughout the growing season to contain growth.

# JASMINUM
## JASMINE

- EVERGREEN, SEMIEVERGREEN, AND DECIDUOUS WOODY VINES OR GROUND COVERS
- ZONES VARY BY SPECIES
- SUN OR PARTIAL SHADE
- REGULAR WATER

To many gardeners, the word "jasmine" immediately recalls fragrance. To others, it suggests flowers in winter, when little else is in bloom. Both images are accurate—but not for all jasmines. The many species offer flowers in all seasons, scented as well as unscented blossoms (usually in white or yellow), and growth habits ranging from vining to vining-shrubby to decidedly shrubby. And some jasmines make fine ground covers, especially for hillsides.

Despite their individual differences, all jasmines share two admirable traits: vigor and ease of culture. They grow more rapidly in good soil and bloom more profusely in sunny locations, but all adapt remarkably well to less-than-perfect conditions with virtually no sacrifice in appearance. They take a range of soils; they tolerate partial shade. For ground cover use, set plants from 1-gallon containers 6 to 8 feet apart; whenever established plants become tangled or untidy, cut them back heavily just before the growing season begins. Jasmines grown as vines will need pruning and training, as well as periodic thinning of tangled stems—a job best done after flowering, though you can remove superfluous new growth as it develops. The vining shrubs must be tied to their supports; thereafter, pruning removes stems that grow in unwanted directions and cannot be trained into place.

A number of species are presented on the facing page, grouped according to the two prevailing growth habits.

*Jasminum polyanthum*

*Jasminum nitidum*

**VINING JASMINES.** These are the true vines, which climb by twining stems; the group includes most (but not all) of the familiar fragrant sorts. The flowers are pinwheel shaped, in pure white or in white with a pink to purplish tinge on the petal backs.

Spanish jasmine, *J. grandiflorum*, and common white (or poet's) jasmine, *J. officinale*, grow in Zones 5−9, 12−24, 28, 29, and 31. Size is the chief difference between the two: Spanish jasmine can reach 15 feet, while common white jasmine attains twice that size. Both are semievergreen in the warmer parts of their range, deciduous in the colder areas. Clusters of fragrant white flowers (1½ inches across in Spanish jasmine, 1 inch wide in common white jasmine) bloom during summer. The rich green leaves are composed of narrow leaflets, giving the vines a fine-textured look.

Evergreen *J. polyanthum* grows in Zones 5−9, 12−24, 28, 31. It climbs quickly to 20 feet—or scrambles briskly over the soil as a frothy ground cover. Fragrant, rose-backed blossoms nearly an inch across are borne in clusters; they mount a major display in late winter and early spring, but can appear sporadically at other times of year as well. Leaves are finely divided into narrow leaflets.

Angelwing (or shining) jasmine, *J. nitidum*, is a late spring and summer bloomer that grows in Zones 12, 13, 16, 19−21, 26; it is semievergreen in the colder regions, evergreen where winters are milder. Purplish buds, borne in clusters of three, open to powerfully fragrant, 1-inch flowers with narrow, pointed petals. Shiny, ovate, 3-inch leaves adorn a plant that grows at a moderate rate; it's equally successful as a 10- to 20-foot vine or an informal ground cover.

Evergreen South African jasmine, *J. angulare*, is suited to Zones 16−24, 28. From summer into fall, scentless, inch-wide flowers carried in clusters of three decorate a vine of modest size with three-leafleted leaves.

Downy jasmine, *J. multiflorum*, grows in Zones 21−24, 26, 28. Its evergreen, 2-inch, ovate leaves have a downy coating that gives the foliage a distinctly gray-green look. Faintly fragrant, 1-inch-wide flowers appear primarily in late winter and early spring. As a vine, this species can reach about 15 feet; in the Southeast (where it may be called star jasmine, though that name really belongs to *Trachelospermum jasminoides*, page 95), it often is pruned to grow as a shrub.

**VINELIKE SHRUBBY JASMINES.** Though the species profiled below can be used as vines, none climbs by twining. All send out very long, slender, lax stems that must be tied into place if the plants are to function as vines; otherwise, they'll flop over to make green haystacks of foliage. As vines, these are best used on walls and trellises or trained up over arbors and pergolas. Flowers are yellow and (except in the case of Italian jasmine) unscented.

Winter jasmine, *J. nudiflorum*, grows in Zones 3−21, 30−34. The bare green stems are a decorative element in the winter landscape all on their own, and the bright, inch-wide blossoms provide further adornment before the foliage emerges. Leaves are glossy green, with three leaflets. Left to its own devices, winter jasmine forms a broadly mounding shrub about 4 feet high; if you tie stems to a support, however, the plant can ascend to about 15 feet, its branches spilling outward. Because stems root where they touch soil, this species is a good choice for covering sloping ground where you also want to control erosion.

Primrose jasmine, *J. mesnyi* (formerly *J. primulinum),* does well in Zones 3 (if sheltered), 4−24, 26, 28−31. In many respects, it is an evergreen version of winter jasmine, but the differences are notable. Stems are much longer (to 10 feet), making primrose jasmine a candidate for covering an arbor. Flowers are semidouble to double and reach 2 inches across; bloom is heaviest from winter to early spring, sporadic throughout the rest of the year.

Italian jasmine, *J. humile*, succeeds in Zones 5−10, 12−24, 28−31. The largest of the shrubby vines, it is also the only one with scented blossoms. The slender stems can reach 20 feet. For vine use, train them on an arbor or pergola; left to themselves, they'll grow upward and arch over to form a huge fountain of greenery. Leaves are light green, composed of three to seven leaflets to 2 inches long; blossoms are just ½ inch in diameter but come in large clusters throughout summer. 'Revolutum' has larger flowers (to 1 inch wide) and larger, darker green leaves than the species.

*Jasminum nudiflorum*

# JUNIPERUS
JUNIPER

- ✿ EVERGREEN WOODY GROUND COVERS
- ✎ ZONES VARY BY SPECIES
- ☀ ◑ SUN OR PARTIAL SHADE
- ◐ ◑ REGULAR TO LITTLE WATER

Junipers are the universal ground covers, flourishing from Maine to California, Minnesota to Florida. At least three points account for their popularity: ease of culture, neat appearance, and an enormous number of varieties.

These plants have two kinds of foliage. The juvenile leaves are short, spiky needles; the mature ones are tiny, overlapping scales. Some varieties bear only juvenile foliage, some only mature foliage, and some a combination of the two. Foliage may be monotonal or variegated, in colors ranging from silvery blue through many shades of green to bright yellow. Junipers are coniferous plants, but the fleshy cones they bear don't resemble the familiar pine or fir cones—they look more like blue to black, berrylike fruits.

One of juniper's strong points is adaptability. As its geographic range makes clear, there's a kind for almost any climatic combination of cool and hot, moist and dry; and beyond that, it takes soils ranging from light to heavy, acid to alkaline. Where summers are hot (especially if they're dry as well), junipers prefer partial shade; in cooler regions, they'll accept some shade but will grow better in full sun. In warm-summer areas, moderate watering will see

*Juniperus conferta*

LEFT: *Juniperus communis* 'Repanda'  TOP: *Juniperus squamata* 'Blue Carpet'
BOTTOM: *Juniperus communis* 'Depressa Aurea'

most junipers through the dry months; in cool-summer regions, plants growing in loamy to claylike soil may be able to get by with no supplemental moisture at all. All junipers are intolerant of waterlogged soil, which will rot their roots.

Though junipers usually spread at a slow to moderate rate, it's best to set out plants from 1-gallon containers 5 to 6 feet apart to avoid overcrowding in the future. Or set plants 3 to 4 feet apart for a faster cover, then remove every other one when they start to crowd each other.

The eight species described here (presented in alphabetical order) have prostrate forms suitable for ground cover use. Among the many varieties of each, we discuss a number of popular choices; you're sure to find others, since new selections enter the nursery trade almost every year. (*Note:* We do not list *J. davurica*, though you may encounter plants labeled as such: there is some disagreement in the nursery trade over which varieties belong to this species, which to *J. chinensis, J. horizontalis,* or *J. squamata.* The variety sometimes sold as *J. davurica* 'Parsonii' is described below under *J. chinensis.*)

*J. chinensis* grows (with the exception noted below) in Zones 1–24, 26, 28–43. Its variety 'Parsonii', commonly called prostrata juniper (and sometimes sold as *J. davurica* 'Parsonii' or 'Expansa'), is a slow grower to 8 feet across and 1½ feet high, with stiffly horizontal main limbs densely clothed in dark foliage. A variegated form ('Expansa Variegata', 'Aureovariegata') has foliage splashed with creamy white. Dense, slow-growing 'San Jose' bears foliage in dark sage green; it reaches 2 feet high and 6 or more feet across. 'Saybrook Gold', the only member of *J. chinensis* with bright gold foliage, is taller and chunkier (to 2 to 3 feet high, 6 feet across) than most of the other ground cover types. Sargent juniper or shimpaku, *J. c. sargentii,* has feathery gray-green foliage on plants to 1 foot high and 10 feet across; its variety 'Glauca' has blue-green foliage, while 'Viridis' is bright green.

Slightly more limited in range than the other members of *J. chinensis* is Japanese garden juniper, *J. c. procumbens;* it does not grow in Zone 26. It has feathery blue-green foliage and reaches to 3 feet high, up to 20 feet across. Its variety 'Nana' is smaller in all respects, with short needles on a foot-high, 4- to 5-foot-wide plant.

*J. communis* grows in Zones 1–24, 31–45. All its ground cover forms are flat and carpetlike. 'Effusa' has silver-banded foliage on a foot-high, 6-foot-wide plant. Similar to 'Effusa' are 'Windsor Gem' (which is lower growing and less dense) and 'Repanda', with soft medium green foliage that turns bronzy in winter. Spreading to 8 feet wide and eventually building to 3 feet tall are 'Depressa', with light green foliage (bronze tinted in winter), and 'Depressa Aurea' (yellow new growth). Mountain juniper, *J. c. saxatilis*, has gray to gray-green foliage and spreads to 8 feet, with secondary branches that grow upward to 1 foot.

*J. conferta*, shore juniper, grows in Zones 3–9, 14–24, 26–28, 31–34, 39. Soft, bright green needles clothe a trailing plant to 8 feet across and 1 foot high. Though its native climate is cool and moist, it will grow in regions with dry, hot summers if given regular watering in well-drained soil. Varieties include heat-tolerant 'Blue Pacific', with especially dense blue-green foliage, and bright green 'Emerald Sea'.

*J. horizontalis* offers the greatest number of choices for ground cover use. Its varieties grow primarily in Zones 1–24, 31–45; those followed by "(28)" also thrive in the humid warmth of Zone 28.

*Juniperus sabina*
'Tamariscifolia'

The tallest of the spreaders, to 1½ feet, is 'Plumosa' (28), usually called Andorra juniper. Its main limbs spread to 10 feet; secondary branches provide the vertical growth. The gray-green foliage turns plum colored in winter. 'Youngstown' looks much the same, but it's lower (to 1 foot), flatter, and spreads to just 6 feet.

Choices abound among varieties about 1 foot tall. 'Bar Harbor' (28), with feathery blue-gray foliage that turns plum purple in winter, spreads quickly to 10

feet; on older plants, foliage dies back in the center to expose the main limbs. Silvery blue 'Blue Chip' creeps to 8 to 10 feet. 'Blue Mat' makes a dense gray-green mat up to 7 feet across. Waukegan juniper, 'Douglasii' (28), spreads to 10 feet; its foliage is rich green when new, then matures to steel blue and turns plum colored in the colder months. 'Huntington Blue', to 7 feet across, has dense foliage in a bright blue gray.

A number of *J. horizontalis* varieties are true ground-huggers that never exceed 6 inches in height. 'Emerald Spreader' is described by its name. 'Glomerata' has deep green foliage that turns plum purple in cold weather. 'Hughes' and 'Yukon Belle' have silvery blue foliage; 'Marcellus' is blue gray. 'Turquoise Spreader' (28) forms a dense mat of turquoise green. Lowest of all—to just 4 inches—are 'Wiltonii' and its sport 'Mother Lode' (both 28). The former makes a dense carpet of intense silvery blue; the latter is brilliant yellow, turning to bronzy yellow in winter.

*J. sabina* grows in Zones 1–24, 31–45. Of its many named selections, none is taller than 1½ feet. Widest spreading is 'Tamariscifolia', called tamarix juniper or tam. This long-time favorite spreads to 20 feet across, its dense blue-green foliage sprays reaching 1½ feet tall. 'Blue Danube' is almost shrubby looking, forming a lacy blue-green mound to about 5 feet across and 1½ feet high; 'Arcadia' has a similar lacy look, but it's wider spreading (to 10 feet) and just 1 foot tall. 'Broadmoor' has soft, bright green foliage on a dense, mounding plant to 10 feet across and just over 1 foot high; the similar 'Moor-dense' reaches 1½ feet high, its foliage growing in a layered fashion. Another soft green

choice is 6- to 9-inch-high 'Calgary Carpet'. 'Buffalo' (to 8 feet wide, 8 to 12 inches high) and 'Scandia' (8 feet by 1 foot) have bright green, feathery to lacy foliage.

*J. scopulorum*, the Rocky Mountain juniper, grows in Zones 1–24, 35, 41, 43. It has several prostrate forms. One of the best is 'White's Silver King', a foot-high, 6- to 8-foot-wide plant with dense, scalelike foliage in pale silvery blue. 'Blue Creeper' is similar but a bit taller (to 2 feet) and not so silvery looking.

*J. squamata* grows in Zones 2–24, 31–41. Its slow-growing variety 'Blue Carpet', spreading to 5 feet across but reaching no higher than 1 foot, has leaves of a rich blue-toned gray green.

*J. virginiana*, called Eastern red cedar, grows in Zones 1–24, 28, 31–43. Its variety 'Silver Spreader' features feathery, fine-textured, silvery green foliage on plants to 8 feet across, 1½ feet high. This species and its varieties provide an alternate host for cedar-apple rust, so do not plant them where apples are an important home or commercial crop.

## LAMPRANTHUS. See page 69

## LANTANA

🌿 EVERGREEN WOODY GROUND COVER

✄ ZONES 8–10, 12–30

☀ SUN

💧 MODERATE TO LITTLE WATER

Where frost is rare or light, easy-to-grow lantana provides reliable color for most of the year. And even in the colder parts of its range, you'd be hard pressed to find a ground cover with a longer flowering period. Individual blossoms are small, but they're packed into nosegaylike clusters about 1½ inches across. The leaves are dark green and ovate, with a crinkled, sandpapery surface; when crushed, they give off a pungent scent that some people find objectionable. Plants grow at a moderate to rapid rate.

The most familiar ground cover lantana is *L. montevidensis* (formerly *L.*

*Lantana montevidensis*

*sellowiana*), a lax, trailing plant that may spread to 6 feet but rises no higher than 1 to 1½ feet. Its dark green, inch-long leaves often have a purplish tinge. The species bears lavender blooms; for color variants, try 'White Lightnin', with pure white flowers, and 'Lavender Swirl', with larger blossom clusters in lavender, white, and a mix of both.

A number of shrubby but spreading lantanas can be used as ground covers, though they lack the truly trailing growth of the previous species. Some are hybrids derived from *L. montevidensis* and the shrubby *L. camara;* some are simply *L. camara* selections. Lowest growing—to 2 feet high and about 6 feet across—is 'Gold Rush', with golden yellow blooms. Reaching 2 to 3 feet high with a spread of 6 to 8 feet are 'Confetti' (with flower clusters in a mix of yellow, pink, and purple), 'Cream Carpet' (cream and yellow), 'Spreading Sunset' (orange red), 'Spreading Sunshine' (yellow), 'Sunburst' (golden yellow), and 'Tangerine' (orange).

Lantanas have no soil preference and need only infrequent (but deep) watering. They're particularly effective on sloping, sunny ground, where they can both control erosion and make a blanket of color. *L. montevidensis* is an excellent choice for raised beds, where its trailing stems will spill over the edges. Space plants from 1-gallon containers about 4 feet apart. To keep established plantings low and well foliaged, cut out dead branches and old, woody stems in early spring.

## LAPAGERIA rosea
### CHILEAN BELLFLOWER

- ⚘ EVERGREEN WOODY VINE
- 🌿 ZONES 5, 6, 15–17, 23, 24
- ◐ PARTIAL SHADE
- 💧 REGULAR WATER

This plant's botanical name commemorates an historic and glamorous personage: Marie Rose Josephine Tascher de la Pagerie, Napoleon's famous Empress Josephine. And as befits its name, the vine is elegant and refined, a delightful choice for display on a post, trellis, or tree trunk.

Stems twine to as high as 20 feet, outfitted in glossy, thick-textured, oval leaves to 4 inches long. The flowers, suspended from thin stalks, are 3-inch-long bells that are so thick and waxy they look

*Lapageria rosea*

almost artificial. The typical flower color is dark rosy red (often spotted with white), but pink and pure white forms are sometimes available. The blossoms never mount an overwhelming display, but they appear over a long season—from spring through summer and into fall.

For best results, provide Chilean bellflower with good, moist, well-drained soil amended with plenty of organic matter before planting. Locate plants in partial shade, choosing a wind-sheltered spot that will not receive reflected heat from sunny walls.

## LATHYRUS odoratus. See page 41

## LIRIOPE spicata
### CREEPING LILY TURF

- ⚘ EVERGREEN PERENNIAL GROUND COVER
- 🌿 ZONES 2–41
- ☀◐● SUN OR SHADE
- 💧 MODERATE WATER

You can't walk on this "turf," but you can enjoy the illusion of coarse, shaggy grass—plus a bonus of flowers that resemble those of grape hyacinth (*Muscari*). Rather lax, strap-shaped, dark green leaves are just ¼ inch wide and about a foot long, forming mounds to around 9 inches high; they grow from underground stems that solidly colonize the soil in the manner of a spreading turf grass, proceeding at a slow to moderate pace. In summer, dark stalks send up spikelike clusters of pale lilac to white flowers which peek through the foliage; they're attractive but not particularly showy. Berrylike black fruits may form after the flowers fade. During the cold months, the foliage takes on a bronzy cast. 'Silver Dragon' has lengthwise white stripes on its dark green leaves; if you see any all-green shoots, remove them.

Creeping lily turf is tough. It can survive in heavy soil, and its fleshy, water-storing roots will carry it through dry periods. For the healthiest growth, though, provide average, well-drained soil and moderate watering during the growing season. Where summers are cool to mild, a full-sun location is fine; in hot-summer regions, partial to full (but not heavy) shade is best. Space plants from flats or pots 1 foot apart. Creeping lily turf is evergreen, but old foliage looks shabby after the first year. To keep plantings looking fresh, mow or shear in late winter or early spring, before growth begins.

*Liriope spicata* 'Silver Dragon'

# LONICERA
## HONEYSUCKLE

🌿 🌺 EVERGREEN, SEMIEVERGREEN, AND DECIDUOUS WOODY VINES OR GROUND COVERS

✂ ZONES VARY BY SPECIES

☼ ◐ SUN OR PARTIAL SHADE

💧 MODERATE WATER

*Lonicera japonica*

Honeysuckle belongs to that group of old-fashioned favorites beloved of country- and cottage-garden tradition. And many members of the group evoke not only nostalgia, but an air of romance—thanks to the penetratingly sweet perfume that proclaims their presence even before they come into view. Individual differences aside, all honeysuckles share certain general characteristics. The clustered flowers are tubular; some have two flaring and unequal lips, while others are essentially straight tubes, looking rather like firecrackers. In some honeysuckles, the blossoms are followed by pea-size fruits in red, dark blue, or black. The oval leaves, often bluish green in color, come in opposing pairs on flexible stems that climb by twining. Though most honeysuckles are used strictly as upward-growing vines, one species—*L. japonica*—can be grown as a casual ground cover as well.

Deciduous *L. × brownii* grows in Zones 1–7, 31–45. This hybrid honeysuckle is represented in the nursery trade by its superior selection 'Dropmore Scarlet', a modest climber to about 10 feet that produces scentless, fire engine red (and firecracker-shaped) flowers from late spring into fall. The blue-green leaves are virtually triangular, and the leaf pairs look to be joined at their bases.

Successful in Zones 2–41 is Japanese honeysuckle, *L. japonica*, a plant loved by gardeners who want carefree exuberance but cursed by those who want an easily managed vine. This species is rampancy personified: in the Southeast, it has become a naturalized weed.

For garden success, proper placement is crucial. Keep in mind that the vine can reach 30 feet, and do not give it the chance to smother shrubs and vulnerable garden plantings; instead, position it where it can cover a wire fence or clamber over an arbor. It can also be used as a ground cover that will reach 1 to 2 feet high; it's especially appropriate on large, sloping expanses where you need a carefree erosion-control blanket.

Japanese honeysuckle blooms from late spring into fall, bearing powerfully sweet-scented flowers of purple-tinted white. 'Halliana' (Hall's honeysuckle) is the most widely grown variety; its flowers open white, then age to chamois yellow. 'Purpurea' has purple-tinted leaf undersides and white blossoms that are purple on their outer surfaces. 'Aureoreticulata', called goldnet honeysuckle, is a far more modest grower than the species. Its foliage is striking: the green leaves are heavily netted with gold veining.

The species and its varieties are evergreen, semievergreen, or deciduous, depending on the severity of winter cold.

*Lonicera sempervirens*

Trumpet honeysuckle, *L. sempervirens*, is another species suited to Zones 2–41. The deciduous to semievergreen, 10- to 20-foot vine leafs out early in spring, producing heavily purple-flushed new growth that matures to blue green. Clus-

*Lonicera × heckrottii*

ters of unscented blossoms appear from midspring into summer. The basic species has orange-red blooms with a yellow throat; 'Sulphurea' ('Flava') bears pure yellow blossoms, while 'Cedar Lane', 'Magnifica', and 'Superba' all have solid red flowers. Red berries follow the blossoms.

Gardeners who want a less exuberant version of Japanese honeysuckle should look instead to woodbine, *L. periclymenum*. This 20-foot vine grows in Zones 2–24, 30–41; it is evergreen in the mildest zones, totally deciduous in the coldest areas. Scented blossoms shaped like flaring tubes come in summer and early fall; they're typically creamy white flushed with purple. Red berries can make a good show in fall. Nurseries offer several superior named forms. Flowers of 'Serotina' are purple on the outside, yellow inside; those of 'Serotina Florida' are red outside, cream within. 'Belgica' has the purple-and-yellow combination of 'Serotina' on a smaller plant with purple-tinted leaves and stems. Yellow flowers of 'Berries Jubilee' are followed by a heavy crop of red fruits. 'Graham Thomas' is farther reaching than the species (to 30 feet or more), with creamy white flowers that age to copper-tinted yellow.

Gold flame (or coral) honeysuckle, *L. × heckrottii*, grows in Zones 3–24, 30–35. It is a vigorous but modest grower to about 15 feet, lovely on pillars and posts. Opening from carmine buds, the two-lipped flowers are warm pink on the outside, yellow inside; bloom time runs from midspring until frost. Blue-green leaves are semievergreen in the warmest zones, deciduous elsewhere.

Giant Burmese honeysuckle, *L. hildebrandiana,* is adapted to Zones 9, 14–17, 19–28. The familiar two-lipped, fragrant flowers identify it as a honeysuckle, but its giant size sets it apart from the rest. Stems are like thick ropes, set with thick, oval evergreen leaves to 6 inches long. The summer flowers may reach 7 inches long; they open white, then age through yellow to buff orange. Climbing as far as 30 feet, this is a striking vine to scale an arbor or wall or to twine along eaves, but be sure to give it sturdy support.

Honeysuckles are not particular about soil quality or type. The less vigorous growers may turn in a marginally better performance with good soil and regular watering, but the truly rampant ones don't really warrant any special attention. All require some training and thinning; the ideal time for this job is after flowering, but in colder zones it's best to wait until early spring (though you will sacrifice some bloom).

If you're using Japanese honeysuckle as a ground cover, set out plants from 1-gallon containers 6 to 8 feet apart. Once the planting is established, shear or mow it nearly to the ground annually or every other year to prevent a thick, flammable thatch of dead stems from building up beneath the foliage.

## MACFADYENA unguis-cati
CAT'S CLAW,
YELLOW TRUMPET VINE

🌿 🌱 Evergreen to deciduous woody
      vine or ground cover

    ✂ Zones 8–29, 31

    ☼ ◑ Sun or partial shade

    💧 Moderate water

Forked tendrils with clawlike hooks give this handsome vine both its climbing

ability and one of its common names. Each leaf consists of two oval, glossy light green leaflets to 2 inches long; the hooked tendril is centered between them. Springtime brings lemon yellow flowers with an irregular trumpet shape, somewhat reminiscent of foxglove blossoms with distinct lobes. Each bloom may be up 2 inches long and 4 inches wide. Thanks to its tenacious tendrils, cat's claw can climb all but slick surfaces, and its rapid growth to as much as 40 feet puts it high on the list of vines for quick coverage. Stems root where they touch the earth, recommending the plant for erosion control on sloping ground. Where frost is light or absent, cat's claw is evergreen; in colder zones, it is partially to almost wholly deciduous.

Cat's claw is not particular about soil; any type will do. For ground cover use, set out plants from 1-gallon containers about 10 feet apart. Plants growing as vines tend to lose the foliage at their bases and carry their leaves and flowers toward the stem ends. After flowering finishes, you can prune plants both to direct growth and to encourage new foliage to sprout lower down, where it will fill in the bare spaces.

*Note:* This plant was formerly known as *Doxantha unguis-cati* and may still be sold by some nurseries under that name.

*Mahonia aquifolium* 'Compacta'

*Macfadyena unguis-cati*

## MAHONIA

👑 Evergreen woody ground covers

    ✂ Zones vary by species

    ☼ ◑ Sun or partial shade

    💧💧 Regular to moderate water

These relatives of barberry *(Berberis)* retain their neat, tailored good looks throughout the year. Plants spread at a moderate rate, advancing by underground stems that send up more or less upright branches decked out in handsome foliage. Each leaf consists of spiny-edged, oval leaflets that are arranged feather fashion—one leaflet at the leafstalk tip, the others arrayed down either side. Small, cup-shaped yellow flowers appear in showy clusters at branch tips in spring; pea-size blue berries often follow.

Most widely available of the three ground cover mahonias is compact Oregon grape, *M. aquifolium* 'Compacta', successful in Zones 2–12, 14–21, 31–41. Each leaf has five to nine glossy, 3-inch, oval leaflets; new growth is a striking copper color, later maturing to dark green. In cold climates, the foliage takes on purple tones in winter. Plantings rise to about 2 feet high.

Creeping mahonia, *M. repens,* grows in Zones 1–21, 32–34. It is taller than the other ground cover mahonias (to 3 feet) and bears leaves with just three to seven rounded, dull bluish green leaflets; in winter, foliage takes on a distinctly reddish bronze cast.

Longleaf mahonia, *M. nervosa,* is adapted to Zones 2–9, 14–19, 32, 34. It has the most elaborate foliage of the ground cover types: each leaf has as many as 21 glossy, ovate leaflets to 4 inches long. The leaves tend to cluster toward the tips of stems that usually reach no more than 2 feet high.

Mahonias are accommodating plants that will grow in virtually any soil. They do fine with moderate watering, but will accept regular moisture if soil is well drained. Compact Oregon grape and creeping mahonia enjoy full sun except in hot-summer or desert climates, where they prefer some shade. Longleaf mahonia does well in light or partial shade in all its zones; in cool-summer areas, it will also grow compactly and well in sunny spots. Set plants from 1-gallon containers about 2 feet apart. These are essentially maintenance-free plants; prune them only to curb overly long stems that disrupt the evenness of a planting.

## MANDEVILLA

- 🌿 EVERGREEN, SEMIEVERGREEN, AND DECIDUOUS WOODY VINES
- 🗡 ZONES VARY BY SPECIES
- ☼ ◑ SUN OR PARTIAL SHADE
- 💧 REGULAR WATER

The strongest-willed nursery shopper may be able to pass up a blooming mandevilla—but for most gardeners, the showy flowers, glossy leaves, and overall look of robust good health make these twining vines hard to resist. The smaller ones rate prominent placement on fences, walls, trellises, or posts; the larger Chilean jasmine is a natural for covering arbors and pergolas. M. 'Alice du Pont' and the M. splendens varieties are often enjoyed outside their hardiness range as pot plants; when weather turns frosty, they can simply be moved to a sheltered location. All mandevillas have trumpet-shaped flowers that flare widely.

Chilean jasmine, M. laxa, grows in Zones 4–9, 14–21, 28, 29, 31. Its common name alludes to the fragrance of its

*Mandevilla* 'Alice du Pont'

blooms, though the scent is more like gardenia than jasmine. This heady perfume wafts into the summer garden from clusters of 2-inch white trumpets that are carried aloft on vines to 15 feet or more. Narrowly heart-shaped, 6-inch leaves densely cover the stems; foliage is reddish purple when new, matures to rich green, and, in colder zones, may turn bronzy red in fall. Chilean jasmine may be deciduous, semievergreen, or evergreen, depending on the depth of winter cold.

Evergreen *M.* 'Alice du Pont' grows in Zones 21–25. Given a warm location and no frost, it is capable of reaching 20 to 30 feet. The bold leaves—dark, leathery ovals to 8 inches long—make a perfect background for the 4-inch-wide, red-throated hot pink flowers that bloom from spring into fall. This is an excellent subject for large containers, where its preference for "gourmet" soil can be indulged (though the confinement will limit its growth). Also adapted to Zones 21–25 is *M. splendens*, called pink allamanda; it shares the looks and bloom season of *M.* 'Alice du Pont' and is, in fact, one of the latter's parents. Its varieties include 'My Fair Lady' (pink-blushed white blooms), 'Red Riding Hood' (dark reddish pink), and 'Scarlet Pimpernel' (yellow-throated dark red).

Evergreen *M. boliviensis* grows only in Zones 24 and 25. In these essentially frostless climates it blooms almost all year, bearing clusters of yellow-throated white trumpets to 3 inches across. Blooms of 'Summer Snow' are similar, but tinged with pink. The vine twines to 12 to 20 feet; its leaves are pointed and about 4 inches long.

Good soil, well amended with organic matter, encourages peak performance from the mandevillas. All require regular moisture in all climates—with the exception of Chilean jasmine, which will accept reduced watering where summers are

cool to mild (in warmer regions, though, it too must have regular water). Tangled growth may need thinning from time to time. Prune *M.* 'Alice du Pont' only during the growing season; prune all others in winter.

*Millettia reticulata*

## MILLETTIA reticulata
### EVERGREEN WISTERIA

- 🌿 EVERGREEN WOODY VINE
- 🗡 ZONES 20–24
- ☼ SUN
- 💧 REGULAR WATER

As the common name suggests, this vine bears a general resemblance to wisteria: it's a vigorous, twining plant of virtually unlimited size, with leaves composed of numerous leaflets and elongated clusters of sweet pea–like blossoms. But evergreen wisteria lacks something of true wisteria's languid grace; its leaflets are darker, glossier, and thicker than those of true wisteria, and the late-summer clusters of reddish purple blossoms are likely to be upright or projecting instead of pendent. This vine does have the notorious wisteria rampancy, and the uses and cautions outlined for wisteria (see page 98) apply.

Evergreen wisteria is a "plant it and stand back" vine that offers no cultural challenges; your attention will be largely devoted to control. Thin out excess and tangling growth on an as-needed basis; winter is the best time for significant pruning, but you can remove superfluous growth throughout the growing season.

## MYOSOTIS scorpioides
FORGET-ME-NOT

- 🌿 EVERGREEN PERENNIAL GROUND COVER
- ✂ ZONES 1–24, 32–45
- ◐ PARTIAL SHADE
- 💧 REGULAR WATER

Forget-me-not's small flowers of purest light blue cloak woodland and shaded gardens with a luminous azure haze in spring and summer. Borne in elongated, curving clusters, the sparkling yellow-centered blooms rise above spreading, 6- to 12-inch-high plants with narrow bright green leaves about 2 inches long. Specialists in perennials carry named varieties with flowers in pink, white, and various blue shades.

Grown in reasonably good soil amended with organic matter, forget-me-not will persist for years, spreading by creeping roots. Space plants from pots about 1 foot apart. In colder zones, plants die to the ground over winter but regrow from the roots in spring.

*Myosotis scorpioides*

## NANDINA domestica
HEAVENLY BAMBOO

- 🌿 EVERGREEN WOODY GROUND COVER
- ✂ ZONES 4–33
- ☀◐● SUN OR SHADE
- 💧💧💧 REGULAR TO MODERATE WATER

Heavenly bamboo is one of the most dependable evergreen landscape shrubs, appreciated for the bamboolike clusters of stems that form tall, upright to vase-shaped clumps of fine-textured, almost feathery foliage. In its lower-growing

*Nandina domestica* 'Harbour Dwarf'

selections, it's an equally dependable ground cover, suited to a variety of locations. The best of these lower sorts for ground-cover use is 'Harbour Dwarf', since it spreads by underground stems. It grows at a moderate rate, reaching 1½ to 2 feet high; leaves are carried almost parallel to the ground, with each leaf made up of numerous narrow, pointed leaflets in groups of three. New spring growth is pinkish green; in fall, cold weather turns leaves to shades of orange to bronzy red.

Heavenly bamboo looks best if grown in good soil and given regular watering during dry spells. However, it performs passably in poorer soils and with less water, even when competing with tree roots. Set out plants from 1-gallon containers about 1½ feet apart. The best winter foliage color comes in full sun, but plants can tolerate such an exposure only where summers are cool. In desert gardens and hot-summer Western valleys, choose a location in partial to full shade. Where soil is alkaline, chlorosis—evidenced by yellowed leaves with green veins—may be a problem; treat affected plants with iron chelates or iron sulfate.

## OENOTHERA speciosa
MEXICAN EVENING PRIMROSE

- 🌿 DECIDUOUS PERENNIAL GROUND COVER
- ✂ ZONES 3–24, 29, 30, 33
- ☀ SUN
- 💧 MODERATE TO LITTLE WATER

Perhaps no other ground cover offers so much color for so little care. But this bounty comes at a price: once happily established, Mexican evening primrose spreads relentlessly by underground stems. In well-ordered gardens, it is a

pest—but in more naturalistic settings with imprecise boundaries (especially on sunny slopes), it's a star.

Despite the common name, Mexican evening primrose opens in the daylight hours. Each 2-inch, chalice-shaped blossom lasts just one day, but the blooms come in enormous profusion from late spring into summer. They're carried on slender, 10- to 15-inch stems with narrow, 3-inch leaves. The usual color is rose pink, paling toward the flower center. 'Alba' and 'Woodside White' have white blossoms (aging to pink in the latter); 'Siskiyou' is lower than the species, bearing light pink flowers on stems to 8 inches high. After bloom, the flowering stems die back to the ground.

Mexican evening primrose is strictly unfussy, prospering in poor soils as well as in better ones. It doesn't like too much moisture around its roots, however, so plants in heavier soils should be watered only infrequently (those in well-drained soil will take moderate watering). Set out plants from pots about 1½ feet apart. At some point after flowering and before the next year's growth begins, shear off the spent flower stems.

*Oenothera speciosa*

*Note:* You may also find this plant sold as *O. berlandieri* or *O. speciosa childsii.*

*Ophiopogon japonicus*

## OPHIOPOGON japonicus
### MONDO GRASS

- 🌱 EVERGREEN PERENNIAL GROUND COVER
- ✂ ZONES 5–9, 14–31, WARMER PARTS OF 32
- ☼ ◑ ● SUN OR SHADE
- 💧 ◌ REGULAR TO MODERATE WATER

Mondo grass is closely related to creeping lily turf (*Liriope spicata,* page 74) and, as the name implies, it is even more grasslike in appearance. It forms dense clumps of lax, dark green leaves ⅛ inch wide and 8 to 12 inches long, spreading slowly by underground stems to form a solid, shaggy "turf" 6 to 8 inches high. Short spikes of small, pale lavender flowers bloom in summer, largely hidden among the leaves; pea-size blue fruits form after the flowers fade. 'Kyoto Dwarf' and 'Nana' are about half the size of the species and spread more slowly.

For the best-looking cover, plant mondo grass in good, well-drained soil and provide regular moisture during dry periods. In cool-summer regions, it will tolerate sun, but in all other areas it needs some shade. Set out plants from pots about 8 inches apart. If plantings start to look shabby from the accumulation of old, dead foliage, mow or shear them back in early spring, before new growth begins.

## OSTEOSPERMUM fruticosum
### TRAILING AFRICAN DAISY

- 🌱 EVERGREEN PERENNIAL GROUND COVER
- ✂ ZONES 8, 9, 12–26
- ☼ SUN
- 💧 ◌ REGULAR TO MODERATE WATER

Trailing African daisy blooms throughout the year on sunny days—but its main flowering period runs from midfall through winter, giving you sheets of purple and white at the very time of year when garden color is most conspicuously lacking. Each blossom is a 2- to 3-inch, purple-centered daisy; the petals are lavender fading to white on their upper surfaces, deeper lilac on their undersides. Variations include 'African Queen' and 'Burgundy', both with purple blooms, as well as the unusual 'Whirligig'—a white-and-blue combination with each petal nipped in at the center, giving it the look of a white spoon with a blue handle. Species and varieties all have oval, gray-green leaves to 4 inches long on foot-tall, trailing plants that root along the stems as they spread. Growth is rapid: one plant can achieve a 4-foot spread in a single year.

Trailing African daisy is adaptable, thriving at the seashore as well as in hot inland regions. Provide reasonably good, well-drained soil; set out plants from flats or pots, spacing them 2 feet apart. Established plantings are fairly drought tolerant but look better with at least moderate watering. In warmer areas, regular watering will yield the best appearance—and in fact, a routinely watered large planting can serve as a fire retardant. When established plantings begin to look untidy, cut plants back to healthy new growth after the main flowering period is over.

*Osteospermum fruticosum*

*Pachysandra terminalis*

## PACHYSANDRA terminalis
### PACHYSANDRA, JAPANESE SPURGE

- 🌱 EVERGREEN PERENNIAL GROUND COVER
- ✂ ZONES 1–10, 14–21, 31–43
- ◑ ● PARTIAL TO FULL SHADE
- 💧 REGULAR WATER

Count on pachysandra to bring a touch of elegance to shaded gardens. Lustrous, oval, deep green leaves, carried in whorls toward the ends of upright stems, form an even carpet about 10 inches high in full shade, about 6 inches tall with more light. The plant spreads by underground stems at a moderate rate, even competing well with tree roots. In late spring or early summer, fluffy spikes of tiny white flowers appear at stem tips; small white fruits may follow. 'Silver Edge' ('Variegata'), a selection with creamy white leaf margins, lends an attractive sparkle to fully shaded locations. Several green-leafed named varieties also offer worthwhile variations on the basic species. 'Green Carpet' features darker, glossier, denser foliage on stems to about 4 inches tall; 'Green Sheen' has notably shiny foliage; and fast-growing 'Cut Leaf' has deeply dissected leaf margins.

Plant pachysandra in good, slightly acid, organically amended soil; set out plants from flats or pots about 1 foot apart. Appearance is enhanced by an annual fertilizer application in early spring.

*Pandorea pandorana*

# PANDOREA

- 🌿 EVERGREEN WOODY VINES
- ❄ ZONES 16–27
- ☼ ◐ SUN OR PARTIAL SHADE
- 💧 💧 REGULAR TO MODERATE WATER

These two twining vines are worth planting for foliage alone—but they bear lovely flowers, too, making them even more appealing. Bower vine, *P. jasminoides,* is the shorter of the two (to 20 feet) but has larger flowers. Foliage is a rich glossy green, with each leaf consisting of up to nine pointed, oval leaflets to 2 inches long. Clusters of 2-inch-wide, trumpet-shaped flowers appear from late spring to early fall. The typical blossom is white with a pink throat, but 'Alba' and the stronger-growing 'Lady D' bear pure white blooms, while 'Rosea' offers flowers in a soft, milky pink with nearly red throats.

Wonga-wonga vine, *P. pandorana,* covers about twice the space of bower vine. Its foliage is the same shiny green, but the 1- to 3-inch-long leaflets are narrower. The clustered, trumpet-shaped flowers make a pleasing spring display; they're a bit under an inch across, in pinkish white or creamy white, often spotted brownish purple in the throat.

Both species grow best with good, organically enriched soil. Bower vine is excellent on posts, trellises, and low walls; be sure it is sheltered from strong wind. Wonga-wonga vine will tackle larger walls and makes a fine cover for arbors and pergolas. Do any pruning needed to shape or thin vines after flowering has finished.

# PARTHENOCISSUS

- 🌿 🌱 DECIDUOUS WOODY VINES OR GROUND COVERS
- ❄ ZONES VARY BY SPECIES
- ☼ ◐ ● SUN OR SHADE
- 💧 MODERATE WATER

Some vines are treasured for their floral displays. These three, however, are valued for their foliage: demure green throughout spring and summer, turning to dazzling orange and red in fall. The blossoms they bear are inconspicuous; you notice only the clusters of small blue-black fruits that form later. The first two species described below are famed for their vigor and potential size; they can cover multistory walls and clothe tree trunks, and Virginia creeper can also blanket open ground. The third species is something of a wimp by comparison, but its leaves are individually more decorative. All climb by means of tendrils tipped with holdfast discs.

Virginia creeper, *P. quinquefolia,* is the most widely adapted, growing in Zones 1–24, 26–43; it and *P. tricuspidata* are the "ivy" of the Ivy League. Each leaf consists of five 6-inch leaflets with pointed tips. Foliage is bronze tinted when new, matures to a semiglossy dark green by summer, and turns to vibrant crimson and burgundy early in fall. Though the foliage is ample, vines always have a see-through appearance; they decorate rather than obscure their supports. 'Engelmannii' has smaller leaves and makes a denser foliage cover than the species.

*Parthenocissus quinquefolia*

Young plants may need initial support or tying, but the disc-tipped tendrils soon make the stems fully self-attaching. Let Virginia creeper decorate walls, arbors, or tree trunks; or use it as a free-rambling ground cover. Of the two large-growing species, this one is the better choice for arbors and other overhead structures.

*Parthenocissus tricuspidata*

Boston ivy, *P. tricuspidata,* grows in Zones 2–24, 31–41. Leaves are broad (up to 8 inches across) and three lobed. Like Virginia creeper, Boston ivy turns from bronzy green to glossy deep green as spring turns to summer—but its range of fall color is wider, varying from orange to wine. The plant is just as far reaching as Virginia creeper, but it produces a solid foliage cover. Holdfast discs and stem rootlets give Boston ivy a tenacious grip on vertical surfaces, so think twice before letting it attach to shingle, clapboard, or mortared brick or stone—the firm attachment accelerates the deterioration of wood and mortar. 'Beverly Brooks' and 'Green Showers' are large-leafed selections, the former offering especially bright fall color. 'Robusta' is larger leafed, the leaves often fully divided into three leaflets. For smaller leaves on less rampant vines, look for 'Lowii' and 'Veitchii'.

Silvervein creeper, *P. henryana,* grows in Zones 4–9, 14–17, 31, and warmer parts of 32. This is the species of choice where space is limited; growth is vigorous, but ultimate size is only about 20 feet. Leaves look like those of Virginia creeper, but their leaflets are smaller (to just 2 inches long). The most striking difference, however, is in the coloration: leaves are purplish when new, then mature to dark bronzy green with a network of pronounced silver veining. (Foliage color is best on plants growing in part or full shade.) Leaves turn a rich red in fall. Like Virginia creeper, this species can serve as a ground cover; it's good in small spaces and where it can spill over a retaining wall.

In nature, these are woodland plants, and as such they thrive in organically enriched soil and dappled sun. But they also grow well in heavy to light (but not alkaline) soils and in exposures ranging from full sun (in mild-summer regions) to full shade. For ground cover plantings of Virginia or silvervein creeper, set gallon-size plants 4 feet apart. Plants of all species need regular moisture to become established; older vines easily get by on moderate watering. Thin and prune as needed for training and untangling before leaf-out in spring.

## PASSIFLORA
PASSION FLOWER

- EVERGREEN, SEMIEVERGREEN, AND DECIDUOUS WOODY VINES OR GROUND COVERS
- ZONES VARY BY SPECIES
- SUN OR PARTIAL SHADE
- REGULAR TO MODERATE WATER

Sixteenth century Spanish missionaries to South America found religious significance in the floral structure of these vines, hence the name "passion flower." You might also see the blooms as a designer's delight, a perfect motif for jewelry or textiles. The flower's virtually identical petals and sepals spread starlike in a flat plane, with a corona of long, threadlike filaments above them; rising from the flower's center, as though on a pedestal, is an elaborate structure containing the reproductive parts. (To the missionaries, the lacy corona represented the crown of thorns; the five stamens, the five wounds; and the 10 petals and sepals, the 10 faithful apostles.) Some species bear egg-shaped edible fruits. Vines climb by tendrils; most are rampant and tangling, reaching as far as 30 feet. The leaves are a favorite food of caterpillars of the gulf fritillary butterfly.

There are numerous *Passiflora* species; a great many are quite intolerant of frost. Nurseries in the mildest-winter regions may offer some of the more unusual tender types. The first four passion flowers described below are the most widely adapted and thus the most widely grown; the remaining five are for mild regions only. All bloom in summer unless otherwise noted.

Maypop or wild passion vine, *P. incarnata*, is the most cold-tolerant species. Native to the southeastern United States, it will grow in Zones 4–10, 12–33. Its 3-inch flowers are white to pale lavender with a showy corona of filaments banded in pink to purple; the yellow, 2-inch fruits are edible. Large, three-lobed, deep green leaves can reach 6 inches wide and long. The vine is deciduous; it dies to the ground in winter in the coldest parts of its range.

The next hardiest choice is *P.* 'Incense' (a hybrid of *P. incarnata*), suited to Zones 5–31. Like its parent, it is a deciduous vine that dies to the ground in the coldest zones. Its flowers are larger,

TOP: *Passiflora incarnata*
BOTTOM: *Passiflora mollissima*

though, reaching 5 inches across; they're violet with a paler purple corona and have a sweet pea–like perfume. The edible, 2- to 3-inch fruits are yellow green when ripe.

Two species will grow in Zones 5–9, 12–29. Blue crown passion flower, *P. caerulea*, is an evergreen to semievergreen vine that dies to the ground in its coldest zones. Its 2- to 4-inch-wide flowers, greenish white with a purple corona, bloom from summer to fall. The 4-inch leaves have three to nine lobes. Yellow to orange, 2½-inch fruits are edible. *P. × alatocaerulea* (a hybrid of *P. caerulea*) has fragrant, 4-inch blossoms in a combination of white with pink or purple; the corona is deep purple. It doesn't bear fruit. The three-lobed leaves reach 3 inches long. Like its parent, this is an evergreen to semievergreen plant that dies to the ground in the coldest parts of its range. It seems to be the least appealing of the passion flowers to gulf fritillary caterpillars.

The following species and hybrids are strictly for mildwinter gardens. Banana passion vine, *P. mollissima*, is a spring-to-fall bloomer for Zones 12–27; it's a particularly aggressive individual, good for cloaking expanses of bare, sloping ground. The three-lobed, 4-inch leaves are evergreen. Pendulous flowers of a lovely rose pink are about 3 inches across and lack a conspicuous corona; the floral segments are carried at the end of a long tube. Edible, 2½-inch fruits are yellow. >

Evergreen *P. jamesonii* is successful in Zones 14–28. Even brighter than the previous species, it bears similar flowers to 4 inches across in glowing salmon pink (you may find it sold as *P.* 'Coral Seas'). The glossy leaves are three lobed, to about 3½ inches long. Like banana passion vine, it makes a fast-growing bank cover.

Evergreen *P.* 'Lavender Lady', growing in Zones 16–25, 27, offers the typical

*Passiflora jamesonii*

flower form in showy, 4-inch lavender blooms with a dark violet corona. Passion fruit or purple granadilla, *P. edulis,* is a semievergreen species adapted to Zones 15–17, 21–25, 27. Its deep purple, 3-inch fruits, ripening in both spring and fall, are the passion fruits raised commercially. White, 3-inch flowers emblazoned with a purple corona come in spring and summer, displayed against light green, three-lobed leaves to 4 inches long. Nurseries in the warmest zones may offer named selections with superior fruits or showier flowers.

The most colorful species of the lot, *P. vitifolia,* is also the most tender, growing only in Zones 16, 17, 21–25. As the specific name suggests, the leaves resemble those of a grapevine—they are deeply lobed, dark green, to 6 inches

long. Sparkling against this backdrop are brilliant scarlet, 3½-inch blossoms with red to yellow coronas; the 2-inch, greenish yellow fruits are edible.

The passion flowers are vigorous regardless of soil type; provide merely average, well-drained soil and you'll get all the vine you need. Use them to cover wire fences or provide shade on an arbor or pergola; two species (*P. mollissima* and *P. jamesonii*) make good covers for sloping ground. For this use, space plants from 1-gallon containers 8 to 10 feet apart. Maintenance of vines entails rigorous thinning and untangling. Winter and early spring are the best times for major thinning, but you can thin excess new growth any time during the growing season.

## PAXISTIMA canbyi

- ☙ EVERGREEN WOODY GROUND COVER
- ☀ ZONES 1–10, 14–21, 32–43
- ☀ ◑ SUN OR PARTIAL SHADE
- ◌ REGULAR WATER

This plant won't catch your eye from across the garden: no showy flowers beckon, no unusual foliage asserts itself. Paxistima's virtue is, instead, in the fine-textured neatness which provides an attractive foil to more visually striking shrubs and trees. The very narrow, inch-long, leathery leaves are a rich, glossy dark green; when chilly weather arrives

*Paxistima canbyi*

in fall, they take on pleasing bronzy tones. The densely foliaged plant grows at a slow to moderate rate, reaching no higher than 1 foot but spreading to 5 or more feet. Branches may root here and there as they touch the soil.

Paxistima doesn't need good soil, but it does require good drainage. It will take full sun (and grow more compactly there) where summers are cool to moderate; where summers are fairly hot, choose a planting spot in dappled sun or partial shade. Set out plants from 1-gallon containers about 2 feet apart.

## PELARGONIUM peltatum
IVY GERANIUM

- ☙ EVERGREEN SHRUBBY PERENNIAL GROUND COVER
- ☀ ZONES 8, 9, 12–24
- ☀ SUN
- ◌ MODERATE WATER

In mild-winter climates, vigorous but noninvasive ivy geranium is virtually unbeatable for providing month after month of color in return for little care. The heaviest bloom comes from mid-spring to midfall, but flowering continues (albeit less profusely) throughout winter unless stopped by frost. Plants have trailing, semiwoody stems that spread rapidly to 2 to 3 feet and build up to about 1 foot high. Glossy, five-lobed leaves to 3 inches across are shaped like those of English ivy (*Hedera helix,* page 64), but they're succulent and thick textured. Carried in rounded clusters of up to 10, the single or double flowers are about 1 inch across; colors run from white through pink shades, red, magenta, lavender, and some striped combinations. Retail nurseries sometimes offer named varieties, but you're more likely to find plants labeled by color alone. For specific named selections—and ones like 'L'Elegante', with variegated leaves—seek out a specialty *Pelargonium* grower. The mixed-color Summer Showers strain can be raised from seed.

*Pelargonium peltatum* 'Mini Pink'

Ivy geranium prefers well-drained, fairly light soil. If soil is alkaline, incorporate acid organic amendments such as fortified redwood bark or peat moss. Set out plants from flats or pots, spacing them 1½ to 2 feet apart. Water plantings only when the top inch of soil is dry. Plants growing in sandy soil will benefit from two or three applications of fertilizer during the growing season, but those in reasonably good soil may prosper without any supplemental nutrients.

## PETREA volubilis
QUEEN'S WREATH

- 🌿 EVERGREEN WOODY VINE
- ✂ ZONES 19–25
- ☼ ☾ SUN OR PARTIAL SHADE
- 💧 REGULAR WATER

Were it not for its tenderness to frost, this twining vine would be a favorite everywhere. In general appearance, it's an evergreen stand-in for wisteria—with the added advantage of bloom several times per year. It grows vigorously to as far as 40 feet, decked out in elliptical, 8-inch, dark green leaves with a rough texture that's responsible for another of the plant's common names, "sandpaper vine." Star-shaped, blue-purple flowers to about 1½ inches across are carried in wisterialike clusters—dense, pendent, up to a foot long. The main bloom season comes in late spring and early summer, but lesser displays occur later during the warm months.

Set out young plants in organically enriched, well-drained soil. Queen's wreath is a fine choice to for any spot where its blossom clusters can be displayed effectively—covering an arbor or pergola, twining along eaves, trained up a high wall. Prune and thin growth as needed during winter.

*Petrea volubilis*

## PHYLA nodiflora
LIPPIA

- 🌿 EVERGREEN PERENNIAL GROUND COVER
- ✂ ZONES 8–29
- ☼ SUN
- 💧 💧 REGULAR TO LITTLE WATER

Its appearance is not at all grasslike— but lippia's ground-hugging growth and ability to endure foot traffic have established its use as a lawn substitute in some areas where a traditional lawn is impractical. Clothed in oval, grayish green leaves to ¾ inch long, the stems creep along briskly, forming a sort of "turf" no higher than 2 inches. Rounded, ½-inch heads of tiny lavender pink flowers appear from spring to fall. They're a magnet for bees; if this trait doesn't appeal to you, mow plantings periodically to remove blossoms.

Lippia grows easily in a wide range of soils, though its performance will suffer wherever nematodes are a problem. It accepts regular moisture in well-drained soil, but moderate or even little watering is entirely sufficient, depending on the weather. You can set out established clumps (from pots) 2 feet apart or plant rooted sprigs at 1-foot intervals. Lippia is an especially satisfactory ground cover in desert areas and equally good in coastal gardens. Plantings tend to look shabby in winter, but an application of fertilizer in early spring will promote fast new growth to cover the last season's scruffy foliage.

*Phyla nodiflora*

## PLEIOBLASTUS

- 🌿 EVERGREEN PERENNIAL GROUND COVERS
- ✂ ZONES VARY BY SPECIES
- ☼ ☾ SUN OR PARTIAL SHADE
- 💧 💧 REGULAR TO MODERATE WATER

Most bamboos are upright, feathery plants, typically used as accent clumps, screening hedges, or grove plantings. Several species, however, are low growing enough to serve as ground covers. Rising more or less vertically from underground rootstocks, their stems (called *culms*) show conspicuous rings *(nodes)* at regular intervals all along their length. From these nodes come short branches bearing linear, almost grasslike foliage. All the ground cover types are so-called running bamboos: they spread by underground stems to colonize the soil. In fact, they spread very aggressively—an asset or a liability, depending on your garden setup. All have been botanically reclassified several times, and nurseries may not have caught up with the current nomenclature. In our descriptions, the former names for each are given in parentheses. >

*Pleioblastus auricoma*

The shortest grower is pygmy bamboo, *P. pygmaeus (Arundinaria pygmaea, Sasa pygmaea)*. It's suited to Zones 4–9, 14–24, 28–32. Pencil-thick culms average a bit less than 1 foot high and are well clothed in 5-inch, bright green leaves. Dwarf fernleaf bamboo, *P. pygmaeus distichus (P. distichus, Arundinaria disticha, Sasa disticha)* looks like a larger version of pygmy bamboo; it reaches about 2 feet. It has a slightly more limited range: Zones 5–9, 14–24, 28–31.

Two species adapted to Zones 5–9, 14–24, 28–31 feature especially decorative foliage. In the garden, they look more like seas of tall grass than low ground covers. *P. auricoma (P. viridistriatus, Arundinaria auricoma, A. viridistriatus)* has 2-foot-tall culms bearing narrow, 8-inch leaves in striking longitudinal stripes of green and gold. Dwarf whitestripe bamboo, *P. variegatus (Sasa fortunei, S. variegata)*, has green-and-white-striped leaves to 8 inches long and 1 inch wide, carried on culms to 2½ feet high.

Although bamboos tolerate adversity, they grow best in reasonably good, organically enriched soil. Unlike most other plants, they establish faster if rootbound, so if possible buy plants that crowd their containers. Set out those from pots 1 foot apart, those from 1-gallon containers 2 feet apart. Because they are invasive, these bamboos are best used in naturalistic settings where they can colonize freely without actually invading other plantings; they make fine erosion-control covers on slopes. If you do use them in more closely controlled situations, curb their spread with sturdy concrete, metal, or wood barriers, making sure these extend at least 1 foot below ground. To keep plantings neat, mow or shear them in fall, after the growing season is finished. Fertilize at least once annually, at the start of the growing season.

## PODRANEA ricasoliana
PINK TRUMPET VINE

- EVERGREEN TO DECIDUOUS WOODY VINE
- ZONES 9, 12, 13, 19–27
- SUN OR PARTIAL SHADE
- REGULAR TO MODERATE WATER

An aura of refinement surrounds this twining vine. It grows at a moderate rate to 20 feet, bearing glossy, somewhat feathery foliage and colorful but not gaudy blossoms. Each leaf consists of two to five opposite pairs of 2-inch, elliptical leaflets plus one terminal leaflet. Summer flowers come in elongated trusses on new growth; blossoms are trumpet shaped, ending in five unequal lobes that flare to nearly 2 inches across. The color is a soft but lively warm pink, with red lines extending into a yellowish throat. The vine makes a lovely warm-season focal point; it's excellent trained on posts, arbors, trellises, trunks of high-branching trees, and sunny walls.

*Podranea ricasoliana*

Give pink trumpet vine reasonably good, well-drained soil. Light frost may cause foliage to drop, but stems will later put out a new crop of leaves. Heavier frosts may kill a vine to the ground, but regrowth is almost certain as long as soil doesn't freeze. Train vines as they grow; thin out any tangling growth during winter. Florida growers should keep in mind that this plant is very susceptible to nematodes.

*Polygonum capitatum*

## POLYGONUM
KNOTWEED

- EVERGREEN TO DECIDUOUS WOODY AND PERENNIAL VINES AND GROUND COVERS
- ZONES VARY BY SPECIES
- SUN OR PARTIAL SHADE
- REGULAR TO MODERATE WATER

When the going gets tough, the knotweeds get going: they're noted for good performance even in the face of indifferent soil, capricious watering, and considerable inattention from the gardener. In fact, they tend to respond to assiduous care a little too enthusiastically—the vines climbing by leaps and bounds, the ground cover species *P. capitatum* aggressively invading neighboring plantings. But their good looks compensate for their rampant exuberance.

The vining knotweeds look much alike and can be used interchangeably; the main difference is a slight variation in flower color and size. Both species have slender, twining stems, wavy-edged, heart-shaped leaves to 2½ inches long, and

*Polygonum aubertii*

tiny, fragrant blossoms borne in large, elongated clusters that produce a veritable froth of bloom from late spring into fall. White-flowered silver lace vine, *P. aubertii,* grows in Zones 2–24, 28–41. It is evergreen in the warmest zones, partially to totally deciduous in colder regions. Even in the coldest zones, it can reach 20 feet in a single growing season, and in warmer areas it may attain twice that size. Growth tends to form an impenetrable tangle—an asset when you want to cover unsightly structures, wire fences, or bare and sloping ground. You can use this vine to great effect on arbors and pergolas, but sooner or later it will require thinning and general tidying. Bokhara fleece flower, *P. baldschuanicum,* grows in Zones 2–24, 31–41. It differs from silver lace vine only in having slightly larger blossoms that turn pinkish as they age.

Two ground cover knotweeds could hardly look less like their vining relatives. Rugged evergreen *P. capitatum* grows in Zones 8, 9, 12–24, performing equally well in sun or light shade. The reddish stems grow in a thick network, rooting as they spread to produce a solid foliage cover to 8 inches high. The oval, 1½-inch leaves start out dark green with a reddish brown crescent pattern, then take on a pink tinge with age. Cloverlike heads of tiny pink blossoms bloom throughout the warmer months. Leaves and stems may be killed at 28°F/–2°C, but the planting will regrow from the roots in spring.

Evergreen *P. vacciniifolium* grows in Zones 4–7, 31, 32. In habit and foliage, it suggests a smaller and more refined version of the previous species. The flowers, though, are markedly differ-

ent: the late summer display of tiny pink blossoms comes in foxtail-like, 3-inch spikes on 6- to 9-inch stems. With the onset of chilly fall weather, the dark green leaves turn red.

*P. aubertii* and *P. baldschuanicum* are quite unparticular about soil. Both are fairly drought tolerant but look better with at least moderate watering. Whenever growth becomes too tangled for easy pruning, you can cut plants to the ground in late winter or early spring; regrowth is fast, with bloom delayed until mid- to late summer. Both tend to colonize a bit by underground stems. If you want to use *P. aubertii* as a ground cover on slopes, space plants from 1-gallon containers about 15 feet apart.

*P. capitatum* and *P. vacciniifolium* perform best with average, well-drained soil and regular to moderate watering (though *P. capitatum* will survive with little). Set out plants from pots, spacing them 1 foot apart.

## POTENTILLA neumanniana
### SPRING CINQUEFOIL

- 🌿 EVERGREEN PERENNIAL GROUND COVER
- ❄ ZONES 1–24, 31–43
- ☀ ◑ SUN OR PARTIAL SHADE
- 💧 MODERATE WATER

This attractive plant may also be sold as *P. tabernaemontanii* or *P. verna* 'Nana'. By any name, it's an appealing low ground cover that, despite its almost delicate looks, is a rugged and relentless spreader. In general appearance, it's reminiscent of a strawberry plant: inch-long, toothedged, glossy leaflets come in fives at the ends of leafstalks carried on creeping stems that root as they spread. In spring and summer, five-petaled, ¼-inch flowers—like tiny wild roses in bright butter yellow—are lavishly scattered over the 3- to 6-inch-high foliage carpet. Growth is fast but not threatening; foliage covers the ground completely, yet plantings are permeable enough to allow spring-flowering

*Potentilla neumanniana*

bulbs to grow beneath. Established plantings will endure limited foot traffic.

Average, well-drained soil suits spring cinquefoil. Set out plants from pots or flats, spacing them 1 foot apart. In hot-summer regions, plants look best when lightly shaded during the heat of the afternoon. Established plantings look better and more uniform if mowed annually before spring growth begins; in the colder zones, mowing also serves to remove the browned winter leaves.

## PYRACANTHA
### FIRETHORN

- 🌿 EVERGREEN WOODY GROUND COVERS
- ❄ ZONES VARY BY SPECIES
- ☀ SUN
- 💧💧 REGULAR TO MODERATE WATER

The large, shrubby firethorns are a staple of the nursery trade. Rugged and durable, they're widely grown for their springtime show of small, scented white flowers and striking fall display of pea-size, orange to red berries. Luckily, a number of prostrate to low, spreading ground cover varieties offer the same seasonal interest. All are tough plants with small, glossy, oval leaves and needlelike thorns that make them effective barriers. They grow at a moderate to rapid rate.

*Pyracantha*

The hybrid 'Lowboy' (listed by some nurseries as a variety of *P. coccinea*) is the most cold tolerant, growing in Zones 3–24, 29–33. Rich green leaves and showy orange fruits are displayed on a spreading plant to around 8 feet across and under 3 feet high. *P. koidzumii* 'Santa Cruz' is a red-berried variety suited to Zones 4–24, 29–32; it is easily kept to 3 feet or lower with occasional pruning. Spreading branches originate from the plant's base and extend to about 6 feet. *P. koidzumii* 'Walderi' (also sold as 'Walderi Prostrata'), suited to Zones 4–24, 29–31, is another spreading, red-berried selection to about 6 feet across; it will reach 3 feet high but can be kept to about half that height. The red-berried hybrid 'Ruby Mound' grows in Zones 4–9, 12–24, 29–31. It's less stiff in habit than other ground cover pyracanthas, with long, arching, flexible branches that spread to about 10 feet and mound to about 2½ feet high.

All firethorns are easy to grow in a wide variety of soils. If soil is well drained, they'll accept regular moisture, though moderate watering is entirely adequate. In more claylike soils with slower drainage, however, give them no more than moderate watering to avoid the risk of root rot. Set out plants from 1-gallon containers, spacing them 4 to 5 feet apart (use the wider spacing for the wider-spreading varieties). Prune only to remove errant growth that shoots up above the desired foliage level. Several potential pests are worth noting. Scale, spider mites, and woolly aphids can all be problems when conditions favor their development. During cool, moist spring weather, fireblight can destroy branches and disfigure plants. A sure sign of this disease is blackened, sooty-looking terminal growth. To control the problem once it has appeared, prune out afflicted branches (cutting 6 inches below the infection), then burn the prunings.

*Pyracantha* 'Ruby Mound'

# PYROSTEGIA venusta
## FLAME VINE

🌿 EVERGREEN WOODY VINE

✍ ZONES 13, 16, 21–27

☼ SUN

💧 MODERATE WATER

The common name describes not only this plant's flower color, but also its preference for heat. And if coolness is its enemy, frost surely is its nemesis—its main flowering period comes in winter! Starting in autumn (in the warmest gardens) and continuing into spring, orange flowers in drooping clusters of 15 to 20 lavishly decorate a vigorous plant that will quickly exceed 20 feet. Individual flowers look much like those of honeysuckle (*Lonicera*, page 75); they're slender,

*Pyrostegia venusta*

3-inch-long tubes flaring into four narrow lobes. Blossom clusters are borne on new growth. In the warmest climates, a scattering of foot-long seed capsules may form after flowers fade. Vines climb by twining and by tendrils: each leaf consists of two or three oval, 2-inch leaflets, and the two-leafleted leaves have a tendril between them rather than a third leaflet.

Flame vine needs just average soil with good drainage. It actually revels in the reflected heat of walls, fences, even rooftops. With its vigor and floral profusion, it makes a striking statement on an arbor or along house eaves or the top of a wall. Do any significant pruning and thinning during warm weather, after bloom has finished.

*Ranunculus repens* 'Pleniflorus'

# RANUNCULUS repens
## CREEPING BUTTERCUP

🌿 DECIDUOUS PERENNIAL GROUND COVER

✍ ZONES 1–11, 14–24, 28–43

☼ ◐ ● SUN OR SHADE

💧💧 💧 AMPLE TO REGULAR WATER

Given constantly moist soil, creeping buttercup makes a lush, foot-high cover that spreads rapidly by creeping stems that root at the joints. The long-stalked, glossy, rounded leaves are deeply cut into numerous segments. In spring, bright yellow flowers are held above the foliage on 1- to 2-foot stems. The basic species has single flowers—showy, but less interesting than those of 'Pleniflorus', which bears button-like, inch-wide double blooms.

Set out plants from pots or 1-gallon containers, spacing them 1½ to 2 feet apart. They'll take any exposure—from full sun to full shade—but where summers are hot, a sunny location will demand special attention to watering. Where conditions are encouraging, plants spread aggressively and will even successfully invade a lawn. In closely maintained gardens, head back exploratory runners as they exceed their allotted bounds.

# RHUS aromatica
## FRAGRANT SUMAC

🌿 DECIDUOUS WOODY GROUND COVER

✍ ZONES 1–3, 10, 31–43

☼ ◐ SUN OR PARTIAL SHADE

💧 MODERATE TO LITTLE WATER

Many gardeners dismiss the sumacs as attractive weeds. True, they do fall into the "abuseproof" category (only saturated soil can do them in), but this very toughness is a virtue in less-than-ideal situations where you want an organized planting but can't (or won't) amend soil or attend to regular watering.

One selection in particular—*R. aromatica* 'Gro-low'—lends itself to ground cover use at garden fringes and anywhere you need a soil-binding plant for seldom-watered sloping ground. It spreads slowly at first, then at a moderate rate as it becomes established. From its network of shallow roots, sparsely-branched stems to 2 feet tall arise in a thicketlike mass. Three-leafleted leaves of a glossy dark green are triangular in outline, each composed of two opposite leaflets with a larger one between them; overall, each leaf reaches 3 inches long and wide. The leaf margins are jagged to lightly lobed. Foliage is pleasantly aromatic when crushed and turns a blazing orange red in autumn. Dense clusters of small red fruits ripen in late summer or early fall.

Although fragrant sumac's virtue is adaptability, it grows best in soil that is slightly acid and reasonably well drained. Grown in heavy soil, it spreads more slowly. Set out plants from 1-gallon containers, spacing them 3 to 4 feet apart. In hot-summer regions, full-sun plantings look better if watered occasionally throughout the summer.

*Rhus aromatica* 'Gro-low'

# ROSA
ROSE

- DECIDUOUS (WITH FEW EXCEPTIONS) WOODY VINES AND GROUND COVERS
- ZONES VARY BY SPECIES
- SUN OR PARTIAL SHADE
- REGULAR WATER

The wide world of climbing roses includes demure sorts that will decorate a post as well as galumphing giants determined to beautify treetops. Various climbers also have been pressed into service as ground cover roses; the common trait among these is canes that are lax enough to sprawl. Recent years, however, have seen the introduction of breeding programs aimed at creating plants expressly for ground cover use. Choices in climbers have increased as well, with nurseries now offering not only newly developed varieties but also ever more species, heritage, and antique roses of climbing habit.

CLIMBING ROSES. The single characteristic that unites climbing roses (and separates them from their shrubby kin) is the nature of their canes: long and somewhat flexible to nearly lax. Most have thorns which, in nature, would help them clamber through shrubs and trees.

Aside from the similarity in their canes, climbing roses are amazingly diverse. Some flower only in spring, while others are repeat bloomers. Blossoms may be of small or modest size (just 1 to about 2 inches across) or almost as large as full-size hybrid tea blooms. Some put out a great number of slender canes, while others establish a framework of just a few canes that, in time, may become arm-thick trunks. Many species roses are climbers, and many of the historic rose classes include climbing individuals. Modern breeding has concentrated on producing plants with larger, more refined flowers and, more recently, with increased cold tolerance.

In general, you can assume that any rose called a "rambler" will have rather thin, limber canes that are easily guided

*Rosa* 'American Pillar'

into place; most flower only in spring, on plants that reach 15 to 25 feet. Many are derived from a Japanese species that is a trailing ground cover. Roses classed as large-flowered climber (LCL), climbing hybrid tea, climbing grandiflora, or climbing floribunda usually have thicker, stiffer canes; in size, they vary from semi-climbers around 8 feet fall to rampant numbers reaching 25 feet or more. These last four groups tend to have the showiest individual flowers, but they're the most likely to suffer from the standard assortment of foliage diseases afflicting hybrid teas. Some shrub roses (notably the hybrid musks) and a number of the so-called English roses will grow like climbers in mild-winter regions.

To acquaint yourself with the range of possibilities, visit public gardens and well-stocked nurseries; consult *Sunset's Roses* (1998), where you'll also find pruning instructions and information on especially cold-tolerant varieties.

GROUND COVER ROSES. Until recently, roses for ground cover use were drawn from the group of plants which would sprawl on the ground if denied support—chiefly the lax-caned ramblers and a few individual climbers ( such as 'Max

Graf' and 'Sea Foam'). But today's gardeners will find an ever-increasing number of roses bred specifically as ground covers. These plants have the desired lax canes, but unlike the long-caned climbers, they have shorter main canes that branch freely yet maintain a plant mass under 2 feet high. The series that began with 'Flower Carpet' is the most widely promoted of these; its members are available in containers at nurseries, garden centers, and home-improvement emporia. The original offering, deep pink 'Flower Carpet', has been joined by two versions in different colors: 'White Flower Carpet' and 'Apple-blossom Flower Carpet'. Among other available ground cover varieties are 'Magic Carpet' (lilac pink), 'Red Ribbons', 'Snow Owl' ('White Pavement'), and 'Watermelon Ice' (deep pink).

## ROSE CULTURE AND PRUNING

When you grow the ever-popular shrubby hybrid tea roses, you'll encounter specific directions for fertilizing, pest control, and annual pruning—all efforts aimed at producing the largest possible quantity of the

*Rosa* 'Flower Carpet'

most perfect blossoms possible. But culture is easier for ground cover roses and many climbing sorts. Most are vigorous plants grown for mass effect, and care is aimed just at keeping the plants healthy and growing. Unless you have a disease-prone climber that needs periodic applications of fungicide, caring for these roses is simple—attend to their water needs during dry periods, fertilize at the start of the growing season, and remove old and superfluous stems each year.

All roses grow best in average to good soil that is at least reasonably well drained. If the soil is fairly light, dig organic matter into it before planting to get the new plant off to a good start. Once roots have grown beyond the prepared area, though, the plant will make do with the native soil. For the most satisfying performance, pay attention to watering: roses prefer regular moisture, though soil should not become water-logged.

*Rosa* 'Coral Dawn'

Pruning any rose is most easily done in winter or early spring (depending on the climate), when plants are dormant and usually leafless: the bare stems make it easy to see what you're doing. And for repeat-flowering roses, the dormant season is the best time to prune. For roses that flower only in spring, however, pruning before bloom will remove at least some potential flowers. To prune these spring-only bloomers, remove dead stems and weak or played-out wood in winter; then wait until after the plant has flowered to take out superfluous but productive growth.

Though roses are grown in all climate zones, keeping them alive over winter in the coldest regions requires consid-

erable effort and determination. Cold tolerance varies greatly among varieties and rose classes, but winter protection is generally recommended where lows normally dip to 0°F/−18°C or lower. Ground cover plants can be protected by a loose blanket of evergreen boughs, and snow itself is an effective insulator. Protecting climbing roses, however, presents a significant problem, due both to the plants' size and to their exposed position. In you live in an area where winter cold is severe, look for the relatively few climbers developed to survive cold winters (some of the Canadian Explorer roses, for example).

## ROSMARINUS officinalis
### ROSEMARY

- EVERGREEN WOODY GROUND COVER
- ZONES 4–24, 26–32
- SUN
- MODERATE TO LITTLE WATER

This plant—the familiar culinary rosemary—is a variable species. The selections most often grown for culinary use are upright shrubs, but several varieties have low, spreading growth and make excellent low-maintenance ground covers that grow at a moderate rate. All have narrow, almost needlelike leaves that are pungently scented and slightly sticky; in color, they're medium to dark green above, gray beneath. Small blue blossoms appear from fall into spring, with the peak display period varying by variety. Stems root as they spread, so that one plant becomes a colony. On seldom-watered hillsides, rosemary is a superlative choice for erosion control.

The original and most widely grown ground cover selection is 'Prostratus'. It hugs the ground at first, but the secondary stems arch, curve, or twist, giving mass plantings a tumbled appearance. Plants spread 4 to 8 feet wide and may reach 2 feet high, though they can be kept lower with selective pruning (you even can shear them into a tabletop of foliage). If they're grown at the edge of a raised bed, their stems will trail over the side in waterfall fashion. Flowers are pale gray blue (French blue).

Similar to 'Prostratus' is 'Lockwood de Forest', distinguished by its lighter and brighter green foliage and clear blue blossoms. 'Ken Taylor' has the arching-trailing habit of 'Prostratus', but it's less dense and bears striking violet-blue blossoms. Two others with intense blue blooms are 'Severn Sea' and bright green–leafed 'Irene'. The lowest grower of all, reaching no higher than 1½ feet, is 'Huntington Carpet', with pale blue flowers.

*Rosmarinus officinalis* 'Irene'

Rosemary grows best in well-drained (even poor) soil; if not overwatered, it will prosper in heavier soils as well. Set out plants from pots or 1-gallon containers, spacing them about 2 feet apart. Provide moderate water during the first year, as plants become established. Thereafter, their water needs are minimal. Plantings in cool-summer gardens remain attractive throughout the year with little or no supplemental water; those in hot-summer regions need occasional summer water to keep them looking fresh. (In desert heat, plants need periodic summer watering to survive.) Prune as needed to remove branches that depart from the desired silhouette. Be sure to make all cuts to side branches or into leafy stems; if you cut back into old stems below foliage, no regrowth will occur.

*Rubus pentalobus*

## RUBUS pentalobus

- ⬆ EVERGREEN WOODY GROUND COVER
- ✂ ZONES 4–6, 14–17, 31, 32
- ☼ ◐ SUN OR PARTIAL SHADE
- ◐ ◑ REGULAR TO MODERATE WATER

Native to the mountains of Taiwan (and sometimes called Taiwan bramble), this blackberry relative is esteemed for handsome foliage rather than fruits. The 1- to 1½-inch leaves are rounded, with three to five broad, ruffle-edged lobes; they are lustrous dark green and rough textured above, grayish white and felted beneath. Creeping thornless stems spread at a moderate rate to form a dense cover up to 1 foot high. The small white springtime flowers, largely hidden in the foliage, resemble strawberry blossoms—but the salmon-colored fruits that follow are unmistakably of the blackberry type. They're tasty, but fall short of pie or jam quality. 'Emerald Carpet' is a widely sold variety with superior foliage.

This plant doesn't care about soil type, but it does need good drainage. Set out plants from 1-gallon containers about 2 feet apart. In all zones, plants thrive in light shade; where summers are cool to mild, they also do well in full sun.

*Note:* Many nurseries still offer this plant as *R. calycinoides.*

*Rubus pentalobus*

## SANTOLINA

- ⬆ EVERGREEN SHRUBBY PERENNIAL GROUND COVERS
- ✂ ZONES VARY BY SPECIES
- ☼ SUN
- ◐ MODERATE TO LITTLE WATER

Adaptability is one of santolina's outstanding traits: it grows happily in cool, dry climates as well as in hot regions with some humidity. The several species and named selections differ in detail but fit a general pattern. Foliage is dense, aromatic, and narrow to needlelike. Plants spread widely unless checked, rooting as they spread; the horizontal stems send up branches that arch upward, producing a billowy effect. In late spring, wire-thin stems bear buttonlike flowers that look like petal-less daisies.

*Santolina chamaecyparissus*

Two species grow in Zones 3–24, 27, 29, 30, 32–36, 39. The more widely grown is *S. chamaecyparissus*, commonly known as lavender cotton. Each gray-white leaf is very narrow and no more than 1 inch long, its margins finely divided into feathery segments. If unclipped, plants will bear brassy yellow flowers; 'Lemon Queen' offers blossoms of a softer lemon yellow. *S. pinnata* has the same narrow, feathery leaves, but in green; its blooms are a light cream. Its variety 'Edward Bowles' has gray-green leaves and light yellow flowers, while 'Sulfurea' bears pale yellow blossoms and silvery foliage.

Well-named *S. rosmarinifolia* grows in Zones 4–24, 27–29, 30, 32. Its 2-inch leaves are rosemarylike needles of medium green, providing a bright contrast to the marigold yellow flowers. 'Primrose Gem' is similar, but with the flower color toned down to a much lighter shade.

All species and varieties will grow in virtually any soil. Moderate watering is best (especially in heavier soils), and where summers are cool, plants can go through the warm months without any supplemental moisture. Set out plants from pots or 1-gallon containers, spacing them about 3 feet apart. Without shearing or trimming, established plantings can mound up to 2 feet high; if you prefer a more formal appearance, you can shear them to tabletop flatness. When older plantings start to show bare patches or simply begin to look shabby, cut them back heavily or shear them in early spring; dense new growth will fill in within the next few months. Shear off spent flowers to keep things looking neat.

*Sarcococca hookerana humilis*

## SARCOCOCCA
### hookerana humilis
SARCOCOCCA, SWEET BOX

- EVERGREEN WOODY GROUND COVER
- ZONES 3–9, 14–24, 31, 32
- PARTIAL TO FULL SHADE
- REGULAR TO MODERATE WATER

It may not look like boxwood *(Buxus)* — but sarcococca is a boxwood relative, and it shares boxwood's renowned neatness

and polish. The glossy dark green leaves, set closely on the stems, are pointed ovals to 3 inches long. The plant colonizes slowly by underground stems, eventually reaching over 6 feet wide and about 1½ feet tall. Tiny white flowers appear among the leaves in late winter to early spring— inconspicuous in appearance, but striking for their penetrating fragrance. Glossy blue-black, pea-size berries come later.

Sarcococca is a first-rate choice for shaded locations that are always on display; in cool-summer regions, it thrives in sun as well. Its slow spread is really its only liability. Set out gallon-size plants in good soil liberally enriched with organic matter, spacing them 1½ feet apart.

## SCHIZOPHRAGMA
### hydrangeoides
JAPANESE HYDRANGEA VINE

- DECIDUOUS WOODY VINE
- ZONES 4–9, 14–17, 31–43, 39
- PARTIAL SHADE
- REGULAR WATER

At first glance, you might mistake this vine for the genuine climbing hydrangea (*Hydrangea*, page 67): it too is a large-leafed plant that will cover shaded walls, clinging tightly with aerial rootlets on stems. When bloom time comes in late summer, though, the differences are obvious. First, all of this vine's growth stays close to the surface it climbs, while climbing hydrangea produces shrubby flowering stems that extend outward. Second, although the flat, white, 8- to 10-inch flower clusters are similar to those of climbing hydrangea, with tiny fertile flowers surrounded by a ring of sterile ones, the sterile blossoms have only a single "petal" (those of climbing hydrangea have four). The ovate to spade-shaped leaves are broader than those of climbing hydrangea, with more deeply toothed margins. The usual foliage color is dark green, but 'Moonlight' has silvery blue-green leaves. 'Rosea' is a rare pink-flowered variety.

*Schizophragma hydrangeoides* 'Rosea'

Plant Japanese hydrangea vine in good, well-drained soil. Throughout the growing season, provide regular moisture during dry periods. You may need to tie young vines into place at first, but in time the stems will begin to attach to the support. Prune only to remove errant growth.

## SENECIO confusus
MEXICAN FLAME VINE

- EVERGREEN TO DECIDUOUS WOODY VINE
- ZONES 13, 16–28
- SUN OR PARTIAL SHADE
- REGULAR TO MODERATE WATER

It may be hard to imagine a climbing daisy, but that's what this is. And what a daisy: though the flowers aren't large (only about an inch across), they're a traffic-stopping orange red with yellow centers. Small clusters of these bright blossoms cover a twining 10- to 15-foot vine from midspring into fall—and sometimes year-round in frostless regions. The broadly lance-shaped,

*Senecio confusus*

bright green leaves are thick and nearly succulent, up to 4 inches long. 'São Paulo' has darker flowers that verge on brick red.

Plant Mexican flame vine in well-drained, sandy to loamy soil. In the mild-climate coastal regions it prefers, it can get by with moderate watering; in warmer regions, you'll need to provide regular moisture. It makes a striking adornment for a trellis or pillar, and can even be planted at the top of a retaining wall to cascade downward. Plants are reliably evergreen in frost-free regions. With light frost, leaves may drop but stems will live; where frosts are harder, the entire plant dies back, then resprouts in spring. Botanists have reclassified this plant as *Pseudogynoxys chenopodiodes,* but the nursery trade may never acknowledge the change.

*Solandra maxima* 'Variegata'

# SOLANDRA maxima
## CUP-OF-GOLD VINE

🌿 EVERGREEN WOODY VINE
✂ ZONES 17, 21–25,
   26 (SOUTHERN PART), 27
☀ SUN
💧 REGULAR WATERING

If ever a vine suggested tropical luxuriance, this is it. It's rampant (to 40 feet), with heavy stems bearing highly polished, broadly oval leaves to 6 inches long. And for size and jungly appeal, the floral offering is second to none: long, inflated buds open to leathery, chalicelike, five-lobed, 6- to 8-inch, banana yellow blossoms with a red-brown stripe running down each

lobe to the flower center. The general impression is of lilies expanded to the size of soup bowls! The main bloom period runs from winter into early spring, but scattered flowering can occur at any time. For variety in foliage, look for rare 'Variegata', with leaves edged in creamy white.

Good, well-drained soil encourages the best growth. Give plants regular deep soakings, letting the soil surface dry between waterings. Cup-of-gold vine is truly spectacular on arbors and pergolas, trained along house eaves or the tops of fences, or as a giant wall decoration. Wherever you use it, you'll need to tie it into place, since it has no means of attachment. It's an excellent seacoast plant, able to tolerate salt spray and salt-laden air. Light frost blackens the leaves, but plants usually recover to put out new growth.

# SOLANUM

🌿 EVERGREEN, SEMIEVERGREEN, AND
   DECIDUOUS WOODY VINES
✂ ZONES VARY BY SPECIES
☀ ◐ SUN OR PARTIAL SHADE
💧 💧 REGULAR TO MODERATE WATER

Any gardener who has grown potatoes (*Solanum tuberosum*) will notice the similarity between that tuber's blossoms and those of these showy vines: all have starlike, five-petaled flowers, with the reproductive parts forming a pointed yellow structure in the blossom's center.

Two species grow in Zones 8, 9, 12–27. Evergreen *S. crispum* is a modest (even shrubby) climber to about 12

*Solanum jasminoides*

*Solanum wendlandii*

feet, with 5-inch, ovate to lance-shaped leaves in soft green. Fragrant, 1-inch, lavender-blue blossoms appear in 4-inch clusters during summer; these are followed by inedible small yellow fruits in fall. 'Glasnevin' has deeper-colored flowers in larger clusters. This species is a slender-stemmed plant that must be attached to its support; it's especially well suited to trellises, walls, and posts. The appropriately (if unromantically) named potato vine, *S. jasminoides,* is a fast-growing evergreen to semievergreen twiner that can reach 30 feet in a tangle of purple-tinted, arrowhead-shaped, 1- to 3-inch leaves. The white, inch-wide flowers, carried on threadlike stalks in clusters of up to 12, are most profuse in spring but appear in lesser quantity throughout the warmer months.

Two frost-tender tropical American species are available to fortunate gardeners in Zones 16, 21–25. Evergreen to semievergreen Brazilian nightshade, *S. seaforthianum,* mounts a summertime display of clustered violet-blue, inch-wide flowers on a slender-stemmed vine to about 15 feet. The oval leaves are 4 to 8 inches long, either undivided or quite deeply cleft into three or more lobes. Pea-size red fruits (appealing to birds) ripen in fall. Like *S. crispum,* this species must be tied to its support.

Deciduous Costa Rican nightshade, *S. wendlandii,* is larger, coarser, and more immediately spectacular than the preceding three species. It can reach 15 to 20 feet, climbing by twining stems and hooked spines. The leaves—ovate or (sometimes) lobed, somewhat boat-shaped, and corrugated in texture—form a lush backdrop for dense, domed clusters of glowing lavender-blue, 2½-inch blossoms during summer. Seen from a short distance, the plant looks like bougainvillea (page 43).

All the above species except potato vine grow best with good, well-drained soil and regular moisture. Potato vine thrives under these conditions, too—but it also performs well in average soil with just moderate watering. Give plants full sun in cool-summer regions; the two hardier species appreciate partial shade where summers are hot. Maintenance consists of pruning and training, with the amount needed depending on the species. Potato vine requires the most attention to pruning and thinning. Do the job whenever growth becomes too interwoven and dead stems start to show—preferably before or after bloom, though vines can be pruned at any time with no ill effects.

## SOLLYA heterophylla
### AUSTRALIAN BLUEBELL CREEPER

- EVERGREEN WOODY VINE OR GROUND COVER
- ZONES 8, 9, 14–28
- SUN OR PARTIAL SHADE
- REGULAR WATER

Versatility is this plant's trademark: you can use it as a modest twining vine, high ground cover, or shrub. In any situation, it offers a summertime bounty of piercingly blue, bell-shaped blossoms in pendent clusters on a plant with a lightweight, fine-textured appearance. The slender, rather lax stems are clothed in glossy, narrow, 2-inch leaves; the small flowers (under 1 inch long) appear on threadlike stalks in clusters of six to 12 at the ends of new growth. 'Alba' is a white-flowered form.

Australian bluebell creeper grows at a moderate rate. As a vine, it reaches just 6 to 8 feet, making it a good choice for

*Sollya heterophylla*

trellises and low walls. Grown as a ground cover, it mounds 2 to 3 feet high and spreads twice as wide; it is most effective on sloping ground or massed atop a retaining wall, where its slender branches will spill gracefully over the edge. This is one of the few plants that grows well beneath eucalyptus trees.

Good drainage is Australian bluebell creeper's most important requirement. Where summers are hot, be sure plantings receive partial shade in summer. For ground cover use, set out plants from 1-gallon containers about 4 feet apart. If the planting looks a bit sparse, you can selectively cut back stems in spring to promote branching. If you're growing Australian bluebell creeper as a vine, select and train the strongest stems, removing any weaker and unneeded shoots that develop at the plant's base.

## STEPHANOTIS floribunda
### MADAGASCAR JASMINE, STEPHANOTIS

- EVERGREEN WOODY VINE
- ZONES 23–25
- SUN OR PARTIAL SHADE
- REGULAR WATER

Legendary fragrance is reason enough to grow this vine—just ask any bride who has carried its flowers in her bouquet. It is related to star jasmine (*Trachelospermum jasminoides,* page 94), and the family connection goes beyond fragrance: the two plants are similar in looks. Leaves are thick, leathery, 2-inch ovals carried on twining stems; clustered, waxy white blos-

soms open to 1½-inch stars from tubular buds. The main flowering period comes in summer, though scattered bloom can occur during other warm months. The vine grows at a moderate rate, climbing to 15 to 25 feet, possibly higher in the most favored locations. Use it to decorate posts, trellises, or arbors—or wherever its beauty and fragrance will be encountered often. Where winter temperatures are too low for survival, grow Madagascar jasmine in a large container and overwinter it in a well-lit shelter where temperatures will remain above freezing.

Madagascar jasmine needs well-drained, organically enriched soil, kept moist but not saturated. Ideally, its roots should be in shade, its stems and leaves in full or dappled sun. Fertilize at the start of the growing season; for the lushest growth, repeat the application 2 months later. Do any necessary thinning or pruning after the main bloom period has finished.

*Stephanotis floribunda*

## STIGMAPHYLLON
### ORCHID VINE

- EVERGREEN WOODY VINES OR GROUND COVERS
- ZONES VARY BY SPECIES
- SUN
- REGULAR WATER

These two twining vines bear clusters of airy yellow blossoms that suggest oncidium orchids in their general structure and their toothed to fringed petal margins. Depending on the species, you can have a smallish vine with small clusters of larger flowers, or a really large one with larger clusters of smaller flowers. Both mount their main show in summer, but they can produce some scattered bloom at other times of year.

Sometimes called Amazon climber, *S. ciliatum* grows in Zones 19–28. It is the more modest climber (to about 15 feet), with 3-inch, heart-shaped leaves that have fringed edges. The foliage cover is open, so the vine makes a tracery of foliage on its support. Flowers are 1½ inches across, presented in clusters of three to seven.

Brazilian *S. littorale* grows in Zones 15–27. Flowers are smaller in this species (1 inch across) but come in clusters of 10 to 20 on an exuberant climber that, if given support, can attain great heights, even reaching the tops of trees. Its appearance is coarser, due in part to the larger (5-inch) oval leaves.

Both orchid vines appreciate good, well-drained soil with added organic matter. Ultimate size dictates use: the smaller vine is best used on posts, trellises, and walls, while the larger species can cover arbors, pergolas, or wire fencing, or even serve as a bank cover for bare, sloping ground (for this use, set out gallon-size plants 10 to 12 feet apart). Thin excess and tangled growth from vines in spring.

*Stigmaphyllon littorale*

*Taxus baccata* 'Repandens'

## TAXUS baccata
### ENGLISH YEW

🌿 EVERGREEN WOODY GROUND COVER

❄ ZONES 3–9, 14–24, 32, 33, WARMEST PARTS OF 34

☀ ◐ SUN OR PARTIAL SHADE

💧 ◐ REGULAR TO LITTLE WATER

Think of English yew, and you probably envision a tall, bulky, dense, and somber shrub, the original darling of topiary artists. But not all members of the species are tall; two prostrate variants number among the finest all-green ground covers. Botanically, English yew is a conifer related to junipers and the like, but it has a softer foliage effect in the landscape. The short, very narrow leaves are dark green and glossy on their upper surfaces, pale beneath; they are arranged spirally around the branches. Small, fleshy fruits, borne only on female plants, are cup shaped and bright red.

Rather small differences separate the ground cover varieties 'Cavendishii' and 'Repandens'. Both put out long, horizontal limbs with slightly drooping branch tips; plants start as small mounds of greenery, then build outward at a slow to moderate pace, eventually reaching 12 feet or so while remaining under 3 feet tall. Of the two, 'Repandens' has the more regular habit and bears straight needles to ¾ inch long; needles of 'Cavendishii' are somewhat sickle shaped and about 1 inch long. Both varieties are

female and will bear fruit if a male plant grows nearby.

English yew takes a variety of soil types, from acid to slightly alkaline, but it must have good drainage. Growth is equally good in sun or partial shade, but avoid planting near south- or west-facing walls, where foliage is likely to burn from reflected heat and light. Set out plants from 1-gallon containers about 3 feet apart. Plants accept regular moisture, but once established, they will get by on moderate watering; in cool-summer climates, they almost qualify as drought tolerant. In subfreezing climates (especially where soil is likely to freeze), protect plants from the desiccating effects of winter wind and sun. In such regions, the best plan is to choose wind-sheltered locations that are relatively shady during winter.

*Tecomaria capensis*

## TECOMARIA capensis
### CAPE HONEYSUCKLE

🌿 EVERGREEN WOODY VINE OR GROUND COVER

❄ ZONES 12, 13, 16, 18–28; WITH PROTECTION IN 14, 15

☀ SUN

💧 ◐ REGULAR TO LITTLE WATER

Its flowers are bright, its foliage glossy— this vine is the picture of robust good health. Rather shrubby by nature (it must be tied to its support), it sends up numerous stems well clothed in feather-shaped leaves that are somewhat reminiscent of rose foliage; each is composed of up to nine ovate, dark green leaflets. The tips of new growth produce spikes of vibrant red-orange, 2-inch blossoms shaped like honeysuckle flowers. If the species sounds too gaudy for your taste, look for 'Aurea', which has clear yellow blossoms and lighter green leaves. Bloom can start as early as late summer and last into winter, depending on the climate. With training and tying, Cape honeysuckle can reach 15 to 25 feet, making a striking adornment for fences, arbors, pergolas, or house eaves. You even can use it as a rough bank cover on hard-to-water hillsides.

Once established, Cape honeysuckle grows easily in just about any soil and with almost any amount of moisture—from regular to scant. To use it as a bank cover, set out plants from 1-gallon containers about 10 feet apart. It thrives in heat and warmth; in cooler zones, give it the warmest location possible. Prune in winter (after flowering) to control size and density. The plant can spread from root suckers—and any piece of cut root (or root left after digging) will sprout.

*Teucrium chamaedrys*

## TEUCRIUM chamaedrys
GERMANDER

- EVERGREEN SHRUBBY PERENNIAL GROUND COVER
- ZONES 3–24, 28–34, 39
- SUN
- REGULAR TO LITTLE WATER

Even when soil is poor or watering infrequent, trouble-free germander faithfully provides a carpet of glossy dark green leaves. Plants produce many spreading stems; from these come ascending branches bearing oval, nearly inch-long leaves with conspicuously toothed margins. The basic species grows at a slow to moderate rate, spreading widely and sending up stems to about 1 foot tall; pinkish purple or white flowers appear at stem ends in summer. For a foliage cover just 4 to 6 inches high, look for 'Prostratum'.

Germander is not at all fussy about soil quality, but it does demand good drainage to keep roots from becoming waterlogged. Set out plants from pots or 1-gallon containers, spacing them about 1½ feet apart. As long as soil is well drained, germander will accept regular moisture but grow just as well with moderate to little water (more in warmer climates, less in cooler ones). If soil is heavy, though, water infrequently (in any climate). If plantings become straggly, shear them back in late winter to early spring, before new growth begins.

## THUNBERGIA

- EVERGREEN TO DECIDUOUS PERENNIAL VINES
- ZONES 16, 21–27
- SUN OR PARTIAL SHADE
- REGULAR WATER

The popular annual black-eyed Susan vine, *Thunbergia alata,* is profiled on page 41. Here we cover two of its perennial relatives, species from subtropical India that are just adaptable enough to persist from year to year in the mildest-winter regions. Both are twining climbers—and there the similarity ends.

*Thunbergia grandiflora*

Sky flower, *T. grandiflora,* is a vigorous, 20-foot vine densely clothed in heart-shaped, 8-inch leaves. True to the common name, the trumpet-shaped flowers are sky blue; each flares into five lobes and reaches about 3 inches across. Blossoms appear through summer and into fall, carried in small, drooping clusters or individually. Sky flower is a good choice for growing on an arbor, large trellis, or wire fence; on a freestanding trellis, it can provide a wall of leaves and flowers in an outdoor-living area.

*T. mysorensis* bears drooping, 1- to 1½-foot flower clusters that are best displayed on an arbor or pergola, where they can dangle decoratively both overhead and from the walls. In bud, the blooms suggest wisteria; but as they open (from the base of the cluster downward), the red, olive-shaped buds turn upward and split to reveal yellow blossoms reminiscent of a gaping birds' beaks. The vine

*Thunbergia mysorensis*

reaches 15 to 20 feet and has rather narrow, elliptical leaves to 6 inches long.

Both thunbergias need good, well-drained soil, preferably amended with organic matter before planting. In frost-free regions, their stems may live from year to year. In the cooler parts of their hardiness range, the tops may be killed by light frost, but the roots should remain alive to send up new stems.

## TRACHELOSPERMUM

- ★ ❦ EVERGREEN WOODY VINES OR GROUND COVERS
- ☊ ZONES VARY BY SPECIES
- ☼ ☽ SUN OR PARTIAL SHADE
- ❂ REGULAR WATER

Despite the common name, it isn't a true jasmine (see *Jasminum,* page 70)—but star or Confederate jasmine, *T. jasminoides,* has a similar and equally penetrating perfume, a heady fragrance that carries for some distance. Adapted to Zones 8–31 and the warmer parts of Zone 32, the plant is a twining vine with oval, leathery, 3-inch-long leaves that are glossy light green when new, maturing to a polished darker green. Against this handsome backdrop appear clusters of 1-inch, pinwheel-shaped white blossoms in summer (late spring in warmer regions). For variety in foliage, look for 'Variegatum', with leaves bordered and blotched in white.

*T. asiaticum* is similar to *T. jasminoides* in perfume and overall looks, but it has smaller, duller green leaves and smaller blossoms in cream to light yellow. It is also more widely adapted, growing in Zones 6–24, 26, 28–32.

Both species prefer well-drained soil. Where summers are hot, choose a location in light shade or a spot that is sunny in the morning, shaded in the afternoon. Plants grow at a moderate pace. Used as vines, they will eventually cover an area 20 feet high and wide. Grown as a ground cover, each plant spreads to 10 feet across and builds up to 2 feet high; set out plants from 1-gallon

*Trachelospermum jasminoides*

containers about 5 feet apart. Both species are wonderfully effective planted at the edges of retaining walls, where the lax stems will spill over the side in streamerlike fashion. To encourage lush growth, fertilize when the growing season begins, then again after flowering. Chlorosis (characterized by yellow leaves with dark veins) may be a problem in alkaline soils; treat affected plants with iron chelates or iron sulfate.

## TROPAEOLUM. See page 41

## VANCOUVERIA

- ❦ EVERGREEN TO DECIDUOUS PERENNIAL GROUND COVERS
- ☊ ZONES VARY BY SPECIES
- ☽ PARTIAL SHADE
- ❂ ❂ REGULAR TO LITTLE WATER

Although related closely to *Epimedium* (page 57) and more distantly to *Mahonia* (page 76), the vancouverias manage to look most like overgrown maidenhair fern *(Adiantum).* Wiry leafstalks grow directly from creeping underground stems; leaves are made up of numerous broad leaflets that resemble small ivy leaves. Threadlike flower stalks rise above the foliage in late spring or early

summer, bearing pendent clusters of small blossoms; petals and sepals are sharply reflexed, giving the flowers a windswept appearance. Plants spread slowly from an ever-enlarging mat of roots, forming sizable patches in time.

Deciduous *V. hexandra* is the most widely adapted, growing in Zones 4–7, 14–17, 19–24. Stems clothed in light green, 2½-inch leaflets make a foliage mass that averages about 1 foot high. Airy clusters of white, ½-inch flowers look like a swarm of insects hovering above the leaves.

Inside-out-flower, *V. planipetala,* grows in Zones 4–7, 14–17; leaves are evergreen in Zones 14–17 but may be deciduous in Zones 4–7. The 1½-inch leaflets are shallowly lobed; the foliage makes a somewhat layered-looking carpet to as high as 2 feet. This species, too, has "swarms" of white flowers, in clusters larger than those of *V. hexandra.*

Evergreen *V. chrysantha,* reaching up to 16 inches high, grows in Zones 5, 6, 14–17. Two characteristics immediately set this species apart from the preceding two: its foliage is a bronzed gray green, and the ½-inch flowers are yellow and come in clusters of up to 15.

*Vancouveria hexandra*

All these refined Western natives grow best in a woodland-type soil—well drained, with plenty of organic matter—but they'll also thrive (though spreading a bit more slowly) in heavier soils, as long as their roots don't get waterlogged. Set out plants from pots about 1½ feet apart. Water regularly during the first year or two, while plants are getting established; thereafter, it's sufficient to provide merely occasional summer watering in cool-summer regions, moderate to regular watering during dry periods where summers are dry and warm or hot.

*Vinca minor*

# VINCA
## PERIWINKLE

- EVERGREEN PERENNIAL GROUND COVERS
- ZONES VARY BY SPECIES
- SUN OR SHADE
- MODERATE TO LITTLE WATER

Periwinkle's charming looks mask a thoroughly tough constitution. The two species differ in size but resemble each other in foliage, flower, and habit. Spreading or arching green stems, clothed in paired shiny, oval leaves, may root at the joints or even at the tips when they touch moist soil; each newly rooted part is then another plant, ready to send out additional stems. Bloom time comes in early spring, when the foliage cover is adorned with single, phloxlike flowers of a medium-light lilac blue—the color known as periwinkle blue.

Dwarf periwinkle, *V. minor*, grows in Zones 1–24, 28–43. It is the more widely adapted species and also the more useful one, thanks to its smaller size and better behavior; it's available in more varieties, too. Dark green, narrowly oval leaves are ¾ to 1¾ inches long, spaced fairly closely on the prostrate stems; plants make a car-

pet of stems and leaves 4 to 6 inches high, against which the 1-inch blossoms stage a bountiful show. With some searching, you can find named varieties with flowers in white and various shades of blue; some have double blooms. Choices include 'Alba' (with white flowers); 'Atropurpurea' (deep purple blooms, smaller leaves); 'Aureola' (light blue blossoms, leaves with yellow central veins); 'Bowles' Variety' (deeper blue flowers, larger leaves; may be the same plant as 'La Grave'); 'Miss Jekyll' (white blooms on a lower-growing plant); 'Ralph Shugert' (reblooms in fall; white-margined leaves); and 'Sterling Silver' (cream-edged green leaves speckled in paler green).

The larger *V. major* grows in Zones 5–24, 28–31, and warmer parts of 32 and 33. Broadly oval, bright green leaves to 3 inches long appear on stems that can build up to a dense, 2-foot-high cover as they arch and spread. Blossoms are 2 inches across. A variant with irregular, creamy yellow leaf margins is available and nicely enlivens shady areas. Wherever it grows, this species spreads relentlessly unless controlled; the better the conditions, the faster the planting advances, infiltrating flower beds, lawns, even native woodland. If you're willing to make the effort to contain it (never turn your back on it!), you'll

*Vinca major* 'Variegata'

have an otherwise carefree cover that, given moderate water in hot weather, will always look good.

Neither species has any soil preference; they even compete well with surface tree roots. In cool-summer regions, plants will take full sun as well as any amount of shade; where summers are hot, partial to full shade is needed for good appearance (in shade, established plantings of *V. major* can survive the summer with no water). Set out plants from pots, spacing *V. minor* 1½ feet apart, *V. major* 2 to 2½ feet apart. Whenever plantings mound too high or become layered with old stems, shear or mow them in late winter to stimulate new growth from ground level.

*Viola odorata* varieties

# VIOLA
## VIOLET

- EVERGREEN AND DECIDUOUS PERENNIAL GROUND COVERS
- ZONES VARY BY SPECIES
- SUN OR SHADE
- REGULAR WATER

When you think of ground covers, violets may not come to mind—but this staple of romantic nosegays is borne on plants with good-looking foliage, well suited to blanketing the ground. Several species, in fact, are vigorous enough to colonize sizable areas, where they'll roll out a colorful floral carpet at bloom time. All have rounded leaves borne at the ends of slender leafstalks; flowers rise just above the foliage mass.

Evergreen *V. odorata,* the sweet violet, grows in Zones 1–24, 29–43. Its legendarily fragrant flowers come in late winter or early spring, depending on the climate. The basic species is purple flowered, but you can find named varieties with blossoms in white (sometimes with bluish centers), pink, dark red, lavender, and blue. Among the most widely available are 'Royal Elk' (long-stemmed violet flowers), 'Royal Robe' (deep purple), and 'Rosina' (deep pink). An established planting of sweet violets rises 4 to 8 inches high (shaded locations encourage the taller growth). Plants spread like strawberries do, forming new plants at the ends of runners. Volunteer seedlings increase plantings, too—sometimes into areas where they're not wanted.

Most widely adapted of the ground cover species is evergreen Labrador violet, *V. labradorica;* it grows in Zones 1–24, 29–45. The adjective "cute" certainly applies to this one, with its 1-inch, purple-tinted leaves and 1-inch purple (but scentless) summer flowers. Plants spread by runners and reach about 3 inches high. Unfortunately, Labrador violet recognizes no limits, and countless volunteer seedlings assist in its attempts at garden conquest. Plant it only if you're willing to thwart its takeover bids.

Another summer bloomer is Australian violet, *V. hederacea,* which grows in Zones 7–9, 14–24, 29, 30; with a few degrees of frost, plants will lose their leaves. Ovate to kidney-shaped leaves rise to 4 inches tall on a plant that spreads

*Viola labradorica*

rather slowly in comparison to sweet violet. The typically scentless flowers are usually blue, fading out to broad white margin.

All violets do best in good soil amended with organic matter, but they'll grow fairly well in poorer, less enriched soil if given supplemental water during dry spells. Where summers are cool, plants can take sunny locations; in hot-summer regions, they need at least afternoon shade. Set out plants from pots, spacing them about 1 foot apart. Fertilize established plantings in early spring to enhance bloom and general appearance.

# VITIS
### GRAPE
🌿 DECIDUOUS WOODY VINES
☼ ZONES VARY BY SPECIES
☼◑ SUN OR PARTIAL SHADE
◐◖ REGULAR TO MODERATE WATER

Mention the word "grape," and several other words come to mind—"jelly," "juice," and "wine," for example. Another such word is "arbor," and for good reason: grapes are classic choices for growing on arbors, where their far-reaching stems can be accommodated and their hanging clusters of fruit can be easily picked.

When you buy grapevines, you can choose from three broad categories. First are the table grapes, those you grow for their edible fruits (good for eating fresh and making jelly). Second are the wine grapes; their fruit, while tasty in itself (but often small and seedy), is used for the range of familiar wines, from red to white. Finally, some grapes are grown for foliage alone; their fruit is of no importance.

The plants in all these categories are similar in basic habit and appearance. They are strong-growing vines that climb by tenacious, spiraling tendrils. The hand-size leaves have distinctly serrated margins; they may be nearly circular but more often are lobed to some extent. Clusters of insignificant flowers appear as the leaves are emerging; by late summer,

the fruits—from pea-size to marble-size—will have ripened. Most vines have showy fall foliage.

*Vitis*

You can grow any grape informally by guiding its growth wherever you want leafy cover. But if fruit production is your principal goal, you'll need to choose the general category—and then a specific variety within it—that will do well in your area. You will also need to guide the vine's structural development along definite lines, following a specific pruning plan each year. For detailed pruning information and descriptions of grape varieties, consult *Sunset's National Garden Book.*

For purely ornamental use, one species stands out: *V. coignetiae,* sometimes called crimson glory vine. Suited to Zones 3–10, 14–21, 28–41, it's a very fast, very tall grower (to at least 50 feet if not checked), outfitted in foot-long leaves that look like huge versions of Boston ivy foliage (*Parthenocissus tricuspidata,* page 80). The "glory" in the common name refers to the fall foliage color—and leaves turn not only crimson, but orange and coppery as well. Fruit is insignificant.          >

*Vitis coignetiae*

Plant grapes in good, well drained soil. For fruit production, locate them in sun; if you want a vine just for leafy cover, you can plant it in partial shade (though mildew may appear on the leaves). Tie stems in place to develop the framework you want. Established vines perform well with just moderate water. Prune as needed in winter to early spring, while vines are leafless and before buds start to swell.

# WISTERIA

- DECIDUOUS WOODY VINES OR GROUND COVERS
- ZONES VARY BY SPECIES
- SUN; *W. SINENSIS* ALSO ACCEPTS PARTIAL SHADE
- REGULAR TO MODERATE WATER

Along with clematis (page 50) and climbing roses (page 87), wisteria is a top contender for the title of "favorite vine." With its elongated, pendent flower clusters and feathery, languid foliage, it is the embodiment of elegance; add the heavy, sinuous limbs of mature plants and you have an arresting combination of beauty and strength. And nothing could be easier to grow.

Wisterias are aggressively vigorous twining vines. There is no true limit on their size or extent of coverage. All have divided leaves constructed feather fashion: narrowly elliptical leaflets are arrayed in pairs on either side of a central leafstalk, with a single leaflet at the leafstalk tip. The foliage is fresh green, the leaflets rather thin and (usually) wavy margined. In fall, leaves turn to glowing but not brilliant shades of yellow and tawny gold before they drop. Carried in long, drooping, foxtail-like clusters, the fragrant flowers look like small sweet pea blossoms; they appear before or as leaves emerge. A wisteria in full bloom is breathtaking, rather like a pastel beaded curtain. Later in the season, long, flattened seedpods may appear, suspended from old flower stalks.

Japanese wisteria, *W. floribunda*, grows in Zones 2–24, 26, 28–41. It has the distinction of producing the longest flower clusters of any wisteria: those of one variety have been recorded at over 3 feet! On most vines, though, 1 to 1½ feet is a more typical length. The blossom clusters open from the base (stem end) downward; this makes for a longer bloom period than other wisterias offer, but blooming plants may look a bit less striking than those in which all the flowers in a cluster open at once. Foliage emerges as vines are flowering; the individual leaves can reach 16 inches long, composed of up to 19 leaflets 1½ to 3 inches long. Stems twine clockwise. The standard flower color is light to medium violet, but a number of named varieties give you specific color choices. 'Macrobotrys' ('Longissima') is the variety mentioned above with 3-foot-plus blossom clusters; its flowers are lilac. White forms include 'Longissima Alba' (with clusters to about 15 inches) and 'Ivory Tower'. 'Violacea Plena' ('Plena') has average-length clusters of double blossoms (like double violets) in a mixture of lilac and purple; young vines may need many years

*Wisteria in autumn*

to establish before they bloom. 'Texas Purple', on the other hand, flowers at an early age. 'Rosea' ('Honbeni') has flowers of a distinct rosy lilac.

Chinese wisteria, *W. sinensis*, grows in Zones 3–24, 26, 28–35, 37, 39. Despite its slightly more limited adaptability, this species is more widely planted than Japanese wisteria. Compared to the latter, it has shorter leaves (to 1 foot) with fewer leaflets (to 13), though its leaflets, too, reach 3 inches long. Stems twine counterclockwise. Flower clusters reach about 1 foot, with all flowers opening at once; flowering occurs before leaves emerge. If you buy a plant simply labeled "Chinese wisteria," you'll be taking potluck on flower color and quality—and if it is a seed-grown plant, you may wait for years before you see the blossoms. Named varieties are a better bet. 'Alba' has white flowers; 'Cooke's Special' has longer-than-average clusters of medium-violet blossoms.

Two less well-known species offer flower clusters to just 6 inches long. Silky wisteria, *W. venusta*, grows in Zones 3–24, 32–45, 37, 39. It resembles an especially heavy-blooming Chinese wisteria with stubby clusters of large flowers. Color selections include 'Alba' (white) and 'Violacea' (blue purple). It blooms as leaves are emerging. Stems twine counterclockwise.

American wisteria, *W. frutescens*, is native to the southeastern and Gulf Coast states and grows in Zones 28–34. Foot-long leaves contain up to 15 about 2½-inch leaflets; stems twine counterclockwise. In contrast to the preceding three species, this one flowers in late

*Wisteria floribunda*

spring to early summer, after leaves are fully formed. The standard color is lilac with yellow markings; 'Nivea' has white flowers that bloom a bit earlier in spring.

With the exception of *W. sinensis,* which will bloom well in partial shade, wisterias must have full sun to flower—so choose planting sites carefully. Soil type is not as important; you can find wisterias growing vigorously in all soils, though they prefer reasonably good drainage. In alkaline soil, chlorosis (evidenced by yellow leaves with green veins) may be a problem; treat with iron chelates or iron sulfate. Unless soil is especially poor, wisterias need no fertilizer.

These vines require attention to guidance and control. When you buy a new plant, decide what sort of framework you want: a single trunk up to a certain height, or multiple stems from the base or close to it. Let the plant grow for 2 years or so; then select vigorous stems for the framework, cut out all others, and rub off all unwanted emerging new shoots. Once the framework has been established, your work will involve directing additional shoots and removing superfluous growth. And there is *always* superfluous growth! Established vines send out quantities of long streamers that twine around anything within reach—in particular, around other stems on the very same vine. If you're not vigilant, nearby trees will eventually be adorned with wisteria foliage and flowers.

Do structural pruning in winter, before buds begin to swell: remove poorly placed stems, dead growth, and any tangling stems that you didn't cut out the previous summer. At this time of year, remove as little as necessary, since you will inevitably be cutting out some wood that would produce blossoms.

The greater amount of thinning should occur during the growing season, when plants produce volumes of new shoots. Soon after flowering is a good time to remove unneeded young growth before it becomes long and tangling. Four to 6 weeks after that, assess the vine again and cut out more new growth if needed. Within the body of the vine, you can cut new stems back to about three leaves rather than to the branch from which they emerge; flower buds for the next year may form on these branch stubs. Because it flowers on new, leafy stems, delay pruning new growth on *W. frutescens* until flowering has finished.

If you have a steep bank that needs a foliage cover, wisterias will do the job nicely. Simply set gallon-size plants about 10 feet apart at the top of the slope, then let the stems cascade downhill. Prune and thin these plants just to keep the coverage looking neat; remove stems that go astray or depart from the evenness you want.

*Wisteria sinensis*

*Some plants require virtually no care under some conditions—and some gardeners opt for low-maintenance landscapes composed solely of such plants. But many of us design our gardens according to the more emotional criteria of*

VINES AND
GROUND COVERS

# PLANTING AND CARE

*beauty and sentiment, accepting the need for routine care as part of the equation.*

*Fortunately, most vines and ground covers offer both good looks and ease of maintenance. If you want them to thrive, however, you'll need to observe two important guidelines. First, choose plants that grow well in your climate. Each description in the encyclopedia (pages 33–99) lists the Sunset climate zones where that plant does best; determine your zone (see pages 108–111), then consider only plants suited to it. Second, be sure you have a clear idea of each plant's maintenance needs, including both routine tasks—those covered in this chapter—and any special care noted in the encyclopedia entries. With the right climate and the right care, your vines and ground covers will flourish.*

A ground cover planting need not be boring. A variety of plants, including bishop's weed
*(Aegopodium)* and violet *(Viola)*, make this carpet of greenery
a study in contrasting tone, size, and texture.

# PREPARATION AND PLANTING

*To achieve a top-notch performance from any vine or ground cover, start by evaluating the garden's soil and taking steps to control weeds. Following that, put plants into the ground the right way, at the right time of year.*

## WEED CONTROL

Only one thing is more unpleasant than a weedy ground cover: having to remove the weeds from it! Fortunately, you can largely avoid the problem if you take a few preliminary steps.

Clear weeds completely from the area you intend to plant. Tilling or hoeing will easily dispatch shallow-rooted annual types, but deep-rooted perennial sorts such as dandelions and Bermuda grass must be dug out by hand (they can regrow from root fragments, and deep hand-digging is the best way to be sure you've removed all the roots).

Herbicides offer an alternative method of weed removal: spray the pest plants with a product such as the systemic herbicide glyphosate, then prepare the soil once the weeds are dead. After your vine or ground cover is in place, you can apply a pre-emergence herbicide to prevent the germination of any weed seeds brought to the surface during cultivation and planting. Mulches (see page 104) offer a further hedge against weed resurgence.

Bermuda grass

## GOOD EARTH

Many gardeners take garden soil for granted—and get away with it! The majority of popular plants are quite adaptable, able to grow in soils of various types that have had little or no preparation before planting (maybe that's why they're popular). It's wise to know something about soils, though, so you can tell if yours needs any special attention. Knowing your soil type helps you plan the right watering program, too.

In general terms, most soil types can be described as heavy (claylike), light (sandy), or somewhere in between the two. The lightness or heaviness stems from the types and sizes of the particles that make up the soil; these, in turn, determine the soil's capacity to hold water and air.

When applied to the soil surface, water percolates downward through the pore spaces between particles. At first it completely fills these spaces, but in time it is depleted—pulled down by gravity, absorbed by plant roots, lost to surface evaporation. As water leaves the pores, air returns to them, until just a thin film of water (unavailable to roots) clings to each particle. This movement of water into and through soil is known as drainage.

Heavy, claylike soil has tiny, flattened particles that pack tightly together. It retains moisture well, because the surface area of the particles is high in proportion to the volume of soil they occupy—but it drains slowly, since pore spaces are so minute. Clay soil is relatively difficult for roots to penetrate, and during prolonged moist spells it remains airless and saturated, even to the point of rotting roots.

Light, sandy soil has relatively large, irregularly rounded particles that pack together fairly loosely, like pebbles or marbles. The large pore spaces allow free exchange of water and air. Water-holding capacity is poor, but drainage is so efficient that roots are never in danger of saturation.

Most garden soils fall somewhere between the two extremes just described; the best ones include a variety of particle sizes and types. To get a rough idea of your soil type, start with a touch test: take a handful of wet soil and squeeze it. Clay feels slick or slimy; when squeezed, it remains in a lump, with any excess oozing in ribbons from between your fingers. Sand feels gritty; a damp handful falls apart when you release your grip or give it a slight prod.

A simple test for drainage can also give a clue to your soil's composition. Dig a 1½-foot-deep hole in the area where you want to plant, then fill it with water. If any water remains in the hole after 8 hours, or if the water level has barely dropped after an hour, you have a drainage problem. Such difficulties are usually due to clay soil, but they may also result from compaction by heavy equipment or (more rarely) from rock or an impermeable hardpan layer near the surface.

SOIL PREPARATION. Organic matter—the decayed remains of once-living organisms—improves the texture of all soils. Added to heavy kinds, it improves drainage; worked into sandy types, it increases water retention. Compost is probably the best-known organic amendment.

For annuals, vegetables, and some perennials, adding organic matter to the soil before planting can mean the difference between average and superior performance. When you plant vines and ground covers, though, the need for organic amendment depends on the particular plant and on your soil type.

If you're setting in a fairly shallow-rooted ground cover that roots as it spreads or that colonizes by underground stems, add plenty of organic matter to any soil type, working it in thoroughly over the entire planting area. The result will be better-quality soil on the surface, merging into the native soil beneath. Drainage will be uniform over the improved area—a particularly important consideration when you're planting in clay.

When planting vines and woody ground covers that spread from individual root systems, you can generally do without amendments if the soil is on the heavy side. Don't amend only the backfill soil in the planting holes, or you'll end up with a sort of bathtub: water will penetrate easily into the amended soil, but escape only slowly into the heavy clay surrounding it, and the result will be waterlogged roots. After planting in heavy soil, make sure that the plants' bases (the point where roots join aboveground parts) remain slightly above grade.

When setting vines and woody ground covers in sandy soil, in contrast, you *should* add organic matter to the backfill. Far from harming plants, extra amendment in the backfill is beneficial—it effectively slows drainage a bit, so that roots of new plants are less subject to frequent extremes of wetting and drying.

# PLANTING

Vines and ground covers are sold in two ways. Many are available growing in containers during the growing season; some are sold bare-root during dormancy. Perennials are likely to be sold in cell-packs, small pots, and 1- or 2-gallon containers. Woody plants are generally containerized, though a few deciduous types such as roses and grapes are also offered bare-root in their dormant season.

The illustrations at right show you how to plant both bare-root and container-grown vines and ground covers. Note that some stem-rooting ground covers—ivy *(Hedera)*, for example—may be sold in flats containing numerous individual plants. Just cut through the soil between plants with a knife (as though you were cutting a sheet cake into squares) and set out the plants as you would those from small pots or cell-packs.

It's important to time planting properly. Bare-root material must be planted at once—and because these plants are sold when dormant, they'll automatically have an entire growing season to establish themselves in the garden. Early planting is best for containerized plants as well; given the chance to settle in during cooler weather, they'll be better able to cope with summer's heat. Container-grown plants can also be set out in summer, but planting them then carries some disadvantages. They'll need special attention to watering and perhaps to shading as well. Unless summers are cool, they'll get off to a slower start than plants set out in spring and may not be well established by fall—making them more vulnerable to cold damage in harsh-winter climates.

Gardeners in relatively mild-winter regions (Zones 4–9, 12–31) can take advantage of fall and winter planting. Roots will grow during winter, poising plants for a vigorous start when temperatures rise in spring.

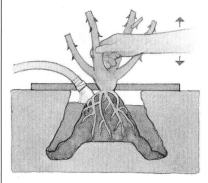

BARE-ROOT. Dig hole deep enough to accommodate root system; form firm soil mound in center. Spread roots over mound; juncture of roots and top growth is at or just above soil grade.

FROM CONTAINERS. Dig hole slightly shallower than rootball at center, slightly deeper than rootball at perimeter. Gently loosen roots; plant in hole with top of rootball just above soil grade.

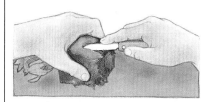

FROM CELL-PACKS. Remove plant from pack (above) and score each face of rootball with a knife to loosen roots. Set plant in hole (below) so that top of rootball is just above soil grade.

# GENERAL CARE

*During the growing season, nurturing your vines and ground covers centers on giving them the water they need. Fertilizing isn't always necessary, but it can improve the performance of some under certain conditions.*

## WATERING

All plants, even drought-tolerant sorts, need water for growth. The descriptions in the encyclopedia (pages 33–99) note each plant's general requirements, but that plant's water needs in your particular garden depend on several other factors as well: soil, climate, the plant's age, and the extent of its root system.

As explained on page 102, the heavier the soil, the more water it can hold, and the longer the allowable interval between waterings. You will, however, need to apply more water to clay than to sand to wet it to a given depth. The rate of application must also suit the soil's drainage speed: apply water slowly to slow-draining clay, more quickly to sand.

Climate and season also influence how long soil remains moist. You'll water less often in cool, moist conditions, more often in hot, dry weather. Consider a plant's age and its root system, too: young or shallow-rooted plants need more frequent watering than established ones and those with deep roots.

APPLYING WATER. There are two basic approaches to watering: sprinkling and irrigation. Likewise, there are two basic methods of application. You can use a hose—either a soaker type (for irrigation) or one with a sprinkler or other device attached to the end—and move it from place to place as needed. Or you can opt for a stationary system with fixed points of water emission—generally a rigid-pipe underground sprinkler system or a drip irrigation setup. The method you choose will depend on what you need to water (an individual vine or an expanse of ground cover, for example), the amount of water at your disposal, and the configuration of the area to be watered.

A swath of ground cover can be covered by sprinklers (hose-end or fixed system) or by a drip irrigation setup outfitted with minisprinklers. These two methods are best for ground covers that root as they spread and for those that colonize by underground stems. If the ground cover consists of widely spaced individual plants, it can also be watered by a drip irrigation system with one or more drip emitters servicing each plant.

The amount of water available for use often influences water-delivery decisions. Where water is scarce or expensive, drip irrigation is fast becoming the top choice. Drip systems offer a variety of emitters and a wide range of delivery rates, letting you apply fairly precise amounts of water to a single plant or a given area, at a rate that suits your soil's absorption ability. And you can customize systems to water irregularly shaped plantings, narrow beds, and widely spaced plants.

For a complete discussion of watering devices and systems, refer to *Sunset's Garden Watering Systems* (1999).

Organic mulch around a juniper helps plant get established by keeping soil cool and moist.

MULCHING. A layer of mulch around and between plants is an important adjunct to any watering system. Spread 1 to 3 inches thick, organic mulches do an impressive job of conserving moisture: the mulch "blanket" shields soil from the drying effects of sun and wind, keeping it (and plants' root zones) cool and moist for a longer period between waterings. These conditions enhance root growth—one reason why mulched new ground cover plantings establish and fill in faster than unmulched ones.

Besides conserving moisture, mulches also suppress weed growth by blocking out the light weed seeds in the soil need for germination. On sloping ground, mulches help prevent erosion and gullying by breaking the force of overhead water from rain or sprinkling.

## FERTILIZING

Some plants need, or at least benefit from, routine fertilizing. Lawns and roses are two familiar examples; they can get by without feeding but grow and look better with it. Many of a garden's more or less permanent plants, however, grow well without supplemental nutrients, as long as the soil is fairly good. The more robust and aggressive vines hardly need additional fuel; similarly, the most vigorous perennial ground covers and the majority of shrubby sorts usually do well just with the nutrients in the soil.

WHAT TO FERTILIZE. Though individual vines and ground covers vary in their nutrient needs, you can still follow a few general rules. First, keep soil in mind. Light, sandy soils are inherently low in nutrients, and applications of fertilizer leach through them quickly; thus, plants growing in sandy soil are likely to need more fertilizer (and more frequent applications of it) than the same plants growing in denser soil with slower drainage. Think about root depth and plant size, too. In all soils, shallow-rooted ground covers (most perennials, for example) often benefit from an annual feeding. Smaller-growing vines, too, may perform better with an annual nutrient boost.

TYPES OF FERTILIZER. Commercial fertilizers are of two general types: dry, water-soluble granules you apply directly to the soil, and concentrates (either dry or liquid) to be mixed with water, then applied in solution.

To use granular types in established plantings, you scatter the pellets over the soil, lightly scratch them in (if possible), and then water thoroughly. How long the fertilizer's benefits will last depends on the type of nitrogen the product contains. Fertilizers containing nitrogen in nitrate form act fastest but are soon spent; sorts with nitrogen in ammonium or organic form offer less immediate results but a more sustained delivery. For the longest-acting dry fertilizer, look for a controlled-release type. The nutrient pellets are enclosed in a permeable coating; with every watering or spell of rainfall, a small quantity of nutrients leaches from the pellets into the soil.

Liquid fertilizers come in the form of soluble crystals or concentrated liquids. Both kinds are diluted in water before application. Such fertilizers provide nutrients immediately, so they're popular for giving plants a quick pick-me-up. Because the nutrients are in solution, though, they soon leach through the soil. Various fertilizer injectors let you siphon liquid fertilizer into watering systems; some cartridge types (more useful in stationary systems) handle tablets or sticks of soluble dry fertilizers. These devices allow you to deliver both fertilizer and water simultaneously to a number of plants.

WHEN TO FERTILIZE. For established plants, fertilize just before the growing season begins, giving the year's first flush of growth a boost. Use a high-nitrogen formula on plants producing meager or spindly-looking growth; their problems are probably the result of nitrogen deficiency. You can apply the same tonic later in spring or in summer to any plants showing this kind of substandard performance. At that time, a liquid formula will give you faster results.

## WHICH FERTILIZER TO USE

Commercial fertilizers contain one, two, or all three of the major nutrients: nitrogen (N), phosphorus (P), and potassium (K). The package label notes the percentage of each nutrient the fertilizer contains, always presenting them in the N-P-K order. A 5-10-10 product, for example, contains 5 percent nitrogen, 10 percent phosphorus, and 10 percent potassium; 0-10-10 fertilizer contains no nitrogen, while an 18-0-0 formulation contains nitrogen alone.

Of the three major nutrients, nitrogen is the one most directly responsible for growth, and thus the one most likely to be needed to improve performance. It is the only one of the three that is water soluble. Rainfall and watering leach it from the soil—more quickly in sand, more slowly in clay. Phosphorus and potassium, in contrast, become chemically "locked" into the soil at the point where they are applied. If roots are to benefit from these elements, they must be placed near the root zone, a job most easily done by digging fertilizer into the soil when you prepare it for planting.

To fertilize most vines and ground covers, choose a general purpose product containing all three nutrients—a 10-5-5 formulation, for example. If you're intent on giving poor performers a quick jolt, though, you may want to choose an all-nitrogen fertilizer (such as the 18-0-0 type mentioned above).

Twining wisteria vine eventually becomes sturdy enough to provide much of its own support.

# TRAINING VINES

While clinging vines such as Boston ivy and Virginia creeper (*Parthenocissus* species) often manage to train themselves, the majority of vines benefit from some guidance to achieve the desired appearance or function. The training needed depends on how the vine climbs and on the support structure provided for it.

TWINING VINES. These are supremely efficient climbers; new growth automatically spirals around any vertical support that's fairly slim (no thicker than your wrist). When plants are young, new stems frequently twine around each other if no other support exists; on established plants, new stems try to ascend by using older ones for support.

To encourage these vines to climb, offer support in the form of wire, cord, rope, stakes, or trelliswork. For wisteria and other twiners that eventually form treelike trunks and limbs, only a temporary support is needed for the plant's initial upward growth. In time, the trunks usually become self-supporting—and by then, the vigorous top growth will be firmly secured (through its own efforts or thanks to the gardener) to some sort of permanent structure.

VINES THAT CLIMB BY COILING TENDRILS OR LEAF-STALKS. Coiling tendrils and leafstalks climb almost as briskly as twining stems; they're less efficient only because they need smaller-diameter supports. Wire mesh, sturdy cord or rope, and plastic netting offer satisfactory initial support. For sturdy vines that become stiff and woody with age (grape, for example), the initial supports merely serve to get the main stems up to the desired height. For wispier individuals (like clematis) or perennials such as hops *(Humulus lupulus)*, the initial supports must usually remain in place permanently.

Tendrils of passion flower *(Passiflora)* coil around supports.

CLAMBERING VINES. It's a classic good news/bad news scenario. The good news is that these vines have no inclination to cling, grasp, and tangle their way upward, so you won't have to worry about them engulfing or hopelessly snarling themselves in whatever is near: you have virtually total control over the positioning of their stems. The bad news is that such vines require close attention to supports and tying if they're to grow as you want. Clamberers are ideal choices for walls and trellises, where you can position stems to suit the shape of the support. If the support has an openwork backing, you can easily tie stems in place with plastic ties or soft twine. If the support is solid (such as a fence or house wall), insert eyescrews into it. Then run ties through the eyes and around vine stems, loosely securing them in place; or run wire between eyescrews, then tie growth to wire.

Wall-grown clambering vine can be tied to wires threaded between eyescrews.

Clambering canes of climbing rose 'Bobbie James' are woven through openwork trellis for support.

## ROUTINE MAINTENANCE

In maintaining vines and ground covers, you assume the role of barber or beautician, providing the periodic combing and clipping these plants need to look their best.

### VINES

Most vines produce enough wayward growth to need some regular pruning to keep their growth organized. Pay particular attention to sorts that have a tendency to tangle; almost all of these require periodic thinning.

Clinging vines are notorious trespassers; be sure to remove poorly placed growth while it is young.

CLINGING VINES. If you're growing ivy *(Hedera)*, creeping fig *(Ficus pumila)*, or another clinging vine, keep an eye on where it's gaining footholds. The beauty of these plants is that they need no tying and can easily blanket vertical surfaces. The danger is that they don't know where to stop or what to avoid; they'll grow right over windows and doors if neglected. As soon as you notice growth beginning to attach in unwanted places, pull it off and cut it back to a safe spot. Trying to remove mature, attached stems is a chore and can damage the surface beneath the vine.

VINES THAT TWINE, CLAMBER, OR GROW BY COILING TENDRILS OR LEAFSTALKS. In general, maintenance pruning of these vines consists of thinning their growth. You'll need to cut out dead, weak, and unproductive stems, and remove any vigorous but tangling stems that create a congested appearance.

How severely or lightly you prune depends on the particular vine involved and, to some extent, on how you are using it. Some honeysuckles *(Lonicera)* and the climbing *Polygonum* species exemplify vines that grow in such exuberant tangles that thinning for exaggerated neatness is futile. Instead, use these sorts of vines where their billowing, impenetrable growth serves a purpose: atop a pergola for shade, on a wire fence for solid cover, swamping an unsightly object to hide it from view. In these situations, pruning will involve only heading back growth as needed to hold the plant to its allotted area—with, perhaps, the occasional scalping all the way back to main stems if growth builds up too densely.

With the majority of these twiners, clamberers, and tendril-coilers, however, you can be a bit more precise. Assess their growth each year during the dormant period (generally winter and earliest spring); pruning won't always be called for, but certain jobs should be tackled when the need arises. Look for and remove dead material and any sizable older stems that are no longer producing strong new growth. Also check the plant for healthy but entangling growth: young stems that twine around or otherwise attach to other huskier stems. If these are not needed for the sake of density, remove them by cutting them back to their points of origin. But if they can be pressed into service to fill gaps in the coverage, detach them by unwinding them or cutting the tendrils; then train them into the desired space.

Vines that bloom only in spring usually produce their flowering stems directly from wood formed the previous year, so dormant-season pruning will inevitably sacrifice some flowers. You can delay any major pruning of these vines until just after blossoms fade but before strong new growth begins.

Deciduous vine has been heavily thinned, then securely tied to support.

If a many-stemmed vine has grown so that most of its leaves and flowers are carried toward the top of the plant, enhance coverage in the bare areas by cutting back some stems to varying degrees; this should encourage production of new, leafy growth toward the middle or bottom of the vine.

During growing season, unwind stems that coil around each other.

You can lessen your dormant-season work if you also keep an eye on growth during spring and summer. When you see stems twining or grasping where they shouldn't, untangle or detach them; then retrain or remove them while they're still pliable and relatively small.

*Note:* For clematis and climbing roses, pruning needs and timing vary with the particular species or class. For specific instructions, consult these plants' encyclopedia entries.

## GROUND COVERS

General ground cover maintenance is covered by one word: grooming. Your goal in all cases is to keep the planting neat and tidy, but the particular plant will determine the way you approach the job.

PRUNING TO SHAPE. Shrubby ground covers are by nature low growing and spreading, but from time to time they send out upright or angling stems that spoil the evenness of a planting. Whenever you see such a stem developing, cut it back to its point of origin or to a horizontally growing lateral branch within the foliage mass.

MOWING. Certain spreading-rooting and colonizing ground covers become so thick and matted in time that only a close trim will restore their attractiveness. Some of these—ivy (Hedera) is a familiar example—accumulate thatch, a tangled mass of stems that gradually raises the height of the foliage cover, harbors slugs, snails, and rodents, and may even be flammable. Others, such as winter creeper *(Euonymus fortunei)* and creeping St. Johnswort *(Hypericum calycinum)*, become rangy and uneven. If the planting is small, you can make a close trim with hedge shears; but for an expanse of any size, the easiest method is simply to mow the plants down with a heavy-duty power mower.

EDGING. A number of ground covers will try to expand their domain unless you periodically restrict them. When shrubby sorts with horizontally spreading stems produce overreaching stems, promptly head the strays back into the foliage mass: the sooner you catch these extensions, the less apparent the pruning will be. For spreading-rooting ground covers, you can maintain an edge with pruning or hedge shears. For underground spreaders, use a shovel or spade to slice the growth back to the desired edge.

REJUVENATION. Many perennial ground covers become overcrowded in time, a condition indicated by flagging growth or the appearance of bare patches in the cover. When this occurs, the best remedy is to dig up the planting and refurbish the soil with organic amendments and fertilizer, then replant—using either the strongest divisions from the original planting or brand-new plants. Do this job at the best time of year for planting in your region (see page 103).

To rejuvenate perennial ground covers, dig up planting, then replant strongest divisions.

# SUNSET'S GARDEN CLIMATE ZONES

A plant's performance is governed by the total climate: length of growing season, timing and amount of rainfall, winter lows, summer highs, humidity. *Sunset's* climate zone maps take all these factors into account—unlike the familiar hardiness zone maps devised by the U.S. Department of Agriculture, which divide the U.S. and Canada into zones based strictly on winter lows. The U.S.D.A. maps tell you only where a plant may survive the winter; our climate zone maps let you see where that plant will thrive year-round. Below are brief descriptions of the 45 zones illustrated on the map on pages 110–111. For more information, consult *Sunset's National Garden Book* and *Western Garden Book.*

### ZONE 1. Coldest Winters in the West and Western Prairie States

Growing season: early June through Aug., but with some variation—the longest seasons are usually found near this zone's large bodies of water. Frost can come any night of the year. Winters are snowy and intensely cold, due to latitude, elevation, and/or influence of continental air mass. There's some summer rainfall.

### ZONE 2. Second-coldest Western Climate

Growing season: early May through Sept. Winters are cold (lows run from –3° to –34°F/–19° to –37°C), but less so than in Zone 1. In northern and interior areas, lower elevations fall into Zone 2, higher areas into Zone 1.

### ZONE 3. West's Mildest High-elevation and Interior Regions

Growing season: early May to late Sept.—shorter than in Zone 2, but offset by milder winters (lows from 13° to –24°F/–11° to –31°C). This is fine territory for plants needing winter chill and dry, hot summers.

### ZONE 4. Cold-winter Western Washington and British Columbia

Growing season: early May to early Oct. Summers are cool, thanks to ocean influence; chilly winters (19° to –7°F/–7° to –22°C) result from elevation, influence of continental air mass, or both. Coolness, ample rain suit many perennials and bulbs.

### ZONE 5. Ocean-influenced Northwest Coast and Puget Sound

Growing season: mid-April to Nov., typically with cool temperatures throughout. Less rain falls here than in Zone 4; winter lows range from 28° to 1°F/–2° to –17°C. This "English garden" climate is ideal for rhododendrons and many rock garden plants.

### ZONE 6. Oregon's Willamette Valley

Growing season: mid-Mar. to mid-Nov., with somewhat warmer temperatures than in Zone 5. Ocean influence keeps winter lows about the same as in Zone 5. Climate suits all but tender plants and those needing hot or dry summers.

### ZONE 7. Oregon's Rogue River Valley, California's High Foothills

Growing season: May to early Oct. Summers are hot and dry; typical winter lows run from 23° to 9°F/–5° to –13°C. The summer-winter contrast suits plants that need dry, hot summers and moist, only moderately cold winters.

### ZONE 8. Cold-air Basins of California's Central Valley

Growing season: mid-Feb. through Nov. This is a valley floor with no maritime influence. Summers are hot; winter lows range from 29° to 13°F/–2° to –11°C. Rain comes in the cooler months, covering just the early part of the growing season.

### ZONE 9. Thermal Belts of California's Central Valley

Growing season: late Feb. through Dec. Zone 9 is located in the higher elevations around Zone 8, but its summers are just as hot; its winter lows are slightly higher (temperatures range from 28° to 18°F/–2° to –8°C). Rainfall pattern is the same as in Zone 8.

### ZONE 10. High Desert Areas of Arizona, New Mexico, West Texas, Oklahoma Panhandle, and Southwest Kansas

Growing season: April to early Nov. Chilly (even snow-dusted) weather rules from late Nov. through Feb., with lows from 31° to 24°F/–1° to –4°C. Rain comes in summer as well as in the cooler seasons.

### ZONE 11. Medium to High Desert of California and Southern Nevada

Growing season: early April to late Oct. Summers are sizzling, with 110 days above 90°F/32°C. Balancing this is a 3½-month winter, with 85 nights below freezing and lows from 11° to 0°F/–12° to –18°C. Scant rainfall comes in winter.

### ZONE 12. Arizona's Intermediate Desert

Growing season: mid-Mar. to late Nov., with scorching midsummer heat. Compared to Zone 13, this region has harder frosts; record low is 6°F/–14°C. Rains come in summer and winter.

### ZONE 13. Low or Subtropical Desert

Growing season: mid-Feb. through Nov., interrupted by nearly 3 months of incandescent, growth-stopping summer heat. Most frosts are light (record lows run from 19° to 13°F/–7° to –11°C); scant rain comes in summer and winter.

### ZONE 14. Inland Northern and Central California with Some Ocean Influence

Growing season: early Mar. to mid-Nov., with rain coming in the remaining months. Periodic intrusions of marine air temper summer heat and winter cold (lows run from 26° to 16°F/–3° to –9°C). Mediterranean-climate plants are at home here.

### ZONE 15. Northern and Central California's Chilly-winter Coast-influenced Areas

Growing season: Mar. to Dec. Rain comes from fall through winter. Typical winter lows range from 28° to 21°F/–2° to –6°C. Maritime air influences the zone much of the time, giving it cooler, moister summers than Zone 14.

### ZONE 16. Northern and Central California Coast Range Thermal Belts

Growing season: late Feb. to late Nov. With cold air draining to lower elevations, winter lows typically run from 32° to 19°F/0° to –7°C. Like Zone 15, this region is dominated by maritime air, but its winters are milder on average.

### ZONE 17. Oceanside Northern and Central California and Southernmost Oregon

Growing season: late Feb. to early Dec. Coolness and fog are hallmarks; summer highs seldom top 75°F/24°C, while winter lows run from 36° to 23°F/2° to –5°C. Heat-loving plants disappoint or dwindle here.

### ZONE 18. Hilltops and Valley Floors of Interior Southern California

Growing season: mid-Mar. through late Nov. Summers are hot and dry; rain comes in winter, when lows reach 28° to 10°F/–2° to –12°C. Plants from the Mediterranean and Near Eastern regions thrive here.

### ZONE 19. Thermal belts around Southern California's Interior Valleys

Growing season: early Mar. through Nov. As in Zone 18, rainy winters and hot, dry summers are the norm—but here, winter lows dip only to 27° to 22°F/–3° to –6°C, allowing some tender evergreen plants to grow outdoors with protection.

### ZONE 20. Hilltops and Valley Floors of Ocean-influenced Inland Southern California

Growing season: late Mar. to late Nov.—but fairly mild winters (lows of 28° to 23°F/–2° to –5°C) allow gardening through much of the year. Cool and moist maritime influence alternates with hot, dry interior air.

### ZONE 21. Thermal belts around Southern California's Ocean-influenced Interior Valleys

Growing season: early Mar. to early Dec., with the same tradeoff of oceanic and interior influence as in Zone 20. During the winter rainy season, lows range from 36° to 23°F/2° to –5°C—warmer than in Zone 20, since the colder air drains to the valleys.

## ZONE 22. Colder-winter Parts of Southern California's Coastal Region

Growing season: Mar. to early Dec. Winter lows seldom fall below 28°F/–2°C (records are around 21°F/–6°C), though colder air sinks to this zone from Zone 23. Summers are warm; rain comes in winter. Climate here is largely oceanic.

## ZONE 23. Thermal Belts of Southern California's Coastal Region

Growing season: almost year-round (all but first half of Jan.). Rain comes in winter. Reliable ocean influence keeps summers mild (except when hot Santa Ana winds come from inland), frosts negligible; 23°F/–5°C is the record low.

## ZONE 24. Marine-dominated Southern California Coast

Growing season: all year, but periodic freezes have dramatic effects (record lows are 33° to 20°F/1° to –7°C). Climate here is oceanic (but warmer than oceanic Zone 17), with cool summers, mild winters. Subtropical plants thrive.

## ZONE 25. South Florida and the Keys

Growing season: all year. Add ample year-round rainfall (least in Dec. through Mar.), high humidity, and overall warmth, and you have a near-tropical climate. The Keys are frost-free; winter lows elsewhere run from 40° to 25°F/4° to –4°C.

## ZONE 26. Central and Interior Florida

Growing season: early Feb. to late Dec., with typically humid, warm to hot weather. Rain is plentiful all year, heaviest in summer and early fall. Lows range from 15°F/–9°C in the north to 27°F/–3°C in the south; arctic air brings periodic hard freezes.

## ZONE 27. Lower Rio Grande Valley

Growing season: early Mar. to mid-Dec.. Summers are hot and humid; winter lows only rarely dip below freezing. Many plants from tropical and subtropical Africa and South America are well adapted here.

## ZONE 28. Gulf Coast, North Florida, Atlantic Coast to Charleston

Growing season: mid-Mar. to early Dec. Humidity and rainfall are year-round phenomena; summers are hot, winters virtually frostless but subject to periodic invasions by frigid arctic air. Azaleas, camellias, many subtropicals flourish.

## ZONE 29. Interior Plains of South Texas

Growing season: mid-Mar. through Nov. Moderate rainfall (to 25" annually) comes year-round. Summers are hot. Winter lows can dip to 26°F/–3°C, with occasional arctic freezes bringing much lower readings.

## ZONE 30. Hill Country of Central Texas

Growing season: mid-Mar. through Nov. Zone 30 has higher annual rainfall than Zone 29 (to 35") and lower winter temperatures, normally to around 20°F/–7°C. Seasonal variations favor many fruit crops, perennials.

## ZONE 31. Interior Plains of Gulf Coast and Coastal Southeast

Growing season: mid-Mar. to early Nov. In this extensive east-west zone, hot and sticky summers contrast with chilly winters (record low temperatures are 7° to 0°F/–14° to –18°C). There's rain all year (an annual average of 50"), with the least falling in Oct.

## ZONE 32. Interior Plains of Mid-Atlantic States; Chesapeake Bay, Southeastern Pennsylvania, Southern New Jersey

Growing season: late Mar. to early Nov. Rain falls year-round (40" to 50" annually); winter lows (moving through the zone from south to north) are 30° to 20°F/–1° to –7°C. Humidity is less oppressive here than in Zone 31.

## ZONE 33. North-Central Texas and Oklahoma Eastward to the Appalachian Foothills

Growing season: mid-April through Oct. Warm Gulf Coast air and colder continental/arctic fronts both play a role; their unpredictable interplay results in a wide range in annual rainfall (22" to 52") and winter lows (20° to 0°F/–7° to –18°C). Summers are muggy and warm to hot.

## ZONE 34. Lowlands and Coast from Gettysburg to North of Boston

Growing season: late April to late Oct. Ample rainfall and humid summers are the norm. Winters are variable—typically fairly mild (around 20°F/–7°C), but with lows down to –3° to –22°F/–19° to –30°C if arctic air swoops in.

## ZONE 35. Ouachita Mountains, Northern Oklahoma and Arkansas, Southern Kansas to North-Central Kentucky and Southern Ohio

Growing season: late April to late Oct. Rain comes in all seasons. Summers can be truly hot and humid. Without arctic fronts, winter lows are around 18°F/–8°C; with them, the coldest weather may bring lows of –20°F/–29°C.

## ZONE 36. Appalachian Mountains

Growing season: May to late Oct. Thanks to greater elevation, summers are cooler and less humid, winters colder (0° to –20°F/–18° to –29°C) than in adjacent, lower zones. Rain comes all year (heaviest in spring). Late frosts are common.

## ZONE 37. Hudson Valley and Appalachian Plateau

Growing season: May to mid-Oct., with rainfall throughout. Lower in elevation than neighboring Zone 42, with warmer winters: lows are 0° to –5°F/–18° to –21°C, unless arctic air moves in. Summer is warm to hot, humid.

## ZONE 38. New England Interior and Lowland Maine

Growing season: May to early Oct. Summers feature reliable rainfall and lack oppressive humidity of lower-elevation, more southerly areas. Winter lows dip to –10° to –20°F/–23° to –29°C, with periodic colder temperatures due to influxes of arctic air.

## ZONE 39. Shoreline Regions of the Great Lakes

Growing season: early May to early Oct. Springs and summers are cooler here, autumns milder than in areas farther from the lakes. Southeast lakeshores get the heaviest snowfalls. Lows reach 0° to –10°F/–18° to –23°C.

## ZONE 40. Inland Plains of Lake Erie and Lake Ontario

Growing season: mid-May to mid-Sept., with rainy, warm, variably humid weather. The lakes help moderate winter lows; temperatures typically range from –10° to –20°F/–23° to –29°C, with occasional colder readings when arctic fronts rush through.

## ZONE 41. Northeast Kansas and Southeast Nebraska to Northern Illinois and Indiana, Southeast Wisconsin, Michigan, Northern Ohio

Growing season: early May to early Oct. Winter brings average lows of –11° to –20°F/–23° to –29°C. Summers in this zone are hotter and longer west of the Mississippi, cooler and shorter nearer the Great Lakes; summer rainfall increases in the same west-to-east direction.

## ZONE 42. Interior Pennsylvania and New York; St. Lawrence Valley

Growing season: late May to late Sept. This zone's elevation gives it colder winters than surrounding zones: lows range from –20° to –40°F/–29° to –40°C, with the colder readings coming in the Canadian portion of the zone. Summers are humid, rainy.

## ZONE 43. Upper Mississippi Valley, Upper Michigan, Southern Ontario and Quebec

Growing season: late May to mid-Sept. The climate is humid from spring through early fall; summer rains are usually dependable. Arctic air dominates in winter, with lows typically from –20° to –30°F/–29° to –34°C.

## ZONE 44. Mountains of New England and Southeastern Quebec

Growing season: June to mid-Sept. Latitude and elevation give fairly cool, rainy summers, cold winters with lows of –20° to –40°F/–29° to –40°C. Choose short-season, low heat-requirement annuals and vegetables.

## ZONE 45. Northern Parts of Minnesota and Wisconsin, Eastern Manitoba through Interior Quebec

Growing season: mid-June through Aug., with rain throughout; rainfall (and humidity) are least in zone's western part, greatest in eastern reaches. Winters are frigid (–30° to –40°F/–34° to –40°C), with snow cover, deeply frozen soil.

# Sunset's Garden Climate Zones

Climate Zones: `▨` | 1 | 2 | 3 | 4 | 5 | 6 | 7 | 8 | 9 | 10 | 11 | 12 | 13 | 14 | 15 | 16 | 17 | 18 | 19 | 20 | 21 | 22

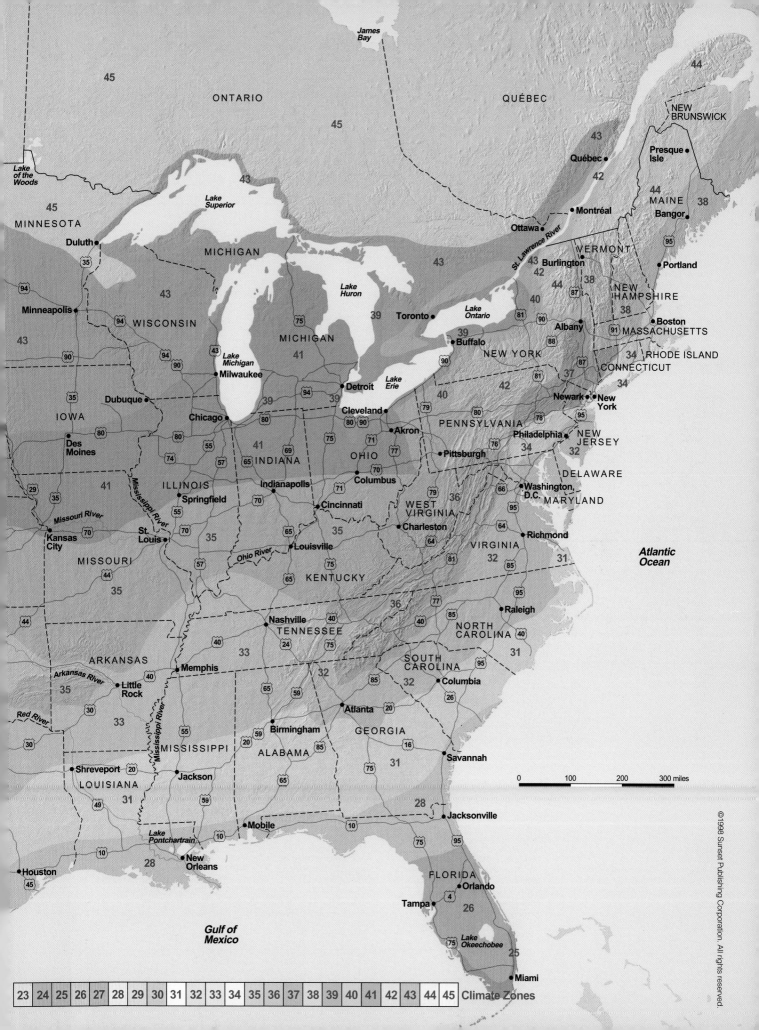

James Bay

ONTARIO
45

QUÉBEC

45

NEW BRUNSWICK
44

Lake of the Woods

MINNESOTA
45

Lake Superior
43

MICHIGAN

43

Québec
43
42

Presque Isle •

MAINE
44
38
Bangor •

Duluth •
35

43

Montréal •

VERMONT

95

• Portland

Minneapolis •
94

WISCONSIN
43

Lake Michigan
43

Lake Huron

39

Ottawa
St. Lawrence River
43
42
Burlington
44
87

NEW HAMPSHIRE
38

Boston •

43
90

MICHIGAN
41

Milwaukee •
94
90

75

Toronto •
Lake Ontario

40
81
90

Albany •
88

91
MASSACHUSETTS

34 RHODE ISLAND

Dubuque •
35

IOWA

41

Des Moines •
80

Chicago •
80

39

Detroit •
94
39
Lake Erie

Cleveland •
80 90
Akron •
71

39
Buffalo •
90

NEW YORK
42

79

PENNSYLVANIA
40

Newark •
78

37
34
87

New York

34 CONNECTICUT

74
57
65
INDIANA
69

75

77

Pittsburgh •
76

Philadelphia •
34

NEW JERSEY
32

29
35
41
Mississippi River
55

Springfield •
70
Indianapolis •

70
Columbus •
71

70

Cincinnati •
35

36

WEST VIRGINIA

66
Washington, D.C. •

DELAWARE

MARYLAND

95

Kansas City •
70
St. Louis •
70
35

55
65
Louisville •
75

Ohio River
KENTUCKY
65

35
Charleston •
64

64
VIRGINIA
32

Richmond •

31

Atlantic Ocean

Missouri River

MISSOURI
44
35

57

79
36

81
85

Little Rock •
30

ARKANSAS
35

Arkansas River
40

Memphis •
65
59

33

Nashville •
40
TENNESSEE
24

40
75
36
77

85

Raleigh •
40

NORTH CAROLINA
31

95

Red River
30

30

33

Mississippi River
55

59

Birmingham •
20
ALABAMA
85

32

SOUTH CAROLINA
85
95

Columbia •
26

31

Shreveport •
20
49
LOUISIANA
31

Jackson •
59

65
GEORGIA
31
16
75

Atlanta •
20

Savannah •

0    100    200    300 miles

Lake Pontchartrain
10

Mobile •
10

28

Jacksonville •

Houston •
45

10

28
New Orleans •

75

95

75

FLORIDA
26
4
Orlando •

Tampa •

Gulf of Mexico

Lake Okeechobee
75

25

Miami •

| 23 | 24 | 25 | 26 | 27 | 28 | 29 | 30 | 31 | 32 | 33 | 34 | 35 | 36 | 37 | 38 | 39 | 40 | 41 | 42 | 43 | 44 | 45 | Climate Zones |

# INDEX